Customer Service in Local Government

Challenges for Planners and Managers

Customer Service in Local Government

Challenges for Planners and Managers

By

Bruce W. McClendon

PLANNERS PRESS
AMERICAN PLANNING ASSOCIATION
Chicago, Illinois
Washington, D.C.

Grateful acknowledgement is given for permission to reprint from the following:

Karl Albrecht and Lawrence Bradford, *The Service Advantage*, reprinted with permission of Dow Jones-Irwin.

Marvin Andrews, "Municipal Productivity Improvements Are a Way of Life in Phoenix," reprinted with permission of the *National Civic Review*.

Edward Banfield, "Ends and Means in Planning," *A Reader in Planning Theory*, copyright 1973, reprinted with permission of Pergamon Press PLC.

W. Barnes and C. Orlebeke, "Scanning the Horizon: Local Response," reprinted with permission from *Nation's Cities Weekly*, official publication of the National League of Cities.

R. Bartley, ed., "The Public Fat Cats" and "Golden Opportunity," reprinted with permission of *The Wall Street Journal*, copyright 1990 Dow Jones & Company, Inc. All rights reserved.

Joseph Bast, "Privatization Works," reprinted with permission of *City & State*.

Howell Baum, *Planners and Public Expectations*, copyright 1983 by Shenkman Books, Inc.

Guy Benveniste, *Mastering the Politics of Planning*. Reprinted by permission of Jossey-Bass Inc.

L. Bernard, "Granger seeks backing for East Side program," reprinted with permission of *Fort Worth Star-Telegram*.

Harry C. Boyte, *Common Wealth: A Return to Citizen Politics*, copyright 1989 by Harry C. Boyte. Reprinted by permission of The Free Press, a division of Macmillan, Inc.

Robert Burchell, "Planning, Power and Politics," *Society*, reprinted with permission of Transaction Publishers.

Stuart Butler, *Privatizing Federal Spending: A Strategy to Eliminate the Deficit*, reprinted with permission from The Heritage Foundation.

Robert Caro, *The Power Broker*, reprinted with permission of Random House, Inc.

Susan Carpenter, "Solving Community Problems by Consensus," *MIS Reports*, International City Management Association, October 1989. Reprinted by permission.

Timothy J. Cartwright, "The Lost Art of Planning," *Long Range Planning*, copyright 1987, reprinted with permission of Pergamon Press PLC.

Anthony Catanese, *Planners and Local Politics* and *The Politics and Planning and Development*, reprinted with permission of Sage Publications, Inc.

Henry Cisneros and John Parr, "Reinvigorating Democratic Values: Challenge and Necessity," reprinted with permission from *National Civic Review*, 79:5, Sept.-Oct. 1990, pp. 408-413.

Steven Cohen, *The Effective Public Manager: Achieving Success in Government*. Reprinted by permission of Jossey-Bass Inc.

T. Darr, "Pondering Privatization May Be Good for Your Government," copyright 1987 by *Governing* magazine.

I. David, "Privatization in America," *The Municipal Yearbook*. Washington, D.C.: International City Management Association, 1988.

T. Denton, ed., "Goals program shows strong leadership," reprinted with permission of the *Fort Worth Star-Telegram*.

Peter F. Drucker, *The New Realities*, reprinted with permission of HarperCollins Publishers.

Gary Enos, "Developers Take SLAPP at Anti-Growth Groups," *City & State*, reprinted with permission of Crain Communications.

A. Freedman, "Amid Ghetto Hunger, Many More Suffer Eating Wrong Foods," reprinted by permission of *The Wall Street Journal*, copyright 1990 Dow Jones & Company, Inc. All rights reserved worldwide.

M. Rogers, *Cold Anger: A Story of Faith and Power Politics,* reprinted with permission of the University of North Texas Press.

M. Scott, *American City Planning,* reprinted with permission of the University of California Press.

David C. Slater, *Management of Local Planning.* Washington, D.C. International City Management Association. 1984.

Gregory Streib, "Dusting Off a Forgotten Management Tool: The Citizen Survey," *Public Management,* reprinted with permission of the International City Management Association.

Costis Toregas, "Electronic Democracy: Some Definitions and a Battle Cry," *Public Management,* reprinted with permission of the International City Management Association.

Michael Lee Vasu, *Politics and Planning: A National Study of American Planners,* reprinted with permission of the University of North Carolina Press.

George Wagenheim and John Reurink, "Customer Service in Public Administration," reprinted with permission from *Public Administration Review,* copyright by the American Society for Public Administration (ASPA), 1120 G Street NW, Suite 500, Washington DC 20005. All rights reserved.

Robert Walker, *The Planning Function in Urban Government,* reprinted with permission of The University of Chicago Press.

Kenneth Webb and Harry P. Hatry, *Obtaining Citizen Feedback: The Application of Citizen Surveys to Local Governments,* 1973, reprinted by permission of The Urban Institute Press, Washington, D.C.

William Whyte, Jr., *City: Rediscovering the Center,* reprinted with permission of Doubleday, Dell Publishing.

Aaron Wildavsky, "Ubiquitous Anomie: Public Service in an Era of Ideological Dissensus," *Public Administration Review,* reprinted with permission of the American Society for Public Administration.

George Will, *Statecraft As Soulcraft,* copyright 1983 by Simon & Schuster, Inc.

Ron Zemke and Dick Schaaf, *The Service Edge,* reprinted with permission of Penguin USA.

R. Zolkos, "State's Troubles Jolt Districts," reprinted with permission of *City & State.*

Copyright 1992 by the American Planning Association
1313 E. 60th St., Chicago, IL 60637
Paperback edition ISBN 0-918286-75-1
Hardbound edition ISBN 0-918286-76-x
Library of Congress Catalog Number 91-75139

Printed in the United States of America

To
my mother
Billie Dee Melton

Contents

Acknowledgments

To begin with, I want to acknowledge and thank John Lewis, director of Goals for Dallas, and Rod Engelen, AICP, director of Phoenix Futures Forum, for their involvement in this book. Both men wrote sections on their respective programs, which are recognized and respected as outstanding examples of citizen participation in visioning and problem solving. The contributions of Lewis and Engelen can be found in Chapter 5.

Next, I want to acknowledge, in no particular order, the following practitioners and academics who contributed to the development of this book: Thomas Christoffel, AICP, executive director of the Lord Fairfax Planning District Commission in Front Royal, Virginia; James Spore, AICP, city manager of Garland, Texas; Linda Dalton, associate professor in the City and Regional Planning Department at California Polytechnic State University; Roger Hedrick, AICP, executive director of the Lafayette Areawide Planning Commission in Lafayette, Louisiana; David Spencer, director of community development in Gillette, Wyoming; George Farmer, AICP, secretary to the City Plan Board of Dayton, Ohio; Charles Hoch, professor in the School of Urban Planning and Policy at the University of Illinois at Chicago; Stuart Meck, AICP, assistant city manager and planning director of Oxford, Ohio; Ron Short, AICP, planning director of Phoenix; Howell Baum, professor in the Institute for Urban Studies at the University of Maryland; Mel Levin, AICP, director of the Community Planning Program at the University of Maryland; Floyd Lapp, AICP, director of the transportation division of the New York City department of city planning; Tom Meeks, AICP, director of planning services for the Greenwood County (S.C.) Planning Commission; Sy Schulman, AICP, president of the Westchester County Association in White Plains, New York; Anthony Catanese, AICP, president of the Florida Atlantic University; Michael Brooks, AICP, dean in the School of Community and Public Affairs at Virginia Commonwealth University; Bob Spaulding, planning director in San Diego, California;

Joel Goldsteen, AICP, professor in the School of Urban and Public Affairs at the University of Texas-Arlington; T. J. Cartwright, associate professor of Environmental Studies at York University; Richard Bernhardt, AICP, the director of planning and development in Orlando, Florida; Jerry Hiebert, AICP, development services director of Richardson, Texas; Jerome Kaufman, AICP, professor in the department of Urban and Regional Planning at the University of Wisconsin-Madison; Norman Krumholz, AICP, professor in the College of Urban Affairs at Cleveland State University; Letha Jacobson, AICP, planning director of Arlington, Texas; Richard Heath, AICP, planning director of Minneapolis, Minnesota; and Joseph L. Rodgers, Jr., AICP, retired director of the Department of Urban and Regional Planning at the University of Oklahoma.

I want to give special acknowledgment and a personal thank you to Bill Kirchhoff, the city manager of Redondo Beach, California. Kirchhoff is courageously leading the charge and challenging the city management profession to institute the radical reforms needed to make city managers more relevant and local governments more effective and responsive to their customers. With missionary zeal and fervor, he is attacking the outdated practices of contemporary managers and giving the following kind of advice:

> The private sector is taking away the management of many services traditionally thought to be the purview of the public manager—hospitals, social service clinics, fire departments, residential security, ambulance service, fleet maintenance, and libraries. This movement clearly demonstrates that much of what we public sector managers do can be done equally well and at a lower cost by entrepreneurs. We will become an extinct profession if we do not ask who our customers are and what they want us to do for them (Kirchhoff 1990).

Kirchhoff's leadership, vision and extraordinary dedication to customer service were an inspiration to me when I worked for him in Arlington, Texas, and his encouragement, support, and protection of my sometimes controversial work will never be forgotten.

I would also like to thank Douglas Harman, president and CEO of the Fort Worth Convention and Visitors Bureau, for contributing the sketches and cartoons found throughout the book.

Finally, I would like to thank Paul Thomas of APA's publications staff, who worked so hard to turn my manuscript into a finished book.

This acknowledgment of the people who gave assistance in my research is simply a way of thanking them for their help. It is not my intent to suggest that these individuals agree with or support any or all of my observations or conclusions.

Foreword

In the decade of the nineties, local governments will be facing massive change. This change is brought about by external as well as internal pressures, and many governments will not be able to weather the transition: they will lose their competitive edge, their local economies will decline, and their citizens will "vote with their feet" and abandon them for other, stronger communities.

What will make the difference in this difficult and dangerous journey of change management? The ability for each contributor in the local government experience (you, the reader) to become a strong participant in evolving partnerships, to appreciate the unifying cry of customer service, and to overhaul the old roles and structures and replace them with new ones that better fit the times of participatory demands, environmental concerns, and deep shifts in the demographics of our communities.

The planning profession is uniquely poised to take a leadership role in such a transition if it can shed its own cultural and intellectual "baggage" and live up to its own competitive strengths. As issues of sustainability, neighborhood redefinition, and cultural diversity dramatically redefine the political and financial landscape of local government, the demands are great for a new type of planning; not for putting together the "bricks and asphalt" of the future, but for assembling political visions and creating blueprints of economic activity for whole regions that will defy the traditional political boundaries of any single municipality or county. The emergence of strategic planning and other process management tools as a vital management instrument of the eighties is no fluke; what should be of concern is the slowness with which some traditional planners have moved towards capturing a role for themselves in this expanded planning approach. Like the Flatlanders of Edwin Abbott's mythical kingdom who lived in two dimensions and could not fathom the magnificence of a sphere (or the way a sphere presented itself in two dimensions), we sometimes continue to live in the two-dimensional world of physical planning and deny ourselves the paradigm-busting (to use a McClendon term) dimension of political action and customer perspective.

In approaching the future, the customer is, indeed, everything. But we must be careful in defining *who* that customer is. And, as in many other challenges, the definition of our objective is not simple. The "formula" that describes the customer may not be the same for all. But the search for a definition must be present everywhere, and its answer unambiguously understood before change can truly be managed. The journey that will snare this definition should follow a roadmap that looks at two different sides of the "skin" of local government: inside the organization, and outside in the community.

A simple truth many times forgotten is that the planning professional is arguably the best "process expert" inside a local government structure. These process skills and the understanding of the importance of anticipating change through a plan or action can be a real asset in a variety of departmental settings. The planner of the future would, therefore, be in a position to assist a potential internal "customer" and establish a stronger grip on the future by creating planning processes that respond to that client's changing environment and pressures. And to the citizen at large, the traditional departmental organization makes less and less sense as time goes on. Voices are being raised: "I don't care who provides the service as long as you help me get what I want . . . and by the way, why are there so many of you all doing small pieces of what I need?" Under such pressures, it will be essential to unify individual departments around a single customer orientation. And the planning process will be indispensable in this redefinition of internal organizational structure.

But we should not stop at the technical, staff dimensions of the internal customer. The political leadership in local government today is beset by clouds of change as well: Term limitations, single-issue special interest groups, and lack of revenues to fund demanded programs are all causing political leaders to search for new ways to approach the task of governance. And the planning professional can be an extremely helpful process creator and facilitator in this search. Whether running a goal-shaping retreat or establishing a joint vision for the community, the planner will be called on to take on new roles by this demanding customer.

The external customer will be very difficult to define. Consider the differing emotions and outlooks associated with these three constituents: the *consumer* of government services, the *inhabitant* of the community and the *taxpayer*. Each has legitimate concerns, and each is viewed differently by the internal elements of the government. And yet, if care is not taken to separate, classify, and organize a community's approach towards each constituent group thus defined, the end result of a customer orientation could well be devastating and counterproductive.

Once this external customer is properly identified, the practical requirements for service may seem overwhelming. Simply finding the customer, and listening to the concerns, needs, and aspirations can be a complex, expensive, and daunting task. Our communities are experiencing dramatic changes in their cultural and ethnic profiles; people with different expectations of government service are besieging us, and with needs that are difficult to describe and link to existing service offerings. The mechanisms we traditionally employ to hear the customer perspective are also not keeping pace with the reality of the "marketplace": surveys are too slow and expensive, and many times are biased by the very questions we are forced to ask. Hearings and community input processes come too late, at inconvenient times, and in physically constraining places that tend to increase the irritation level of our customers. So how can we be professionally responsive to a mandate to "hear the customer"? Through the modern wizardry of computers and telecommunications!

Today, information kiosks placed in grocery stores and shopping malls can inform the customer of needed services and hear their concerns and suggestions around the clock with a few touches of an electronic screen, and in the language of the user's choosing. Telephones can serve as instant polling places through voice mail and audiotex services. Plans and approval forms can be sent by fax lines, payments sped through credit card transactions, and interdepartmental coordination guaranteed through local area networks that force uniform review of plans in a single time frame. All these technologies are not elements of the future; they form the arsenal of today, and the planner who wants to be a player in the local government of the future must accept the challenge and learn the increasingly technology-based vocabulary of customer connections. Indeed, the very cycle of service that is presented in Chapter 6 can be dramatically rethought and made much closer to the customer if we consider the potential of information technology. The moment of truth shifts with a touch of technology. Consider the old: "driving to city hall . . . parking . . . finding a clerk . . . finding a map . . ." Now see the new: "customer picks up phone in home or office . . . dials 'map number' . . . types answers to brief questions using touch tone keys . . . fax machine downloads needed plat." An amazing transformation can indeed occur, if the planning profession is willing to reexamine tradition, form, and structure! This new technology can empower the customer to become more involved in the process of governance. And on the way, it can also create significant opportunities for cost reduction and, happily, revenue production—what has come to be called public enterprise. And at a time when privatization is considered to hold an almost mystical power and to be a golden panacea for all local ills, it is essential to take time and consider the strength, beauty, and responsiveness of public action under a customer orientation.

These new bold thoughts about customer service form part of Bruce McClendon's excellent offering, *Customer Service in Local Government: Challenges for Planners and Managers.* Using example after practical example, highlighting procedures that have actually worked in specific local governments, and with a strong dose of belief in the strength of local government as a relevant actor in shaping the future for society, Bruce has given all of us an excellent guide for the future. Planning is, after all, a process. And many may say that the process of planning far outweighs the value of the end result. If that is true (and I believe it is), then the planner of the future will have to become more of a process builder, a strategic team player perfectly attuned to the emergence of the almighty customer. And the advice within the pages of this guide helps to show the way through the chaos and institutional crises of today to a more logical, practical, and empowering way to find, listen to, and serve that all-important customer of our local government—the citizen of the Spaceship Earth . . .

Dr. Costis Toregas
President
Public Technology, Inc.

Introduction

Eugenie L. Birch, AICP, gave the keynote address at the 1990 annual conference of the American Planning Association. She stated that, based on her experience as coeditor of the *Journal of the American Planning Association*, there has never been a better, more rewarding, or more challenging time to be a planner (Birch 1990). I, too, have observed the growing public interest, recognition, and support for planning and have concluded that planning has never been more visible, more valued, and more effective than it is today. But it is my concern that the planning profession will misread this trend. Yes, there is incredible interest and support for planning. But it is for a new and different kind of planning—a planning that is unlike anything that most planners have been taught, seen, or done before.

Planning is "in," and it's "in" because it is being done better than ever. Some of the most common, essential characteristics of the planners that are responsible for planning's resurgence are:

• They work for their customers, not themselves. They get close to their clients, they listen to them, they care about them, and they involve them in the development, delivery, and ownership of useful, quality products and services. They create in writer and futurist Alvin Toffler's word "prosumers"—meaning they integrate production and consumption.

• They have a moral commitment to empowerment. They trust people and work to empower them to solve their own problems and to make them accountable for their actions.

• They understand and value the political decision-making process and they use consensus-building, conflict-resolution techniques, negotiation, and compromise to develop politically viable, collaborative solutions to tough problems. They respect and trust decision-makers and work hard to earn the trust and respect of those involved in the decision-making process.

• They know that effective planning means solving problems, not producing plans, reports, or studies. They have a bias for action and practice strategic planning. They use logical incrementalism to gradually and systematically achieve far-reaching goals and objectives.

• They deliver high-valued, streamlined plans, reports, and studies that emphasize communication and understandability. By shrinking the size of the product, they increase the ratio of value to product size and thereby increase the value and benefit of their work.

• They are committed to innovation and entrepreneurship. They constantly seek new clients and look for opportunities to develop needed products and services. They enhance existing products and discontinue outdated products and services. They make hard budget choices and "rightsize" their organizations, which maximizes their effectiveness and efficiency. They don't wait for change, they help create it.

• They are network builders, educators, coaches, cheerleaders, and team players. They enjoy their work and are fun to work with. They make others more productive and are considered to be an asset to the decision-making process. They are not lone wolves, isolated, arrogant, or utopian in thought. They are pragmatic problem solvers who believe in making a difference. They are valuable and they do make a difference.

My purpose in writing this book is to urge the planning profession to examine and evaluate itself and then to abandon the seriously flawed theories and practices that have alienated so many planners from the very people they are trying to serve. Most traditional planning theories are increasingly in conflict with the way planning is being practiced and with the results being reported from recent academic research. For planners, the hour is late and the stakes are great. What is now needed, in the words of Judith Innes de Neufville, an associate professor of city and regional planning at the University of California at Berkeley, is for the profession "to develop a new way of seeing the problems and the task of planning—to make a gestalt shift to a paradigm that will provide a more satisfactory mesh with reality, a more usable set of goals for practice, and a more fruitful direction for theoretical inquiry" (Innes 1986).

Innes is not the first, nor will she be the last, to call for a fundamental transformation in the practice of planning. The simple reality is that planning based on traditional theory, principles, and practices has repeatedly failed to produce results and satisfy customers. What is needed is a new framework for practice and a new paradigm that links theory and practice to results.

Just over 10 years ago, Harvey Perloff, then the longtime dean of the School of Architecture and Planning at the University of California at Los Angeles, wrote *Planning the Post-Industrial City* and offered these observations:

> Much of the content and style of urban planning today reflects *departures from* unsuccessful practices in the past—particularly reliance on a relatively rigid physical master plan to guide urban development and a largely intuitive and centralized approach to its creation—rather than *movement toward* any agreed upon new principles or practices. In part, this is a reasonable pulling away from old paradigms suggesting a sensible instinct for experimentation. However, it also reflects inadequate learning from past experience, a lag in practicing concepts that have already been well developed in theory, as well as an inadequate effort to create the new paradigms that hold promise for the future . . . not unexpectedly, a certain amount of confusion has accompanied the moving away from the previous dominant paradigm and the experimental search for effective new approaches to the problems of planning in our complex, troubled cities (Perloff 1980).

According to *Webster's Seventh New Collegiate Dictionary*, a theory is not facts but rather "the analysis of a set of facts in their relationship to one another." Theories are what makes it possible to transfer a large number of factual observations into a logical system of ideas that explains the real world in a coherent and understandable fashion. In science, there is no such thing as a bad theory, because if a theory fails to accommodate the facts and is not proven over time it is rejected and discarded.

Nineteenth-century physicists thought that space was occupied by a substance called ether, which was essential for the transmission of light waves. Michelson and Morley subsequently demonstrated that ether did not exist. Disproving this theory opened the way for Einstein to develop the theory of relativity.

Unproven theories can be dangerous if they mask our lack of understanding and discourage experimentation and progress toward future discoveries. For a long time, Isaac Newton's theory of gravity worked well and was useful to the scientific community. But as our knowledge of astronomy, physics, and mathematics grew, Newton's theory was no longer accurate. New theories were developed that did a better job of explaining and predicting events and relationships. So, too, must traditional planning theories be evaluated for their accuracy and usefulness and better theories developed to replace them. These theories need to be based on an open, receptive analysis of competent practitioners and effective practice.

Theories are more than mere speculative guesses by an investigator on a television mystery show. They must be grounded in facts and expressed in a way that can be tested and verified by observations. The theory itself may even suggest ways to verify its reliability. It may even lead observers to seek previously unknown facts that will support its conclusions.

Theories are shaped by paradigms. A paradigm is a set of beliefs, rules, or regulations that defines boundaries. Strongly held paradigms induce filtering and screening of information coming to the researcher. Paradigms affect our judgments and decisions by influencing our perceptions and the way we are able to look at reality.

During the notorious accident involving the Three Mile Island nuclear power plant, the plant's managers would not accept the data and measurements coming from their instruments. The information was not consistent with their expectations, so it was ignored with disastrous consequences to the plant and subsequently to the whole nuclear power industry.

Today the planning profession is suffering from its own form of meltdown, and it's happening right in front of the eyes of a large number of unseeing or uncaring scholars. Existing paradigms are filtering out incoming real world experiences and blocking the acceptance of new information. We must choose to change our paradigms if we want to see the world anew. Too many in the academic community suffer from paradigm paralysis. We need new theories and paradigm flexibility. In the words of Austrian anthropologist Konrad Lorenz, in his book *Behind the Mirror: A Search for a Natural History of Human Knowledge*, "truth in science can be defined as the working hypothesis best suited to open the way to the next better one." If we can have truth in lending laws, surely we can have truth in planning.

What was once a gap between planning theory and practice has become a gulf and immediate corrective action is now warranted. Many traditional planning theories do not reflect reality and are actually impediments to effective practice and to the development of new theories that are capable of explaining how planning can be made more effective. Don't misunderstand what I am trying to say. I am not suggesting a reduced emphasis on research. In fact, the continued examination of the theory and practice of planning is essential if researchers are to assist practitioners, and vice versa, in their efforts to advance the profession. What is being proposed is that scholars should be placing a higher priority on research and teaching that will improve the skills, capacities, and effectiveness of public sector planners. More courses must be developed that reflect a combination of both theory and practice. The MRCP and other similar degrees are terminal professional degrees and the academic community's failure to fully address the practice needs of planning students is troubling. There is just not enough evidence of a widespread conscious effort to link theory to successful practice.

Today the planning profession is at a true crossroads. Nothing less than the future of the profession may be at stake. We can continue to support the failed utopian theories and practices of the past or we can instead be paradigm busters and lead the way to a more exciting, more rewarding, and more effective profession. A few researchers and practitioners are leading the way and speaking out. They are aggressively discarding failed theories and outdated concepts and developing innovative techniques and practices that produce results. They are becoming effective and they are making a difference.

Based on a combination of almost 25 years of experience as a practicing planner, years of inquisitive research, hundreds of interviews with planners and public officials, and a lot of reading, I have concluded that the paradigm governing traditional planning theory is not consistent with the emerging principles, strategies, and tactics that are being successfully used by effective city planners. It is time for the profession to critically reexamine the traditional theories of planning and to develop new theories and ideas that mesh with the realities of successful practice. This will take courage and a willingness to fail as new paradigms are developed and tested, but it must be done.

I, like many other practitioners, have rejected such mainstay traditional planning theories as the comprehensive rational approach, advocacy planning, and apolitical planning. In their place I have attempted to propose a pragmatic theory of planning based, in Charles Hoch's words, "on human experience, practical activity and democratic community participation, but without the naturalistic bias and liberal pluralism incorporated in mainstream planning theories'' (Hoch 1984). It is a theory based on the following assumptions:

- planning is a service profession that cannot continue to ignore the frustrations, expectations, and demands of customers or the marketplace;
- planning is part of a political process and this country is shifting from a representative democracy to a participatory, collaborative democracy;
- people (the customers) must be trusted to make decisions for themselves and must be encouraged to solve their own problems and to take responsibility for their present condition;
- face-to-face collaborative problem solving is more effective than top-down decision making;
- the public itself should be the primary arbiter of what constitutes the public interest;
- incrementalism and strategic planning are much more effective techniques than traditional comprehensive planning;
- the rational planning theory is irrational;
- advocacy planners were not really advocates;
- the planning process is not a linear sequence but rather is interactive with implementation being intertwined with every part of the process.

Planners need to understand that effective planning means providing needed and useful products and services to their customers and clients. Most public sector planners display a disturbing reluctance to regard the people they are planning with, or for, as "customers." Many of these planners even have a resistance to using the words customer and client. Why is this so? One public agency planner told me that to refer to people as customers would cheapen and demean the practice of planning. He argued, "We're not Wal-Mart," and he was right. Wal-Mart is much more successful and much more effective at serving its customers than most planners are.

Webster's Seventh New Collegiate Dictionary defines client as "a person who engages the professional services of another" and customer as "one that purchases a commodity or service usually systematically or frequently" or "one that patronizes or uses services." It is interesting to note that planning consultants have no hesitation when it comes to treating their contacts as clients or customers. Even elected officials are starting to appreciate the concept of customer service. Henry Cisneros, the former four-term mayor of San Antonio, advises that "government agencies must adopt programs and attitudes that allow them to be much closer and responsive to citizens, their 'customers'" (Cisneros 1991).

Public sector planners need a wake-up call. In addressing the 1990 annual conference of the International City Management Association, Costis Toregas, president of Public Technology, Inc., stated: "Customers are the dominant driving force in the private sector and 'the customer' must become the primary focus and dominant driving force in government." Former San Antonio city manager Lou Fox tells me, "For government, everyone is a customer."

The goal of every planner should be to treat everyone like a customer and to provide them with effective planning services. To me, effective planning is a remarkably simple concept. It is planning that makes a difference, produces results, and, most of all, is satisfying to our customers. It is important, says Guy Benveniste, author of *Mastering the Politics of Planning*, that planning ". . . is worthwhile. That it pleases some, that it helps, that it solves a problem, that it is enduring, that it is esthetic, grand, beautiful. That we like it" (Benveniste 1989).

According to Fred Bair, Jr., one of the planning profession's most respected practitioners, "the only true measure of the success of planning is the amount and kind of action it induces, guides, or prevents" (Bair, Jr. 1970). In the wisdom and words of Harvey Perloff, "planners must look to the effectiveness of implementation as the measure of success. Only when plans and programs are actually carried through, and the outcomes closely approximate those desired, can the whole planning operation be thought to be worthwhile" (Perloff 1980). Unfortunately, after reviewing the annual reports of numerous planning agencies recently, Linda Dalton, associate professor in the city and regional planning department at California Polytechnic State University, concludes that planners "were more concerned with documenting workload than with demonstrating effectiveness in planning" (Dalton 1989).

Effective planning that is customer-oriented is usually measurable and quantifiable through the use of customer surveys and questionnaires. Just as you consider yourself successful if you achieve what you set out to do, so do your customers. Effective planning depends on delivering products and services that are needed, wanted, and valued by customers, and that satisfy them. Satisfaction is the key objective because, as retailing authority Stanley Marcus has said, "if you don't satisfy, the customer doesn't come back."

In my first book, *Mastering Change,* Ray Quay, AICP, and I argued that planners needed to focus as never before on providing problem-solving assistance and services that produce meaningful results. It was pointed out that few, if any, citizens believed planners offered any direct benefits to them or were very effective in solving important local problems. We quoted Howell Baum, an associate professor in the School of Social Work and Community Planning at the University of Maryland, who stated, "in the present public mind 'planners' are linked with the seeming multitude of public programs which cost vast amounts in taxes and accomplish apparently little" (Baum 1983).

I continue to preach that helping and empowering customers to find and solve their own problems is the key to relevance and effectiveness for planners. The negative public perceptions of planning have been improved when results have been produced. Winning is a powerful change agent and planners have been and can be winners. The recent Persian Gulf conflict is an excellent example of what I have been talking about. Before the war, the military was associated with many of the worst characteristics of government bureaucracy. There was a widespread perception of incompetency created by purchasing fiascos, the lack of military success in Vietnam, the failed Iranian hostage rescue attempt, and the Lebanon disaster. Most if not all the negative perceptions of military incompetence have been transformed by the stunningly swift victory over Iraq. The term "military leader" is no longer an oxymoron and Norman Schwarzkopf and other officers are being touted for public office and high-level positions in private industry.

Winning planners are also leading the way to increased relevance and respect for the planning profession. In writing this book I am indebted to the many courageous planners who have taken risks and dared to break the rules in order to provide effective services to their customers. They are in the forefront of what is truly a revolution in the practice of planning. All across this country, paradigms are being smashed and new reality-based theories, procedures, and practices are being developed. For ineffective planners, the days of "drinking that free Bubble Up and eating that rainbow stew" are gone. As one planner warned, "You had better watch out. One moment you're a peacock, and the next you're a feather duster." Effective planners will be put on pedestals and ineffective ones will be put on notice. Who will survive and thrive in this new world?

Successful planners have changed the basic ways they practice in order to increase their effectiveness and are delivering the needed useful products and services and, most importantly, the results that the public is demanding. I believe that their work and the research and findings discussed in this book will lead to the development and acceptance of a new pragmatic theory of planning and new ways of practice that will link the concepts of customer service and effective city planning. The choice is yours. You can lead, you can follow, or you can ask, "What happened?"

REFERENCES

Bair, Jr., F. 1970. *Planning Cities*. Chicago: American Planning Association.

Baum, H. 1983. *Planners and Public Expectations*. Cambridge, Massachusetts: Schenkman Publishing Company, Inc.

Benveniste, G. 1989. *Mastering the Politics of Planning*. San Francisco: Jossey-Bass Publishers.

Birch, E. 1990. "The Bloom Is on the Rose." *Journal of the American Planning Association* Vol. 56, No. 2.

Cisneros, H. 1991. "Reinvigorating Democratic Values: Challenge and Necessity." *Public Management* Vol. 73, No. 2.

Dalton, L. 1989. "The Limits of Regulation—Evidence from Local Plan Implementation in California." *Journal of the American Planning Association* Vol. 55, No. 2.

Hoch, C. 1984. "Doing Good and Being Right." *Journal of the American Planning Association* Vol. 50, No. 3.

Innes, J. 1986. "Visible Planning Theory: An Agenda for Research and Education." *Strategic Perspectives on Planning Practice*. Lexington, Massachusetts: Lexington Books.

Kirchhoff, B. 1990. "Babbitt Could Have Been a Manager." *Public Management* Vol. 72, No. 11.

Perloff, H. 1980. *Planning the Post-Industrial City*. Chicago: Planners Press.

The Concept of Customer Service and Effective City Planning

THE SERVICE CRISIS

It is increasingly being recognized that there is a real crisis in customer service. The business world knows this and so do its clients and customers, who are growing increasingly vocal about the poor service they are receiving. Do you personally know anyone or any organization that is delivering outstanding service? Most of us have heard many more stories about horrible personal service experiences than good reports.

There is general agreement that there has been a significant decline in recent years in quality of service. In response to the question of "How well do service companies meet your needs and concerns as a consumer?" Cambridge Reports found that only eight percent of consumers answered "excellent," 50 percent responded "good," but 42 percent said "fair" or "poor." In addition, more than one in three of those surveyed contended that "service industries care less than they did a few years ago about meeting my needs" (Zemke and Schaaf 1989).

In the movie *Back to the Future*, a young Michael J. Fox was transported back to the early 1950s. He adjusted well to most of the conditions he found but was clearly surprised when he passed a "service station" and saw four uniformed men servicing a car by checking the oil, cleaning the windshields, testing the air pressure in the tires, and filling the car's fuel tank with gasoline. Even those of us who lived in the 1950s and can remember seeing this kind of service were shocked by the contrast to

1

today's self-service stations staffed with an attendant sitting behind bulletproof glass.

Planes, Trains and Automobiles was a more recent movie that ridiculed the transportation service industry. In one scene, Steve Martin is taken by bus from the airport to a distant rent-a-car lot and abandoned with the keys to a nonexistent car. He suffers emotional trauma, damage to his clothing and belongings, and physical injury in his harrowing journey on foot back to the rental agency, which is now out of cars. In response to his mistreatment, Martin directs a violent, emotional outburst at the counter clerk. And when he cannot produce a receipt, the clerk cheerfully replies, "You've been f _ _ _ ed."

This was a very outrageous scene, but it doesn't greatly distort or exaggerate the extent of the perceived decline in the quality of customer service. One of my friends recently told me of the following experience: His children came home from school one day and could not get in their house. They did not have a house key and relied on the garage door opener—which would not work—to get inside. The children spent the afternoon with a neighbor. When their parents came home that evening, they found a note attached to the front door explaining that their electrical service had been cut off for failure to pay their utility bill. But they had the canceled check to prove it had been paid. Later that evening their electricity was restored. Mistakes can happen, but what my friend remembers is that the company expressed no remorse nor offered any apology. But the utility company did say they would be nice guys and not require another security deposit or charge the family for turning their power back on.

When collecting information for this book, I attempted to call the planning director for the city of Los Angeles to arrange an interview. On my first long-distance call, a computer answered and quickly gave a lengthy list of phone numbers for an impressive array of planning functions. At the conclusion of the message, the machine stated that the list would not be repeated. Unfortunately, nothing in the list had sounded anything like administration, so I had not written down any numbers. A second long-distance call was placed, and this time I wrote down the number for zoning information, assuming that this would lead me to someone that might know how to get in touch with the planning director. On my third long-distance call, I again got to listen to a computer and was told that a "telephone technician" would be available only between the hours of 10:00 and 11:30a.m., and then the call was disconnected. I was not a happy camper and wondered what life must be like for a zoning applicant or someone else in Los Angeles that wanted to talk with a live planner. Voice mail and other telecommunication technology can be used to improve public service but, unfortunately, it can also be used to fend off the public and alienate customers.

Recently, a zoning inspector in a major city notified an off-premise sign company that a particular sign was in violation of the zoning ordinance. The company was told to remove the sign or be subject to a fine of $1,000 a day for each day the sign remained. The sign company quickly had the sign taken down at considerable expense. I was surprised to read about a sign company responding so quickly to a violation notice, but that is not the point of this story. What is significant is that when the sign company's representative went to the planning department to verify that all of its other signs were in compliance with zoning, she learned that the inspector had made a mistake and the sign they had just removed was, in fact, a legal sign. This example of poor customer service made the front page of the local newspaper and received national publicity when the sign company subsequently filed a lawsuit for damages against the city.

Boards and commissions have a high visibility service function that can influence the public's perception of local government. A significant number of people have direct involvement with various commissions at public hearings and in many communities these hearings are shown on cable television and covered by the news media. Stuart Meck, past president of the American Planning Association (1990–91) and assistant city manager in Oxford, Ohio, contends that "there are many cities, unfortunately, where the public hearing process is run like a garage sale" (Enos 1991). Meck is particularly concerned about the negative impact that insensitive boards have on the public's image of the regulatory process and on its faith in local government. For example, a well organized neighborhood group recently appeared before a board of adjustment to protest the request for a special exception for a helistop. The planning department staff report recommended denial of the request because it would be incompatible with the adjacent residential area. The applicant was a helicopter pilot, and he readily admitted a helistop was not compatible with a residential environment. The zoning ordinance specified that a special exception could be approved by the board only if it was found to be "wholly compatible" with surrounding development. In approving the special exception, board members reasoned that the public didn't appear to understand the situation, that helicopters don't make as much noise as most people think, and, besides, the applicant has the right to the full enjoyment of his property. At the same meeting, a citizen who asked for the sound system to be turned up was curtly admonished by the board's longtime chairman to move to the front of the chamber. This same chairman also later asked the city council to deny an ordinance that had been developed by "idealistic" planners and that had broad public support, because of the hearing workload it might create for the board. So much for the concept of service to the public.

Here is another anecdote that illustrates poor customer service. Steve Baumhover, a graduate planning student at Iowa State University, was doing research on the city of Ramapo, New York. Ramapo had developed a growth management program in 1966 and, in a landmark legal case, the New York supreme court upheld the system. Several years later, the city ceased using the approved system. Baumhover wanted information on why it was repealed and wanted to know about the growth and development of Ramapo since the action was taken. First he called the information operator to get a number for the planning department. The operator could not find a number for planning but was able to give him a listing for city hall. Baumhover called city hall, and was soon cheerfully transferred to the city attorney's office. Unfortunately, no one in the office had any recollection of the case or anything that resulted from it. Upon further inquiry, he was given the phone number of the consultant that handles the planning for the city. Baumhover called the number and reached the receptionist at the planning firm. She informed him that the planner was in a meeting and that she would leave a message for the planner to call him back. When the call was not returned the next day, Baumhover again called the planning firm and the receptionist explained that the planner was in a meeting and that she would have him return the call.

Over the next several days, Baumhover repeated the process and received the same results each time. On the sixth call, he explained to the receptionist that he only needed five minutes of the consultant's time. She replied, "Mr. . . . was busy and had a lot of meetings and did not want to be bothered between these meetings." Baumhover reported that in a final attempt to get the information he needed, he called city hall one more time. None of the people he talked to could help him, but they did offer to sell him a copy of the zoning ordinance and subdivision regulations for $25 (Baumhover 1990).

In *The Service Advantage*, Karl Albrecht and Lawrence Bradford wonder "do government agencies know what a customer is?" (Albrecht and Bradford 1990). They report that when a governmental office recently surveyed its employees, one responded by complaining about the "public" that always seemed to arrive between 4:30 and 5 p.m., just before closing time. This employee preferred that people would come in at a time more convenient to him.

Albrecht and Bradford, consultants specializing in service management, are especially concerned about the increasingly poor service they are observing in government. In this vein they offer the following damning comments:

> Some government agencies should change their sign from 'take a number' to 'be a number' because that is the way they treat their customers all too frequently—as a faceless number in a long day of faceless numbers. It's a case of being unwilling or unable to view the customer as a source of valuable information for improving the quality of government service. Citizens are not viewed as customers who pay taxes for the government services (there's an oxymoron) that they are supposed to receive. We've reached the point where we hesitate to work with governmental agencies who want to become service-driven because of the near-impossible task of changing bureaucratic systems (Albrecht and Bradford 1990).

I have not seen any planning departments that have a 'take a number' sign, probably because most don't have enough customers. However, I have seen signs in planning departments that suggest an attitude of indifference or insensitivity to the public and a willingness to put the staff first. In one planning department a planner had a sign on his office wall that stated: "If you're in such a hurry, maybe you'd better go away and come back when you have more time." Another sign in another agency read: "This is not Burger King. You don't get it your way. You take it my way or you don't get the son of a bitch."

A critical examination of the effectiveness and efficiency of services that are being provided in most local governments will usually reveal significant shortcomings. If you discover that service is poor, admit it and get on with improving it. Customers can be very forgiving and understanding if they believe you are really repentant and that you are

"FRIENDLY" SERVICE

sincerely trying to make things right. Customers respect and appreciate an apology for poor service and bureaucrats need to be less protective and more trusting in their customer relationships. Sometimes, however, in recognizing and attempting to correct poor service the problem is compounded by an unwillingness to admit to past failings. For example, for two years the city of Austin, Texas, had been publishing *Growth Watch*, a quarterly demographic/statistical publication. On February 1, 1991, subscribers to *Growth Watch* received a mailed notice informing them that the planning department was intending to redefine the scope of the publication and to upgrade the reporting format. The notice stated, "In undertaking this project, we intend to provide, not only a more comprehensive, informative and reliable document, but a more timely and therefore useful product as well. By developing a more integrated and flexible production process, we hope to cut our publication time in half. In order to accomplish this task, we will be temporarily suspending publication for two quarters. The 1990 third and fourth quarter issues will not be published. The annual 1989 issue should be out shortly."

What a mess. Subscribers to *Growth Watch* had not received their last two issues, the annual 1989 issue would be published in 1991, and the planners were suspending publication for six months so they could redefine and upgrade the scope of the publication. I particularly was intrigued by the goal of the publishers to cut their publication time in half. Half of what? Were they going to start publishing an issue every six weeks, or by cutting production time in half did this mean they would try to be an on-time quarterly publication. This notice could not have given the subscribers much confidence in the planning department or the future of *Growth Watch.* Telling their customers that they were suspending publication for six months to improve the product when it had not been published for six months comes across like a weak and transparent excuse for failing to meet their responsibilities. Besides creating doubt about the integrity of the planning staff and the viability of the publication, they further alienated their customers by informing them that the suspension of the publication would not affect their subscription status. Rather than offering customers a clearly deserved refund, the planning department announced that subscribers would continue to receive future issues as they were published for the duration of their subscriptions. Under the circumstances, subscribers should have been given the option of a refund or received an extended subscription as compensation or mitigation for poor service.

People are fed up with excuses for poor service. Increasingly hostile and unforgiving customers are demanding and expecting better products and services from both the public and private sector. The perceived decline in the value and quality of customer service is probably worse in the public sector and city planners are facing challenging times. In many communities, the public's basic attitude toward government is becoming ugly and mean spirited. Frustration, alienation, and skepticism has evolved into cynicism. The term "public servant" seems to be a synonym for "parasitic incompetent."

Many people believe that government at all levels has simply gotten too big and that it is too intrusive into their lives. At one recent council meeting I heard such comments as: "If we hadn't have stood up, you jerks at city hall would've run over us"; "You government people are a joke"; and "I don't want any government input on how to run my personal life."

The public has a general negative opinion of the local government bureaucracy and it is quick to take the side of any complaining citizen. At a recent council meeting a resident lambasted the city staff. She had been given a violation notice to remove her carport, which had been constructed in violation of the front-yard setback ordinance and without benefit of a building permit. The inspector told her the city had received a complaint and that she had 10 days to remove the carport or be subject to a fine of up to $1,000 a day. Addressing the council, she said that 10 days was not adequate notice, and exclaimed, "Heck, in 10 days, I couldn't even find out who I was supposed to talk to at city hall!" She got a big laugh and ovation from a clearly sympathic audience. The public instinctively likes to believe that government employees are incompetent and citizens are quick to accept any testimony which confirms and reinforces their natural inclinations.

THE REBELLION OF THE ELECTORATE

According to four-term former San Antonio mayor Henry Cisneros, citizens in alarming numbers "are becoming increasingly disengaged from public affairs, uninterested in the political process and public institutions, and skeptical that government has the talent, resources, and moral courage to solve problems" (Cisneros 1991). The electorate is growing increasingly sullen and rebellious and citizens are actively searching for opportunities to get even. Unlike many other service industries, there are limited competitive alternatives to many government functions and services. But customers without real choices in the political marketplace are still finding ways to express their anger and register their dissatisfaction. Voters in Oklahoma, Colorado, and California are leading the way. In what can only be interpreted as a no-confidence vote in public officials, voters in these states overwhelmingly decided in 1990 to limit the length of time that individuals can serve in elected office. In Oklahoma, voters decided by a two to one margin to limit state legislators to 12 years in office. Colorado voters have placed a similar 12-year cap on elected service and extended it to include that state's delegation in Congress. And in California, voters have approved an initiative that limits the terms of state officeholders and also mandates a lifetime ban from office once the term limit has been reached. At the local government level, Kansas City voted to limit the mayor and council members to two consecutive four-year terms and to make it retroactive. The public is fed up with a system that protects career politicians and is doing something about it.

It has been argued that one reason the quality of government services has declined is that arrogant public officials are insulated and protected from their everyday customers and clients. A *New York Times* and CBS News poll released in November of 1990 found that 77 percent of those surveyed "believe government is run by a few big interests looking out for themselves rather than for the benefit of all the people." There is a collapse of faith in the belief that government and politicians can make things better and there is pessimism about the future—a characteristic that is contrary to the historically optimistic "can-do" spirit of faith in this nation's ability to solve problems.

Opposition to new taxes and support for cutbacks in government at all levels are also increasing in popularity. I remember a story about an angry taxpayer who exclaimed, "The public's money is a lot like drugs. It's very easy to become addicted to it." His solution: "Send the county supervisors to a tax detox center." The general feeling is that if government can't provide the kind and quality of services that are needed by the average person, then at least the cost of local government and the tax rate can be reduced. All in all, it is a hostile and demanding environment. Local government planners are reporting that the people they are trying to serve are getting smarter, more sophisticated, and more demanding. The public, our clients, wants value and quality for its tax dollars and it is becoming increasingly difficult to satisfy. The general public doesn't know what planners do and, whatever it is, doesn't feel it is relevant to their lives.

Planning is a service profession and planners cannot ignore the frustrations, expectations, and demands of their clients. The profession must come to grips with such basic questions as: What is planning? Who are we planning for? and How can we do a better job of serving and satisfying our customers? Unfortunately, service is ephemeral and good service is difficult to define and hard to explain. Good service is also an elusive target because different customers expect different things and their needs and expectations are constantly changing. But the overwhelming contemporary public image that planners must face and overcome is that the government can't do anything very well.

PLANNING AND PLANNERS ARE UNDER ATTACK

Planning is being attacked both from within the profession and from the outside by the customers of plans—the people. With respect to academia, Norman Krumholz, the former planning director for Cleveland and past president of the American Planning Association (1986–87), tells me, "Most planning scholars are contemptuous of, and offended by, what practitioners actually do as planners." Krumholz and Robert Mier, who is on the faculty at the University of Illinois at Chicago, wrote in a joint commentary for *Planning* magazine that they "were struck at the last annual meeting of the Association of Collegiate Schools of Planning by the widening gap between planning education and practice— between the ideas of teachers of planning and the actions of working planners" (Krumholz and Mier 1987). Mel Levin, the director of the community planning program at the University of Maryland and past president of the American Institute of Certified Planners, complains that within the profession "there is an unfortunate tendency toward self-flagellation with planners excoriating planning," and he laments that "practitioners are less glib and convincing on the defense than their professorial persecutors" (Levin 1987).

Even when planning appears to work it is subject to criticism and rejection. *Planning* magazine reported that Andres Duany, a neotraditionalist planner/architect, told a large audience in Folsom, California, that their award-winning master plan "is a recipe for disaster" and that "you are building yourself a really lousy place" (Knack 1989). He argued that third-rate planning and city planners were the culprits responsible for the mess.

My principal concern and objection to much of the academic and some of the professional criticism of planning is that it is all too often directed at the planners who are taking risks, breaking the rules, and pioneering new strategies and practices. As evidenced by what is found in this book, the main thrust of my criticism is aimed at those planners and academics who have failed to make the needed adjustment from ineffective traditional theories to real world practice. Most of the public's criticism is valid and should be a cause for greater concern within the profession. Our customers are trying to tell us something.

The intended beneficiaries of planning also are increasingly willing to express their dissatisfaction. In May of 1989, Seattle residents voted overwhelmingly to limit annual development of downtown office space and to restrict building heights, despite the adoption of a conflicting comprehensive CBD plan only four years before. In recent years, Sarasota County, Florida, won several awards for its 1981 growth management plan and much praise for its efforts with citizen participation in community planning. Sarasota's state-mandated comprehensive plan was approved in 1989 by the Florida Department of Community Affairs, only to be followed by Florida's first countywide moratorium referendum.

In early November of 1990, the Maryland Chapter of the American Planning Association recognized Uri Avin, AICP, as its planner of the year for his contribution to the profession and his substantial personal commitment to getting the general plan for Howard County approved. Yet later that month, Avin was fired. Days later, the plan received the national APA award for comprehensive planning. Charles Ecker, the newly elected county executive, did not explain the firing other than to say "a lot of these jobs are subject to the whims of the county executive" and that Avin "doesn't know how to deal with people" (Gallagher 1991). In summary, the national award committee liked the general plan and the local committee liked the planner, but unfortunately the public never accepted the plan and the guy who did the hiring and firing rejected the planner. What message do you think this conveys about award-winning planning and planners?

Over the years, the primary challenge for the planning profession has been to provide meaningful and effective products and services to the community and to its clients. Early city planning efforts were clearly associated with "good government" and reformist elements and were based on a desire to protect the community from bossism and corruption in local government. Semiautonomous planning commissions both protected and isolated planners from elected officials and their various plans and studies were easily ignored. These early planning experts were increasingly seen as irrelevant elitists. People are drawn toward power and authority and the profession responded over time by changing its focus from independence and autonomy to linkage with and dependency on the executive branch. More recently, planners have learned they can become more effective by being sensitive and responsive to the needs of the legislative branch and by demonstrating technical competence and value in the production and delivery of useful products and services to the private sector.

Mel Levin advises that planning agencies must be perceived as efficient and useful by the public at large, business and civic groups, and the officials that make budgetary decisions. He contends that, "In general, flourishing planning agencies are not viewed as alien and ideological but as pragmatic and user-friendly. They are seen as approachable and understandable vehicles for doing well the things that elected officials and their constituencies want done. To the neighborhoods and local Rotary Club, the planning director is 'one of us,' not a faceless bureaucrat" (Levin 1985).

What planners need to keep in mind is that change is a natural process and that we should welcome and even seek to accelerate the evolution of the profession. The most positive aspect of the changes happening within the planning profession is the growing recognition of the need to be more responsive and more effective in our relationships with our vast array of possible clients. The very nature of the products and services that are developed and delivered by planners must be shaped by the constantly changing needs of their clients. Only in this way can planners consistently provide meaningful and effective service.

The growing general crisis in customer service and dissatisfaction with traditional ineffective planning services is both a threat and an opportunity for planners. Historically, planners have been able to adjust very well to the changing nature and role of planning. Since the inception of city planning, planners have alternatively functioned as social workers, architects, city managers, regulators, policy analysts, and economic development specialists. The wide range of opportunities for today's planners is partly responsible for much of the existing confusion, concerns, and disagreement within the planning community as to what planning is and what planners should be doing. Change is inevitable. If the planning profession attempts to insulate itself from change and to ignore market realities, then planners are an endangered species. Planning will still be important, it just won't be done by planners.

In the classic movie *Atlantic City*, there is a memorable scene where Burt Lancaster, an aging numbers runner for the mob, remembers what the city was like in its heyday. According to Lancaster everything was bigger, brighter and better in the old days. Walking along the Boardwalk he points out toward the water and exclaims, "The Atlantic Ocean . . . yeah, it was really something then."

During the 1970s and 1980s, planners created problems for themselves because of a failure and inability to render useful and valued customer service. Despair and self-doubt permeated the air at national conferences as older, Lancaster-like planners relived past glories and reported continuing declines in their status as planning drifted toward the bottom of the governmental food chain. UCLA planning professor John Friedmann found in surveys that nine out of 10 planners thought their work was a failure; planners lamented that "we no longer know what to do. Our solutions don't work. The problems are mounting" (Friedmann 1987). This sense of failure was widespread and evident at all levels of practice. Lynnis Jameson, AICP, an experienced assistant director of neighborhood development in Kansas City, Missouri, often tells me that, in government, no one really cares about what planners do except planners. Professor Michael Brooks reported that "the planning office in many communities does little more than administer the local zoning process" and "it is increasingly difficult to identify cities in which professional planners play strong roles in shaping the physical—much less the social and economic—structure of the community" (Brooks 1988). The recently retired and highly respected longtime planning director of a large midwestern city told me that his professional life was a failure. He could point to nothing that resulted from his years of public service. He said he wanted to write a book about his professional life and he was going to call it *Squandered Fortune: The Irrelevant Life and Times of a "701" Planner.*

There are planners, of course, that are making a big difference. Eugenie Birch, the coeditor of the *Journal of the American Planning Association,* entitled her keynote address at the 1990 annual conference of the American Planning Association, "The Bloom is on the Planning Rose" (Birch 1990). She observed that "today's proliferation of planning activities is unprecedented" and that "at this moment popular support for planning is growing by leaps and bounds."

But while noting that planning is ascendant and is positioned as it has never been before, Birch questioned if planners are as well positioned as the profession itself. She asked, "In the coming decade, the demand for our skills will be high, but are we equipped with the technical expertise, vision, political savvy, and salesmanship required to meet the need, or are we going to let others fill it instead of us?"

ARE PLANNERS SERVING THEIR CUSTOMERS OR THEMSELVES?

Once I overheard an associate planner complain as he hung up the phone, "Hell, I wish people would quit interrupting me. I have important work to do." Now this statement was made by a planner whose job required extensive interaction with the public. This planner had no understanding of the linkage between customer service and effective city planning. In talking with him, he made it clear that the most important part of his job was not dealing with the public, but rather producing technical studies, reports, and plans. He whined that if he only had less contact with the public he could be much more productive. Unfortunately, his response is all too typical of many planners. In my experience, most planners, particularly younger ones, don't like working with the public and find this to be the most unsatisfactory and unrewarding aspect of their job. Their primary motivation is to satisfy themselves.

Some of you may be surprised to learn that there are planners who practice and receive a salary without providing useful services to anyone. In reality, it's easy to be a clientless planner. Such planners, regardless of the fact that they report to some higher managerial or political authority, exercise independent thought and judgment. They see themselves as expert visionaries that can't be bothered by the problems of the public, though the public interest is their guiding light. Aaron Wildavsky provides the following warning about such well-intentioned bureaucratic planners: "Bureaucrats are supposed to see themselves as public servants. They serve society by protecting it from itself; they serve the state by protecting it from becoming society. Here we have a concept of a public interest without the public. At long last we know what the public interest is, namely an interest not held by anyone in society" (Wildavsky 1988).

T. J. Kent, Jr., a respected authority on comprehensive planning, found growing popularity among planners in the 1960s for the notion that the principal client of the general plan should be the professional staff. Some planners, according to Kent, consider city planning to be too technical to be understood by laypersons, including those laymen who become elected officials, and believe city planners are best suited to interpret the public interest. Kent noted that planners who hold such views "sometimes prepare plans for themselves to use as a basis for making recommendations to the city planning commission or chief executive, but they do not reveal their plans" (Kent 1964). Another related but more common failing involves preparing a large, complex comprehensive planning document, getting it adopted by an overwhelmed planning commission and city council, and then using it against the adopting body to challenge its decisions. It makes for controversial news stories, bad relations between staff and decision makers, and ineffective planning.

Why make such a big deal over a few independent autocratic planners? My response is that the above characteristics fit a surprisingly large number of planners. In fact, Howell Baum, in his book on *Planners and Public Expectations,* concludes that most planners have followed the traditional model of such professionals as physicians and lawyers (Baum 1983). These planners have attempted to set themselves off as experts who have independence from and power over their customers. They don't need clients but their clients need them. They can pump out solutions to problems without ever having to engage the people they are supposed to be working for. They have succeeded in reversing the relationship between client and staff.

Professor Baum found that *only* 44 percent of all the planners in his surveys "look for supportive feedback from their immediate client or from the constituency for or with whom they are planning." When planners working for private consulting firms were excluded, Baum's responses showed that less than 25 percent of public agency planners used client praise as an indicator of their effectiveness. One planner included the following comment in his or her survey response: "I am concerned about my satisfaction period. . . . Sometimes I am doing bits of work, and I am able to say it is a good piece of work, whether they like it or not." Baum's research confirmed my findings that a large percentage of planners, particularly those working in local governmental planning organizations, are their own best clients. I suspect the percentage may even be higher for planners in federal agencies.

The traditional role of planners as free-lance intellectuals and independent, autonomous professional visionaries is seriously flawed. The Edmund Bacon model of the autocratic and domineering planner trying to "tell" people what to do is no longer a workable strategy for effective planning. Neotraditionalists, such as Miami architect Andres Duany, are only the latest example of planners who attack the physical form of existing cities and impose their own lifestyles, values, and design ideals on others. Noted planner Jane Jacobs has spoken eloquently on behalf of large cities with traditional values: dense, central areas characterized by a mixed-use, mixed-age, three- to six-story urban form focusing on an active corridor-street pedestrian life. She has argued that "people should not scatter in panic from central cities . . . they should build more of them, bigger and better" (Hill 1988). Jacobs views low-density urban areas, suburbs, villages, and rural areas as "urban form examples of life's sometimes greatest vices: stagnation, homogeneity, and boredom."

Over the last quarter-century, Jane Jacobs has unmercifully attacked the planning profession. Since suburbia, not Greenwich Village, has been the dream and preferred urban form for the average American, it must be the planners' fault. David Hill, an authority on Jacobs, seriously questions the psychological basis on which Jacobs concludes that people want diversity in their working and living environment. He asks, "Does a creative, entrepreneurial 'city type' of person exist, or is Jacobs saying we are all potentially 'city types' but that society is so badly organized that some of us must suppress our true desires for city living and settle for suburbia and rural areas" (Hill 1988)?

Hill's questioning of Jacob's philosophy is appropriate. Obviously, there are "city types" that want to be "rural types" or "suburbia types." For example, the Pierce family lives in Chicago's notoriously violent Cabrini Green high-rise housing project. A reporter interviewing the family wrote that after a sudden burst of gunfire was heard from outside the building, 13-year-old Julie said that she wanted to live in the country, where her family could have picnics and not worry about people shooting out windows (Freedman 1990).

Jacobs has also consistently opposed the ideas of such well-known and respected planners as Lewis Mumford, Charles LeCorbusier, and Ebenezer Howard. Frank Lloyd Wright proposed a decentralized urban pattern that he called "Broadacre City" that was the reverse of LeCorbusier's teachings. Broadacre City, a visionary amalgam of country and city, was to be a four-square-mile, self-contained community of approximately 1,400 families, with small farms, small electrically powered factories, small schools, and homes on one-acre lots (Scott 1969). Broadacre City may have been the ultimate horror for Jacobs, but she was also opposed to LeCorbusier because his high-density ideal metropolis called for the radical sorting and separating of land uses.

Lewis Mumford advocated a cellular pattern with a strong central nucleus surrounded by housing and industry at decreasing densities away from the center. Neotraditionalist Andres Duany wants to cluster mixed-use development in rural areas into towns and villages with nonhierarchical grid patterns for streets. Enough already. The point I am trying to make is that the only things most of these physical planning theorists appear to have in common are a belief in the importance of their own views, opposition to other theorists, and an eagerness to criticize and blame planners for most urban ills. Barbara Berlin, AICP, former planning director of Park Forest, Illinois, complains, "We're blamed for everything," and she points out that real estate people and bankers have much more to say about the shape of suburbs than either planners or architects (Knack 1989).

Andres Duany is but the latest in a long line of critics and saviors. He uses confidence, sarcasm, and aggressiveness to deliver a powerful message. But neotraditionalists are not content with representing their clients in the development process. They want to change the rules and impose their vision on planners and communities that have been seduced by the neotraditionalists' shiny package.

Most cities have zoning ordinances that permit planned mixed-use developments. Neotraditionalists want zoning ordinances to be amended to permit mixed uses with far different standards or controls than exist in most communities. I watched one of Duany's presentations and concluded that he was primarily intent on embarrassing local planners, architects, and engineers in order to gain public sympathy and support for changing zoning and other development controls. To the extent that local regulations impede the marketplace or fail to achieve important community objectives, I support his efforts. Unfortunately, many of the regulations he opposes have valid community purposes and serve to protect the public health, safety, and welfare. (For further discussion, see "A Critical Look at Neotraditional Town Planning" in the November 1990 *PAS Memo* published by the American Planning Association.)

Other aspects of neotraditionalism also conflict with the idea of customer service. The idea of mixed uses, for instance, inevitably means a closer proximity between industrial and residential uses. Even modern light industry such as computer manufacturing, says Joel Goldsteen, in his book *Danger All Around,* can house highly toxic waste (Goldsteen 1991). Segregation of land uses is not always romantic, but it does promote and protect the public health and safety.

In addition, surveys have shown that segregation is the urbanization pattern preferred by most people. Richard Heath, AICP, planning director for the city of Minneapolis, says market research conducted in his city revealed that local people's choice of where to live was most strongly influenced by security from crime and by neighborhood appearance (larger yards and bigger houses were favored). Both of these factors indicate a preference for suburban and rural life. The survey also showed that public transportation, convenience to work, and nearby shopping—all deemed important by the neotraditionalists—were far less important than these other factors.

Ruth Knack, senior editor of *Planning* magazine, says that architects like Duany often "discount the nonvisual aspects of planning as being irrelevant or destructive" (Knack 1989). Reed Dunn, Jr., AICP, the director of planning of the York County (Pa.) Planning Commission, finds that Duany and other similar design advocates often make his job more difficult. "It's tough enough as it is in the growth management business without the added burden of these pseudo-planners telling us their design skills will solve all the community development problems that have evolved in the last half century" (Dunn 1990). Furthermore, Sam Hall Kaplan, a Los Angeles-based design critic and lecturer at the Art Center College of Design in Pasadena, contends "there is also something elitist about the neotraditional concept, a designer-knows-best feeling that hints at a repressive, dogmatic approach to planning" (Kaplan 1990).

Who are these visionaries planning for and where is the linkage to the marketplace? Despite all the fulminations of planners and other do-gooders, people continue to move from central cities to exurbia. Arthur Nelson and Kenneth Dueker attribute this to the following: the desire by households to escape urban environmental diseconomies and socioeconomic heterogeneity; the pursuit of the classical "Jeffersonian" rural ethic; the desire to locate within or near open spaces and recreation opportunities; and the ability of households to select locations that offer levels of public services more commensurate with their needs (Nelson and Dueker 1990).

These are real beliefs, and planners who want to save urban America need to respect them and challenge themselves to help cities incorporate some of these important values into the urban environment. Many of our cities are broken and need to be fixed. According to Nelson and Dueker, "a large share of exurbanization exists because of the failure of urban areas to meet their promise as cities." Hans Blumenfeld, a noted researcher in the study of quality of life issues, was on the mark when he concluded many years ago that cities, above all, must have "an orientation toward people" (Blumenfeld 1969). If planners don't have this orientation, then what hope is there for significant change? And change driven by competition and responsiveness to the marketplace is the only hope for urban America.

Some cities are already listening and learning how to change in response to the voices they are hearing. For many years, Dayton, Ohio, has been a leader in surveying its citizens to measure their satisfaction with service delivery and with efforts to meet the unique needs of different neighborhoods. Customer service is clearly the mission and focus of local government in Dayton and much can be learned from their efforts.

In Los Angeles, a city councilwoman has suggested issuing residents a "voucher" that they would exchange for a fixed-dollar value of services. Each resident would be allowed to choose for themselves the mix of products and services they would receive for their tax dollars.

Most recently, the city of Minneapolis has demonstrated an extraordinary commitment to customer service and empowerment. The heart of Minneapolis's newly adopted *Twenty–Year Revitalization Plan* is an incredible commitment allowing individual neighborhoods to develop revitalization plans for themselves and providing $400 million over the next 20 years for implementation. This unprecedented level of support for neighborhood self-determination is based on the assumption "that the neighborhoods know best what their future should be," according to Richard Heath, the Minneapolis planning director (Papatola 1990). Minneapolis has seen the future, and its a future based on customer service, self-help, and neighborhood empowerment.

WHOSE VISION IS IT ANYWAY?

In 1988, the newly elected board of supervisors of Loudoun County, Virginia, initiated a Vision program. It was intended to develop a broad, long-term idea for the ultimate physical form of Loudoun County. Unfortunately, the top-down vision that was developed was not the result of a grass roots citizen initiative, and when hearings were scheduled to inform the public about the results the community responded in anger. The board of supervisors realized their mistake and appointed a Vision Task Force with broad citizen representation in an attempt to allay suspicions and rebuild trust.

Reform and change based on a commitment to customer service and empowerment is the future of the planning profession and local government. The radical architect/planner Robert Goodman argued that "the makeup of a neighborhood commune or whatever it's called should ultimately be based on the free choice of individuals coming together to create a common way to live, not simply because planners are trying to create neighborhoods with bourgeois 'vitality'" (Goodman 1971). Paul

Davidoff charged that the difficulty with many planning programs is that "citizens are more often *reacting* to agency programs than *proposing* their concept of appropriate goals and future action" (Davidoff 1965). Lynnis Jameson admittedly tells me that quite often it's planners who come up with their own vision and who are trying to push it onto someone else.

Very recently, Thomas Jacobson, the planning director of Chesterfield County, Virginia, warned neotraditionalists that "instead of molding people to fit the plan, we need to understand the needs and desires of residents, temper them with community objectives, and mold our plans accordingly" (Jacobson 1989). In a similar vein, Robin Walsh, the director of planning for Plantation, Florida, advises that "city planners must respond to the preferred life-style of the majority of community residents, not to personal preferences" and "in a democratic society, public policy must reflect the public's desires" (Walsh 1989). William H. Whyte, Jr., has successfully argued that cities work best when they are shaped to accommodate people's own views and values—not the planners' (Whyte 1988).

There is a temptation to believe that if only we could become a closed guild and wall ourselves off from the intrusions of the world, we could stop the changes and restore the old certainties. Paolo Soleri has been working for over 20 years building Arcosanti, his model city of tomorrow 70 miles north of Phoenix. He envisions thousands of people moving to his city to live, work, and recreate in closed quarters—the antithesis of the American dream. He has vision all right, and he has critics, who say that the city is a forced vision that does not mesh with the landscape.

In Soleri's view of the world, people exist to live in his city, not vice versa. Soleri has defended his failure by saying he is blessed with ignorance. But ignorance of people and markets is no blessing, it is a contagious disease that is fatal to most experts.

The importance and relevance of visioning has declined in recent years. Angela Moore, AICP, the director of planning for Henrico County Virginia, tells me that it can be dangerous for planners to develop and articulate a community vision. What a planner sees as visioning, the public, she says, can easily interpret as just another example of idealistic or impractical planning. William Fulton, AICP, warns that today's markets demand short-term results and that "in planning now, the cloud-niner is likely to find himself not just out of the loop, but out of a job, no matter how good his ideas are" (Fulton 1989).

Yet visioning has always been one of the most important aspects of planning practice and theory. I concur with Virginia Commonwealth professor Michael Brooks's argument that "the urban planning profession needs a new generation of visionaries, people who dream of a better world, and who are capable of designing the means to attain it" (Brooks 1988). Who are these planning visionaries? They are our clients.

Vision, for today's planners, means having a perspective that sees the vast possibilities of the future and tries to achieve them. It means having an awareness of the big picture, an understanding of critical relationships and linkages, and a sense of priorities. It is a collective, community-based vision, not a singular, fixed picture. It consists of many evolving visions developed through a vigorous, interactive, bottoms-up process.

This type of shared vision is not the traditional autocratic model advocated by visionary experts. And it is not the grand visionary plan advocated by Daniel Burnham, who said: "Make no little plans; they have no magic to stir men's blood and probably themselves will not be realized. Make big plans; aim high in hope and work, remembering that a noble, logical diagram once recorded will never die."

The planner's role is not to create and impose a grand vision, but rather to help his or her customers find the plans and solutions, regardless of scale, that fit the community's image and strivings. People don't want to hear about the planner's vision, they want to develop it themselves. This does not diminish the role of the planner in the vision-setting process. If anything, planners have a much more exciting and challenging responsibility than ever before. In the view of UCLA's John Friedmann, it is "transactive planning" that "involves a process of mutual learning between the expert and the client (citizen) groups," and a basic restructuring of the relationship (Friedmann 1973). Rather than continuing to impose our views on our customers, planners should learn from Michael Jackson, who sings in "Man in the Mirror": "if you want to make the world a better place, take a look at yourself and change."

ADVOCACY PLANNING AND CUSTOMER SERVICE

For experienced planners there should be something vaguely familiar about the call for a stronger and more responsive customer-service orientation in city planning. It reminds one of advocacy planning.

What was advocacy planning? In the 1968 "Green Book" (*Principles and Practice of Urban Planning*), William Goodman, Eric Freund, AICP, and Paul Davidoff wrote that "the essence of advocacy planning is the encouragement of organization on the part of those people who are most often the objects of planning activities—that is, those most often 'planned' for" (Goodman and Freund 1968). This brings to mind the time that Amos asked Andy, on their old radio show, what he thought of the new urban renewal plan. Andy humorously and pointedly responded, "It depends on whether you are the planner or the plannee."

In theory, advocate planners were supposed to organize people and help them in preparing a plan advocating their views and values. Behind this concept was the nagging fear that the expert judgments of professional planners may not be inherently better than those of the people being planned for and, in fact, they might even be harmful to some people. It was argued more specifically that the underprivileged could not successfully participate in the standard planning and political decision-making process because of their apathy, sense of powerlessness, and lack of knowledge. There was no general recognition that most of the people in most communities had the same limitations. Instead, advocacy planning was born and forever linked in most minds with social welfare planning for lower income and minority groups. From this well-intentioned birth came a bastardized vision of customer service. This weakened, deformed species lingers with us today in isolated pockets, but its heritage casts an ominous shadow and stigmatizes any attempt to transform advocacy planning into something more in keeping with the true spirit of customer service. Good luck to the planner that informs his manager or public officials that he is starting an advocacy planning project.

Unfortunately, what begins wrong usually ends up wrong, and this was clearly the case with advocacy planning. There were three primary causes for the failure of advocacy planning. First, advocacy planning did not reflect a philosophical commitment to customer service but rather a paternalistic approach of "planner knows best." Anthony Catanese, president of Florida Atlantic University, tells the story of the planner who dies and awakens to find himself in his vision of the perfect master planned community. When the planner remarks that he always knew that this is what heaven would be like, a creature with horns, a tail, and a pitchfork appears and says, "Wrong again!"

The recent movie *Defending Your Life* provides a similar view of the perfect afterlife, called Judgment City. This smoothly functioning city, which appears to be a cross between Disneyland and Sun City, Arizona, is neither heaven nor hell. It is the netherworld in between where the dead are put on trial to determine their ultimate destination. Every person's needs, from food to transportation, are taken care of. The place is run by an efficient workforce that wears business suits, smiles a lot, and talks about its superiority over the people it is servicing. The sterile environment of this way station to heaven epitomizes the worst attributes of utopian urban perfection as designed and operated by intellectually superior and uncaring bureaucrats.

Most advocate planners were sincere in their desires to serve their disadvantaged clients, but they were also condescending and arrogant and many of their plans reflected this. (Excellent examples of these failures can be found in many books, including: *After the Planner* by Robert Goodman, *The Federal Bulldozer* by Martin Anderson, and *The City Planning Process* by Alan Altshuler.) This relationship of expert to client was doomed to fail. Clients want assistance and advice, but they also want a meaningful role in making decisions. Trust, respect, and sensitivity are essential in any successful volunteer or service relationship, and the clients must have autonomy and ultimate authority. All too often, planners were unwilling to respect and trust the judgment of their clients. These planners weakened the real power of the already weak and disadvantaged by making them even more dependent on the technical knowledge and expertise of the staff. Furthermore, by hiding behind a barrier of professional expertise, many planners alienated themselves from the very people they were trying to serve (Bassin 1990).

The second reason advocacy planning failed is that it was not based on an awareness and understanding of the political decision-making process. Planners who could not get their public interest-based efforts approved by elected officials tried to use the support of their disadvantaged clients to pressure the city council, mayor, or city hall. Adversarial relationships became the norm and, as planning became more political, these politically inept planners became even less effective.

The final mistake of advocacy planning was limiting its application to only a small segment of the community. One of former president Ronald Reagan's favorite stories was about the clerk in the Bureau of Indian Affairs who was seen crying. When asked what was wrong, he replied, "My Indian died."

Unfortunately, advocate planners did not truly understand that apathy, powerlessness, and lack of knowledge were not limited just to lower income and minority residents. The "silent majority" was also ignored by city planners who incorrectly believed that the middle class was fully capable of fending for itself. Like the national Democratic political party of recent years, advocate planners narrowed their client base to such an extreme that they seriously damaged their practical and political effectiveness.

Planners trying to serve only a few groups or classes of people become part of the problem and willing participants in what John Gardner, former secretary of the U.S. Department of Health, Education, and Welfare, calls "the war of the parts against the whole" (Gardner 1990). Planners have to choose between two opposing ideas—the politics of class warfare or President Lincoln's all-embracing vision of boundless democratic opportunity. Fred Bair, Jr., one of the most experienced and respected practitioners in planning, advised planners many years ago to take their thumbs off the scales: "It is time to mean what we have said to serve all the people and not merely a select few. Consider all without giving public special privilege to any, to the end that there are good plans and harmonious regulations for every part of the urban area, so that the whole conserves the health, safety, morals, comfort, convenience and general welfare *of the whole community*" (Bair, Jr. 1970).

In his insightful book, *The New Realities*, Peter Drucker contends that single-cause, special-interest groups are dominating the political decision-making process. These groups know no compromise and hold their cause to be a moral absolute. They do not trade votes. Drucker warns that:

> An organized single-cause minority that can marshal 3 to 5 percent of the vote can rarely provide the margin of victory. Its opposition though often ensures defeat. It thus is rarely a force for positive action, but it succeeds in blocking whatever action it does not approve. . . . as a result, political decisions and actions have to be postponed until there is a "crisis," an "emergency," a "catastrophe." Only under such a threat does the single-cause, special-interest group lose its veto power (Drucker 1989).

In a pluralistic society planners and public officials have many constituencies, each suspicious of the others and each trying to protect its own best interests. The easy way is to take sides and help block change, but the real challenge is to find the shared values and visions in the community and to help develop the leadership that during times of crisis can reconcile the differences between these disparate factions. Achieving a workable unity in a pluralistic environment should be one of the primary objectives of every planning program. One of the late professor Paul Seabury's last great deeds was to commission a small plane to fly over the Earth Day parade in his hometown of Berkeley, California, with a banner telling the mayor to forget radical politics and just fix the potholes. In the final analysis, people don't want ideology, they want results.

In too many conflicts the common ground is there but the prevailing local way of resolving issues works against mediation and resolution. It sometimes appears to us that regulatory processes and public hearing procedures exist to promote adversarial relationships and to encourage deadlock. Some of my experiences in Galveston, Texas, led me to conclude that among many local residents the prevailing attitude was "we don't have it and we won't let anyone else get it either." There is a story that typified my experiences. It seems that a man was fishing on a rock and sand jetty extending into the bay, using live crabs for bait. A tourist walked out to watch the fisherman, and noticed that the crabs were being kept in a shallow hole scooped out in the sand. After several minutes, the tourist inquired of the fisherman what kept his bait from simply climbing out of the hole. His response was that these were Galveston crabs and "whenever one of the crabs tries to climb out of the hole, one of the other crabs reaches up with a claw and pulls him back in."

Disconnected, uncaring, and untrusting communities are not healthy incubators for innovation and initiative, and thereby reduce the potential for both individual progress and mutual gain. Daniel Kemmis, the former minority leader and speaker of the Montana House of Representatives and current mayor of Missoula, Montana, contends that the regulatory bureaucracy in government ". . . represents a major development in the modern project of keeping citizens apart—shielding them from the necessity of direct, face-to-face (republican) problem-solving" (Kemmis 1990). He contends that the mutual blocking of initiatives has clouded the climate of enterprise and frustrated the public interest. Kemmis cites the example of the degeneration of public hearings as a useful forum for the open, positive discussion and exchange of ideas and feelings. He notes:

> . . . next to the courtroom, the public hearing room is our society's favorite arena for the blocking of one another's initiatives. Out of everything that happens at a public hearing—the speaking, the emoting, the efforts to persuade the decisionmaker, the presentation of facts—the one element that

is almost totally lacking is anything that might be characterized as "public hearing" . . . The duty to hear does not extend beyond the decisionmaker; those who testify are not encumbered by any such responsibility. So it is that "public hearings" are curiously devoid of that very quality which their name might seem to imply (Kemmis 1990).

Philosopher and educator John Dewey argued that the release and fulfillment of one's potential could take place only in rich, manifold association with others, with each having "the power to be an individualized self making a distinctive contribution and enjoying in its own way the fruits of association" (Dewey 1927). University of Illinois-Chicago planning professor Charles Hoch contends that Dewey recognized there would be conflict but believed that, "in the face of conflict among different groups, the public interest would be served best through intelligent and reflective transaction. In other words, the primary transactions of a democratic policy would consist of such activities as bargaining, negotiating, and persuasive argument rather than regulations or commands" (Hoch 1984).

After all was said and done, neither the planners, their clients, nor the political decision makers were satisfied with traditional advocacy planning. It was a failure because it was not properly understood or effectively practiced. It was a well-meaning attempt to address the basic issues of inequality and "fairness," but a failure nonetheless. HUD secretary Jack Kemp has said that any true concept of fairness must recognize the necessity of a link between reward and individual human effort.

Government critic Charles Murray, in his book *In Pursuit of Happiness and Good Government*, suggests that "the satisfaction one takes from any activity is a complicated product of the degree of effort one puts into it, the degrees of responsibility one has for the outcome, and the function it serves" (Murray 1988). This means that people with problems must be empowered to solve their own problems. What was and is needed is a combination of John Friedmann's concept of "moral commitment to an ethics of empowerment" (Friedmann 1987) and Daniel Kemmis's development of a "face-to-face, collaborative citizenship" (Kemmis 1990).

Today, successful advocate planners are helping their clients become their own planners by teaching them about networking, conflict resolution, consensus building and the local political decision-making process.

Conditions are being created in which people can act on their own environmental needs and make distinctions between the experts' technical and personal judgments. Intermediaries between the people with problems and those with the power to help solve them are gradually being eliminated. Successful planners are using volunteerism, self-help, and coproduction techniques to ensure that their clients are given actual authority and shared responsibility for working together to solve their problems. These planners are advocates in the truest meaning of the word.

A superb example of planners as advocates comes from the Glenwood Triangle neighborhood of Fort Worth, one of the city's toughest and most run-down areas. There, planners have stood alongside a local neighborhood association as coaches and facilitators, teaching residents how to access services and information from city hall. However, as part of the city's Targeted Area Planning Program, the neighborhood team, not the city staff, formulates and implements its own plan for improving the area. Today, much of Glenwood Triangle has been rehabilitated, and a healthy neighborhood of working class people is emerging (Kirchhoff 1990). There will be more about the progress of citizens in Fort Worth in later chapters.

Adapting to a less "authoritative" approach and assuming a more facilitative style does not diminish the value and importance of the planner in the decision making process. Far from it! T. J. Cartwright, associate professor of Environmental Studies at York University, explains that the facilitative approach requires planners to have a better understanding of social causes and the elements of social change. This approach, he says, won't be easier than an authoritative one, but it will be more effective (Cartwright 1989).

For many planners this is difficult to accept. They intuitively want to take things into their own hands. As tempting as this is, it must not be allowed to get in the way of the more important mission of customer empowerment. Always follow the "Iron Rule" of Ernesto Cortes, the patron saint of community organizers in Texas: "You never, ever, do for people what they can do for themselves" (Rogers 1990). I liken the primary role of the planner in the facilitative approach to that of a football coach. Planners need to prepare their customers to play the "game." They need to: teach them the rules; work on their strength, conditioning, and endurance; expand their capacity and capability to perform; provide them with techniques on how to score points; motivate them; and most importantly of all, help them develop a strategy and game plan for ultimate victory.

Planners must also do what they can to ensure a level playing field, which means creating an open, collective, collaborative planning process and providing increased direct access to decision makers. Customers must learn to play the game themselves, be accountable for their actions and the end results. I reject the criticism of some who contend that empowering means a loss of purpose and relevance for planners and that it demeans their role. Planners must have the courage and faith to trust their customers and they must be committed to the concept of customer empowerment. This is truly ultimate customer service.

TESTING FOR A CUSTOMER SERVICE ORIENTATION

In our workshops on "Planning Agency Management," Ray Quay and I ask each participant to complete the service test exercise shown in Figure 1-1. It would be beneficial if you would stop at this point and take the test yourself.

While almost all the participants fail this test, most demonstrate they are sensitive to their customers and want to help them. Of course our results are skewed because, at the time, we are lecturing on customer service and most of the participants anticipate what kind of answers we are looking for. Yet a significant percentage of those taking this test will reveal their true bureaucratic tendencies and lack of sincere interest in customer service. The standard bureaucratic response to this question is that if the applicant is not back by 5:00, then the office is closed and the staff goes home.

So what is the correct answer? Contrary to what you might be thinking, issuing the permit or allowing the contractor to install the burglar bars without the permit is not the right answer. Many planners tell us that this is what they would do. We then describe a scenario where the permit is issued and the planner has a good weekend, but when he comes to work Monday morning he is met by a newspaper reporter. He is told that there has been a tragic accident resulting in a loss of lives. A house caught on fire Sunday night and the family was trapped inside because burglar bars were installed without an inside safety release mechanism. The reporter wants to know if the contractor received permission to install the bars, and if the city inspected and approved the work.

Figure 1-1. Service Test

Background

It is 4:45 on a Friday afternoon. An unknown contractor is asking your department for a building permit so he can install an extensive set of burglar bars in a residence. He has left some information back at his office that you need in order to correctly process his permit application. He can not go to his office and get back before you close at 5:00 p.m.

Question

What would you do in this situation and why?

Answer

_____

_____

_____

_____

_____

_____

_____

_____

_____

_____

_____

_____

_____

_____

_____

_____

_____

At this point in our workshops, the bureaucrats who denied the permit are feeling pretty good about themselves. We then describe a different scenario. The contractor leaves city hall and doesn't get back before 5:00. The planner goes home and enjoys a nice weekend. On Monday morning the planner reports to work and is met by the contractor and a newspaper reporter. It turns out that an elderly woman had been robbed and badly beaten last week. She was due to get out of the hospital on Saturday and had arranged for the contractor to install burglar bars for her safety. The contractor explained that since no one in the inspection department was willing to wait for him on Friday, he was not allowed to do the work. Unfortunately, the night that the woman came home from the hospital the criminal returned and beat her to death. The reporter wanted to know why the staff had been so picky about the permit and why no one had been willing to stay late in order to help out this older woman.

The correct answer to this test question is that there is not enough information to make a decision. Yet over the years only one person at our workshops has given this response. When the question states that the contractor has left some information back at the office, you don't know what this information happens to be. Is it part of the plans pertaining to the release mechanism or is it something insignificant that won't endanger the public health and safety? What about the person that the contractor is working for? Do they have any needs that might justify special consideration, such as the staff working late on Friday?

The real value of this exercise is that it lets people discuss and justify their natural inclinations. If you like to work 9:00 to 5:00 and you like to follow the rules, then you can justify denying the permit. But if you have a natural predisposition toward customer service, you can ask the right questions, make sure that the public is being protected, work overtime, and issue the permit. My tendency is to prefer planners that are looking for a way to be of service and who want to make a difference in people's lives. However, some managers prefer bureaucrats that follow the rules, don't take risks, and treat everyone the same. I would guess that since you're reading this book you are probably more interested in providing effective customer service than you are in being a safe bureaucrat.

REFERENCES

Albrecht, K., and L. Bradford. 1990. *The Service Advantage.* Homewood, Illinois: Dow Jones Irwin.

Bassin, A. 1990. "Does Capitalist Planning Need Some Glasnost?" *Journal of the American Planning Association* Vol. 56, No. 2.

Baum, H. 1983. *Planners and Public Expectations.* Cambridge, Massachusetts: Schenkman Publishing Company, Inc.

Baumhover, S. 1990. ". . . And One that We Won't Follow Up." *APA Planning and Law Division Newsletter,* December.

Benveniste, G. 1989. *Mastering the Politics of Planning.* San Francisco: Jossey-Bass, Inc.

Birch, E. 1990. "The Bloom is on the Rose." *Journal of the American Planning Association* Vol. 56, No. 2.

Blumenfeld, H. 1969. "Criteria for Judging the Quality of the Urban Environment." *The Quality of Urban Life: Urban Affairs Annual Review.*

Brooks, M. 1988. "Four Critical Junctures in the History of the Urban Planning Profession." *Journal of the American Planning Association* Vol. 54, No. 2.

Cartwright, T. 1989. "Urban Management As a Process Not an Output." *Review of Urban and Regional Studies* Vol. 3, No. 4.

Cisneros, H. 1991. "Reinvigorating Democratic Values: Challenge and Necessity." *Public Management* Vol. 73, No. 2.

Davidoff, P. 1965. "Advocacy and Pluralism in Planning." *Journal of the American Institute of Certified Planners* Vol. 31, No. 5.

Dewey, J. 1927. *The Public and Its Problem.* New York: Henry Holt Company.

Drucker, P. 1989. *The New Realities.* New York: Harper and Row.

Dunn, Jr., R. 1990. "Questioning Cluster." *Planning* Vol. 56, No. 11.

Enos, G. 1991. "Developers take SLAPP at Anti-Growth Groups." *City and State* February 11–24, 1991.

Freedman, A. 1990. "Amid Ghetto Hunger, Many More Suffer Eating Wrong Foods." *The Wall Street Journal* December 18, 1990.

Friedmann, Jr., J. 1973. *Retracking America: A Theory of Transactive Planning.* Garden City, New York: Anchor Books.

Friedmann, Jr., J. 1987. *Planning in the Public Domain.* Princeton, New Jersey: Princeton University Press.

Fulton, W. 1989. "Visionaries, Deal Makers, Incrementalists: The Divided World of Urban Planning." *Governing* Vol. 2, No. 9.

Gallagher, M. 1991. "Maryland County Fires Director." *Planning* Vol. 57, No. 2.

Gardner, J. 1990. *On Leadership.* New York: The Free Press.

Goldsteen, J. 1991. *Danger All Around.* Unpublished.

Goodman, R. 1971. *After the Planners.* New York: Simon and Schuster.

Goodman, W., and E. Freund. 1968. *Principles and Practice of Urban Planning.* Washington, DC: International City Management Association.

Hill, D. 1988. "Jane Jacob's Ideas on Big Diverse Cities: A Review and Commentary." *Journal of the American Planning Association* Vol. 54, No. 3.

Hoch, C. 1984. "Doing Good and Being Right." *Journal of the American Planning Association* Vol. 50, No. 3.

Jacobson, T. 1989. "Sins of the Neotraditionalist." *Planning* Vol. 55, No. 11.

Kaplan, S. 1990. "The Holy Grid: A Skeptic's View." *Planning* Vol. 56, No. 11.

Kemmis, D. 1990. *Community and the Politics of Place.* Norman, Oklahoma: University of Oklahoma Press.

Kent, Jr., T. 1964. *The Urban General Plan.* San Francisco: Chandler Publishing Company.

Kirchhoff, C. 1990. "Potholes, Planners and Police." *Texas Town & City.* October.

Knack, R. 1989. "Repent Ye Sinners, Repent." *Planning* Vol. 55, No. 8.

Krumholz, N., and R. Mier. 1987. "Viewpoint." *Planning* Vol. 53, No. 1.

Levin, M. 1985. "Planning Agencies: Surviving in Hard Times." *Planning* Vol. 51, No. 1.

Levin, M. 1987. *Planning in Government.* Chicago: Planners Press.

Murray, C. 1988. *In Pursuit of Happiness and Good Government.* New York: Simon and Schuster.

Nelson, A., and K. Dueker 1990. "The Exurbanization of America and Its Planning Policy Implications." *Journal of Planning Education and Research* Vol. 9, No. 2.

Papatola, D. 1990. "In Minneapolis, Neighborhoods Know Best." *Planning* Vol. 56, No. 10.

Rogers, M. 1990. *Cold Anger: A Story of Faith and Power Politics,* Denton, Texas: University of North Texas Press.

Scott, M. 1969. *American City Planning.* Berkeley, California: University of California Press.

Walsh, R. 1989. "Cars Forever." *Planning* Vol. 55, No. 10.

Whyte, Jr. W. 1988. *City: Rediscovering the Center.* New York: Doubleday.

Wildavsky, A. 1988. "Ubiquitous Anomie. Public Service in an Era of Ideological Dissensus." *Public Administration Review* Vol. 48, No. 4.

Zemke, R., and D. Schaaf. 1989. *The Service Edge.* New York: NAL Books.

2

The Politics of Customer Service

THE MYTH OF RATIONAL, VALUE-FREE, APOLITICAL PLANNING

One of the most persistent myths of the planning profession is that planning is technical, rational, and apolitical. In the rational model a problem is defined, facts are gathered and objectively analyzed, goals are chosen, courses of action are selected, programs are implemented, and the results are analyzed for future guidance (Banfield 1973). Alan Altshuler noted in the introduction to his classic book, *The City Planning Process,* that many planners' claim to legitimacy is based on a commitment to a comprehensive, systematic, and rational planning process that services the public interest by deriving the best means to achieve objectives (Altshuler 1965). Charles Hoch, a professor in the School of Urban Planning and Policy at the University of Illinois at Chicago, contends that planners want to "do good" and to "be right." He points out that those interested in "being right" focus "on the methodological or technical qualities of planning activity, and they defend their actions by referring to the validity and reliability of the analytical procedures used to justify them" (Hoch 1984).

The premise of the modern city planning profession is that the increasing complexity of society requires expert analysis to comprehend it and expert professional planners to manage it. Yet this very complexity means that top-down technical solutions are doomed to failure. All too often planners deliver macro solutions to micro problems. Furthermore, the solutions are coming from the wrong people. "What are we for,"

Woodrow Wilson once wrote, "if we are to be scientifically taken care of by a small number of gentlemen who are the only men who understand the job?"

Unfortunately, the established style of city planning in this country for many planners is as technical and rationalistic as the engineering design for a bridge, according to professor John Friedmann at UCLA. He sarcastically describes the planning process and the planner's environment as follows: ". . . it proceeds in linear sequence from problem statement to solution. Because the guiding value judgments are implicitly accepted, planning assumes a posture of objective aloofness. Surrounded by the antiseptic walls of his office, the planner measures, analyzes, and projects. The less the outside world intrudes upon his calculations, the happier he is. He strives to reach determinate solutions . . . The reality, he will insist, lies hidden in the data tapes with which he works and not in the confusing babble of the outside world" (Friedmann 1973).

Traditionalists believe that if and when politics and the emotions of the outside world are permitted to intrude into the planning process, then objectivity and rationality are lost and the purity and value of the results are compromised. "Yet," according to William Potapchuk, the executive director of the National League of Cities' Program for Community Problem Solving, "the failure to recognize the political elements often dooms technical-correct solutions to the library of un-implemented reports" (Potapchuk 1991). Following the rational, apolitical model can be likened to practicing in a hermetically sealed jar of pabulum. Leaving the intellectual safety of the jar and learning to practice in the real political world is a wrenching but essential step for planners who want to have a meaningful and rewarding professional life.

Fortunately, it is not necessary to structure the planning process so that you have to choose between reason and emotion. In Japan products are based on the concept of *kansei,* or having an absolute awareness of both reason and emotion. Planning, too, can follow this concept.

As planners attempt to understand and balance the conflicting values of their customers, "planning starts to lose its technical 'virginity' and to get tangled up with subjectivity—attitudes, opinions, perceptions, etc." says T. J. Cartwright (Cartwright 1987). He adds, "in the end, we have to recognize that planning involves judgment as well as technique."

When planners start to talk about "good," objective, or rational planning I run as fast and as far as I can. In a recent comic strip of

"Mother Goose and Grimm," Santa asks the dog Grimm if he's been a good little boy this year. Grimm answers: "Define good." Goodness or rationality, like beauty, is in the eye of the beholder. Justice Oliver Wendell Holmes, Jr. wrote: "A word is not a crystal, transparent and unchanged. It is the skin of a living thought that varies in color and context, according to the light in which it is held." To listen to traditional planning rhetoric you would conclude that planners are rational and that political decision makers are irrational. But to suggest that planners have a corner on rationality or that they are more rational or less irrational than others in the planning process is a dangerous thought. Planners are human, with values, beliefs, and emotions just like anyone else. Noted planner Norton Long points out, "The question is not whether planning will reflect politics, but whose politics will it reflect. What values and whose values will planners seek to implement?" (Long 1972).

Paul Davidoff argued that planners should not only clarify what their values are, but actually affirm them (Davidoff 1965). I do not pretend to be value free, nor do I want to hide what my values are. In fact, I will take this opportunity to follow Davidoff's advice and to affirm these values to you. I believe in the basic competence of the individual and that human dignity must be respected above all. I advocate self-esteem, self-discipline, integrity, responsibility for one's acts, respect for others, moderation and tolerance, perseverance, and a commitment to serving others and the larger community. I am tolerant of differences, but not of unhealthy, self-destructive behavior or of those who are unwilling to try to help themselves. Waiting patiently for assistance usually leads to defeat, pessimism, and despair. Individuals, families, and neighborhoods must use their own resources to influence and support a larger community of common interests.

I am driven by a commitment to serve and empower my customers, all of them. I care when they care and I am willing to blame them when they don't. And I am not "blaming the victims," only trying to help them reach their potential.

Planners do not have a special claim on objectivity or defining the public interest. In fact, much of what passes for objectivity, neutrality, and public interest could not withstand critical evaluation. Fortunately, there are checks and balances in the typical planning process. Public officials are usually accountable for their decisions and the political process is becoming increasingly sensitive to public perceptions. Full public disclosure and extensive community involvement and debate strengthens the value of planning and encourages an informed decision, resulting in what conservative political theorist George Will calls a "good society." According to Will, "A good society is remarkably independent of 'individuals' willing the social good. A good society is a lumpy stew of individuals and groups, each with its own inherent 'principle of motion.' This stew stirs itself, and in the fullness of time, out comes a creamy puree called 'the public interest'" (Will 1983).

Planning and planners are critical ingredients in the political stewing process. It is amazing that planners can claim a planning process is rational when political factors are excluded from the process. If political considerations are ignored, then the process and resulting product can't be rational. In fact, to use such an apolitical process is irrational. It is also insulting to our customers. As Howell Baum says, "Whenever a planner speaks of an issue in a way that ignores interests and emotions, the planner is directly ignoring the people who have interests and feelings, and is truly eliminating them" (Baum 1990).

In my view, planning is a political process, and it is political involvement that creates effective planning. T. J. Cartwright argues that "planning has to incorporate some sort of 'political' process to be able to arbitrate among the competing interests" (Cartwright 1987). Donald Spaid, AICP, former planning coordinator for St. Paul, observed that "it is the political process that causes things to be built" (Spaid 1978).

Furthermore, I concur with Leon Eplan who, as the commissioner of budget and planning for Atlanta in 1978, wrote that "the person who does not realize that every planning decision is a political decision is not going to get very far" (Eplan 1978). And when I say "not very far" I am speaking both in terms of professional advancement and, more importantly, of effective planning and implementation. At its core, rational, apolitical planning is dysfunctional. Yet writer and researcher Robert Burchell, in an article for *Society* magazine, observes that "the rational model . . . by default, continues to stand the test of time" (Burchell 1988).

This growing dichotomy is responsible for the increasing confusion and ambivalence that planners are experiencing as they struggle for relevance and effectiveness. The following comment by a local planning director is typical of such mixed feelings: "I think the political process is a healthy one. It gives a whole lot of people an opportunity to participate. But at the same time, it results in decisions that are counter to good planning or management" (Baum 1983).

I have found that many planners leave school and start their careers with an apolitical philosophy, but modify their views over time and become more appreciative of the value of politics in the planning process. "Young planners just out of school have dreams," says one respected French planner. "They think they can convince with their arguments. Seasoned planners have learned from experience. They pay attention to political reality" (Benveniste 1989).

Charles Hoch, a recognized academic authority on the relationship between planning and politics, has found in his research that approximately 50 percent of planners feel threatened by politics (Hoch 1988a). He concludes that implementing plans places planners at greater risk than making plans. Hoch argues that overcoming the limits associated with rational, apolitical planning "will require taking forms of political action that create constituencies and foster allies—forms of action that enhance the legitimacy and efficacy of planning in ways that now appear wrong or weak" (Hoch 1990).

Many experienced planners have found that most of the fear that planners have of politics can be traced to inexperience and to a shocking lack of knowledge about the political decision-making process. Jerome Kaufman's course on "Strategies for Planning Effectiveness," which he teaches in the Department of Urban and Regional Planning at the University of Wisconsin-Madison, is one of the rare instances where academia attempts to educate planners about the politics of planning.

I admit to being puzzled by the absence of courses on urban politics in so many graduate planning curricula around the country. There is clearly a vast, unchallenged field of literature that documents the case that planning is far more a political craft than laboratory science. (See Benveniste 1989; Beauregard 1990; Catanese 1974, 1984; Patton and Sawicki 1986; Kaufman 1978; Krumholz and Forester 1990).

These authors' advice is clear and consistent. Robert Beauregard, a professor in the department of Urban Planning and Policy Development at Rutgers, contends that contemporary planners have eschewed politics and political positions which, in turn, has contributed to planning's loss of direction, influence, and legitimacy (Beauregard 1987). He also reasons that if planners are going to be effective participants in the process, they "must admit to a political function and abandon ideological claims to objectivity" (Beauregard 1990). Alan Altshuler has complained that past efforts to isolate and protect planners from politics are a major reason behind the long tradition of ineffectiveness in planning in the country (Altshuler 1965). Similarly, Harvey Perloff observed over a decade ago that with respect to political effectiveness and political legitimacy, "the current weakness of urban planning is in no small part related to its narrow relationship to the higher levels of government" (Perloff 1980).

Many other respected academics hold similar views. "If planning is to be successful as measured by the quality of policies, plans and programs developed and actions resulting from such efforts, then planners," according to Anthony Catanese, "will have to adapt to more politicized roles because all of these activities occur within a political process" (Catanese 1974). He adds, "the question is no longer whether planning is a part of a political process, rather how planning can be made part of good politics." Catanese proclaims that "good planning and good politics are an unbeatable combination for a working democracy."

A recent survey of planning departments in the 100 largest cities in America documents the influence of politics in planning (see Table 2-1). The survey, which was conducted in 1990 by Phoenix planning director Ronald Short on behalf of the City Planning and Management Division of the American Planning Association, found that in 18.7 percent of the cities politics had an *extreme* influence on the local planning work program. Another 34.7 percent of the respondents reported that politics had a *moderate* influence on their work program, and 41.3 percent noted that it had *some* influence. Only 5.3 percent of the cities surveyed indicated that politics had *no* influence on their work program. Excluding subdivision regulations, which are basically an administrative function with few discretionary responsibilities, the management of personnel

Table 2-1. Degree That Council Politics Affects Planning Department Activities

Activities	PERCENT REPORTING INFLUENCE			
	Extreme	Moderate	Somewhat	None
Work Program	18.7	34.7	41.3	5.3
Scheduling of Projects	8.0	54.7	29.3	8.0
Planning Recommendations	4.1	32.4	48.6	14.9
Degree of Citizen Involvement	18.7	45.3	29.3	6.7
Implementation Strategies	6.7	50.7	40.0	2.7
Zoning Recommendations	12.2	14.9	44.6	28.4
Subdivision Recommendations	2.7	9.6	30.1	57.5
Personnel Assignments	1.4	5.4	25.7	67.6

Source: *Third Annual City Planning Agency Survey*, City Planning and Management Division, American Planning Association, (1990).

assignments was the only department activity with very limited or no political influence.

John Forester, associate professor of City and Regional Planning at Cornell University, in his well-known 1982 essay on "Planning in the Face of Power," concluded that planners do not have the choice between being technical or political. He found that "the technician is necessarily a political actor; the crucial questions are: In what way? How covertly? Serving whom, excluding whom?" (Forester 1982).

In *Making Equity Planning Work,* Forester and Norman Krumholz make several observations that support the contention that apolitical planners do not provide real customer service:

> These politics-avoiding planners are likely to isolate themselves and subvert their own influence as a result. They are likely to write in a style that only other professionals will understand. They are likely to present the results of their analyses to key actors *after* the important, though perhaps informal, decisions have been made. As a result, their work risks being rigorous but useless, technically superb but unheeded, analytically precise but off-target . . . Despite the care with which they do their job, they serve very few people . . . The pursuit of an apolitical, detached, professional style here produces failure, not competence (Krumholz and Forester 1990).

Planners can't continue to satisfy fewer and fewer people. They need to be actively involved in restoring people's faith in government. Planners and politicians need each other if they want to maximize their effectiveness. "Planning without a political force behind it becomes a paper exercise," says Lisa Peattie, a professor in the Department of Urban Studies and Planning at M.I.T., "and politics without planning becomes a politics of symbols or personalities" (Peattie 1978). Of course planners are also pretty skillful at developing symbols.

The need to develop closer ties between planners and public officials is not a new idea. Robert Walker, a respected political scientist and author of *The Planning Function in Urban Government,* concluded in the 1930s that planning agencies would not be successful unless they could develop harmonious relations with political decision makers and other government personnel. Walker even urged planners "to undertake a role as the *confidential* advisor of incumbent officials" (Walker 1941).

It's not just the academic community that has discovered the linkage between politics and effective planning. Practitioners are speaking out with growing vigor. Ann Leviton, former director of the Whitman

County Regional Planning Commission in Colfax, California, says her hardest lesson to learn was "that people don't always do the rational thing and that almost everything is political" (Knack 1986). Norm Krumholz, the former planning director for Cleveland, Ohio, found that the public decision-making process is generally irrational and always highly politicized (Krumholz 1978). He argues that if planners are going to be effective, they must become willing participants in the political process.

Some planners try to protect themselves by hiding behind a barrier of technical and professional expertise. But Arthur Bassin, AICP, a retired planner and architect who practiced in both the public and private sectors, notes that "any plan that affects the lives of people, for better or worse, is itself an 'ideological' statement" and "anyone who attempts to lay out some aspect of a community's future thereby becomes a political partisan" (Bassin 1990). A majority of planners recognize that planning is value laden. A national survey of American planners conducted by M. L. Vasu in 1979 found that 87.7 percent of the AICP respondents agreed that a plan cannot be politically neutral and that the planning process was value oriented (Vasu 1979).

Richard Bernhardt, the director of the Department of Planning and Development for the City of Orlando, tells me that "almost everything that we planners do is political, so if you want to be effective you have to be political." He adds, "politics is the art of making things happen, and as a planner, I am committed to bringing about positive changes in the community—to making good things happen."

Susan Brody, former planning director for Eugene, Oregon, and current director of the Department of Land Conservation and Development for the state of Oregon, says matter of factly that politics is an integral part of planning. Roger Hedrick, the executive director of the Lafayette Areawide Planning Commission in Lafayette, Louisiana, says that planners who are not sensitive to political factors have the influence and impact of a bug on the windshield of a fast moving car.

Nevertheless, most planners are reluctant or even unwilling to discuss the political aspects of their jobs, having been taught in graduate school that planning is apolitical. They are fearful of political repercussions and also uncomfortable with the work they are doing.

One of the best examples of a politically astute and effective planner is Norm Krumholz, now a professor of urban planning at Cleveland State University. Krumholz's views were shaped in part by his experience as a planner in Pittsburgh, where he worked under two strong planning directors, Cal Hamilton, AICP, and John Mauro, who had different management styles and philosophies. John Forester reports that "Cal Hamilton appeared to pay less attention to politics and decision making than to getting the models right; John Mauro apparently did just the opposite" (Krumholz and Forester 1990). It was Mauro's style and manner of practice that Krumholz adapted and took with him to Cleveland.

Making Equity Planning Work, by Krumholz and Forester, is the impressive history of planning in Cleveland under Krumholz from 1969 to 1979. This detailed case history should be required reading for every planner. With respect to politics, Krumholz took an aggressive and sometimes risky posture. But he balanced his behind-the-scenes political involvement with highly visible, technically competent work. *Publicly,* the department projected an apolitical, conservative stance. Krumholz dressed in a suit and tie, spoke in a cordial but nondeferential manner, and the staff produced solid technical studies and reports. His planners, says Forester, were articulate and persuasive. Krumholz believed that "professional analysis articulated cogently and persistently in the political process could enhance the planning staff's credibility, respect and practical influence" (Krumholz and Forester 1990). He was right.

POLITICAL REALITY, PRAGMATISM, AND CHOICE

Politicians don't want planners to be politicians. They simply want planners to be less idealistic and more relevant, pragmatic, and sensitive to the local political environment. Charles Hoch has suggested that planning theorists should consider a revised pragmatism as a replacement for the rational paradigm. He contends, "informed by a critical assessment of power relations, a revised conception of community, and a persistent focus on practice, a radical pragmatism might offer a promising way not only to conduct inquiry about planning, but to improve our planning conduct as well" (Hoch 1988b).

To be pragmatic, planners must have a working knowledge of the local political system. Ignorance of political factors and political reality is not bliss, it is a prescription for ineffectiveness and failure. Mel Levin, former president of the American Institute of Certified Planners, laments that "too many planners are so out of touch with political reality that they set off bombs without quite knowing what went wrong" (Levin 1987).

Many years ago in Lawrence, Kansas, the experienced building inspector asked the new planning director if he would help him deal with a minor zoning violation. An individual developing a mini-storage complex had fenced in the front yard in violation of the zoning ordinance. The inspector said that the owner had been notified, was very cooperative, and even had asked for assistance on complying with the ordinance. The inspector asked if the director or his new assistant would write the owner a letter explaining the specific requirements of the ordinance. The director eagerly agreed and in short order the assistant director mailed an informative letter to the property owner. Unbeknownst to either planner, the owner was Travis Glass, the longtime chairman of the county commission, and he was, in fact, both uncooperative and angry about the situation. The following is the letter he sent back to the planning director, as well as to the city manager and the mayor.

Dear Mr. McClendon:

As your records will reflect, title to this property is held by a partnership, in care of Mr. John McGrew, 900 Indiana Street. Operation and maintenance of the property is likewise taken care of by Mr. McGrew and any notices of violations should be directed to his attention.

This partnership contracted with Mr. Jack Sprecker to build these units in accordance with the terms of a construction contract and all applicable City of Lawrence regulations and ordinances. The units were finished in July 1969 and upon final inspection by the building inspector's office it was certainly assumed that all requirements had been met. If this was not correct, why was notification not made prior to this date?

I would call to your attention many situations of this same kind in existence throughout the City and would be concerned as to the real motive behind your notice on this particular piece of property. Am I to assume you have made an on-site examination of all such properties within the City and you are advising each owner they are also in violation?

I would like also to be advised why the enforcement of zoning violations is being done by the planning department. It has always been my opinion that these matters were more properly handled by the Building Inspector's staff or the City legal department.

As you may or may not be aware, a portion of the Lawrence-Douglas County planning department funds, including your salary, are paid by Douglas County, under the assumption the efforts put forth by your office are directed toward planning, revision of zoning ordinances and regulations, and most certainly not law enforcement.

If all of the work in the planning department were on a current basis, perhaps this type of activity might be warranted. However, many projects are behind and Douglas County has been waiting months for a revised County sub-division regulation which your office is supposedly working on. I can see why planning is slow if your office is devoting much time to their type of activity in place of your proper work.

It would appear to me that a complete examination of all planning department activities will be warranted prior to the adoption of a 1970 budget, to determine just how much time is being devoted to planning and whether a continuation of the joint City-County planning is warranted.

Yours very truly,

Travis E. Glass

The story of William Gomes, the former city planner for Littleton, New Hampshire, provides another opportunity for city planners to observe and learn about local politics. Gomes, an outsider, was hired in 1987 to set up the town's first planning department. According to Gomes, in an article he wrote for *Planning* magazine, the town manager had decided to hire a nonlocal professional so that code enforcement decisions would not be clouded by family or business interests (Gomes 1991). Gomes acknowledges that the manager's reasoning should have alerted him to possible problems in the town's views of planning and zoning. Over the next few years, Gomes developed and attempted to enforce a revised sign ordinance. His efforts met with persistent local opposition and eventually the ordinance was repealed by an initiative measure. In 1990, after repeated frustration and lack of support from the townspeople and elected officials, he resigned from his position. Preston Gilbert, the executive director of New Hampshire's North County Council, offered the following summary of the lessons to be learned from Gomes's experience: "It seems to me that the whole affair resulted from the installation of an outsider who was asked to enforce land-use controls rigorously, without ever getting a chance to understand the local psyche. He became the town enforcer instead of the town planner" (Lewis 1991).

Political insensitivity is a liability at any level of government in any profession. When Lauro Cavazos was forced to resign as secretary of education under the George Bush administration, critics pointed out that Cavazos was ineffective because he lacked knowledge of Washington politics. One high level government official noted, that Cavazos was totally shocked that he was in trouble. He thought that if he was in trouble, Bush would have called him (Leubsdorf 1990).

It is interesting to note that in the same newspaper that reported the resignation of Cavazos, the editors recommended Texan Tom Luce as his replacement. Luce had a successful track record in dealing with education issues at the state level. It was argued that Luce had a broad and deep grasp of many of the problems of public education and that he would be an active and aggressive education secretary. The only concern I had with the editorial was that it failed to question whether Luce adequately understood the Washington system so that he could be effective in its unique environment. I have the same question whenever a planner accepts a position in a community that he or she doesn't know much about. Experienced planners understand the need to learn about and adapt to the local political environment. Inexperienced planners often see only the technical aspects of the job. Hopefully they at least read the local newspaper.

President Bush eventually named former Tennessee governor and University of Tennessee president Lamar Alexander as education secretary. As governor, Alexander had focused on education and had developed a rapport with many other governors—crucial qualifications because many needed educational reforms will have to take place at the state level. Alexander also had experience in Washington, as a legislative assistant to Senator Howard Baker and as a White House executive assistant. Based on these facts, I predict Alexander will be a very effective education secretary.

When I've talked about politics at various workshops, I am usually asked just what it is that politicians want from planners. In response, I share both my experiences and the findings of others on this subject. In 1973, Dennis Rondinelli, while a member of the faculty of the Graduate School of Management at Vanderbilt University, wrote that "with the increasing complexity of urban decisionmaking, political leaders and urban administrators are demanding from planners pragmatic assistance with policy formulation and implementation" (Rondinelli 1973). Sally Shipman, AICP, a good friend and former member of the Austin, Texas, city council, tells me that "public officials understand and appreciate realistic, 'straight' talk delivered in concise, simple reports and value pragmatic assistance."

Communicating information so that it can be useful to elected officials and others is difficult for many planners. John Friedmann contends that "most planners prefer communicating their ideas in documents complete with charts, tables, graphs, and maps, as well as long appendices containing complex mathematical derivations and statistical analyses" (Friedmann 1973). One reason for this is that many planners are more interested in impressing their peers than in satisfying their clients. Another reason, according to Friedmann, is that "the planner's language is conceptual and mathematical, consciously drained of the lifeblood of human intercourse in its striving for scientific objectivity."

A quick review of almost any planning document exemplifies this point. For example, look at the following introduction to a well-prepared comprehensive plan describing "The Comprehensive Planning Framework" in a southwestern city:

> The ranking system, adopted in 1982, established a hierarchy of plans. The *Comprehensive Plan* is the rank one plan: area and facility plans are rank two plans; and sector development, neighborhood, and corridor plans are rank three plans. All plans must be compatible with higher ranking plans for the same area. (See Appendix B for list of approved plans.) The *Plan* ranking ordinance states: 'Adopted City plans for urban development and conservation are of varying rank importance. Lower ranking plans should be consistent with higher ranking plans, and when this is indesputably not the case, the conflicting provision of the lower ranking plan is null and void.' Rank two plans carry out the *Plan's* general guidelines and policies. Area plans outline issues, relationships, and policies for large areas . . . Rank two plans may recommend *Comprehensive Plan* amendment in order to further refine policies, techniques, or boundaries. . . .

The role of planners in the political system is to enhance the decision-making process, not to show others how smart and superior they are. The knowledge that competent planners possess, if properly presented, can have great influence on public officials. Planners should not fear sharing this expertise. Rather, they should be interested in linking knowledge and power to the advantage of their customers.

John Forester teaches that "planners have to interpret problems and their political contexts together, so they can use whatever techniques are at hand in a practical, timely and politically astute manner" (Krumholz and Forester 1990). According to Anthony Catanese, planners must "understand and recognize the political process and utilize scientific tools in such a manner as to strengthen the basis for decisionmaking" (Catanese 1974).

Guy Benveniste, professor of policy planning in the Graduate School of Education at the University of California at Berkeley, says that a good strategy for the political realist is to "seek the political compromise that makes sense technically" (Benveniste 1989). An important responsibility for the planner is to make sure there is a solid, well-documented, and defensible technical basis for the resulting decisions of the elected officials.

In recent years it appears that many practitioners have become very adept at working within the context of local political systems. Hamid Shirvani, dean of the School of Architecture and Planning at the University of Colorado, has interviewed a number of planning directors and discovered that, "Many planners have become political animals; they know how to try to expand their roles, yet they recognize the built-in limitations they face. They have learned through experience how to be of influence" (Shirvani 1985).

Susan Brody, director of the Oregon Department of Land Conservation and Development, has found that upper-level planners are much more politically astute than when she first started practicing. This is a positive change according to Brody. She has learned from experience that "planners can accomplish so much more when they try to accommodate different political perspectives, present viable alternatives and develop proposals that reflect a political consensus."

Pragmatism on the part of planners requires that elected officials be given politically viable options to choose from. This is a hard concept for some planners and city managers to accept. I know of one city manager who was opposed to presenting alternatives to the city council. His theory was that if given options, the council might select the wrong one. He felt much more comfortable in making the choice for them. He also restricted the council's access to information that conflicted with his views and positions. This was only done, he reasoned, to protect the council from unnecessary conflict and controversy. I am strongly opposed to this strategy because it is contrary to this country's political heritage and the principles on which the city management form of government is based. Yet I must be honest and report that the city manager who used it was very effective and enjoyed a long tenure in several cities.

OPTIMAL SOLUTIONS VERSUS OPTIONS

Some planners believe that for every problem there is a single, technically right, optimal solution waiting to be developed. This partly explains why planning sometimes takes so long. It is because these planners are trying to get it right the first time. They assume that with hard work, plenty of research, sound technical analysis, and detailed supporting documentation the decision makers will accept their optimal solution. Well, I've got bad news for these planners. For almost all problems there are multiple solutions and the best single solution is the one that the decision makers choose. When planners functioning as mediators are able to raise the quality of debate, develop viable options, and facilitate consensus building, then they will be useful and relevant to the problem solving process. "The concept of the planner as a mediator," according to Henry Fagin, one of the elder statesmen of the planning profession, "is different from the idea of the planner as the master designer who alone can perceive the one best plan to fit a situation that he alone grasps" (Fagin 1970). Fagin added that the "notion of mediation among differing interest groups, rather than service to an abstraction called the public interest, squarely recognizes and addresses the fact of cultural, social, and economic diversity among people, and the perpetual presence of validly particular interests."

Howell Baum's surveys of today's practitioners are always insightful. In a random survey of 50 members of the Maryland chapter of the American Planning Association, he asked how often each planner discovered a unique, correct solution to a problem. Forty-four percent replied that they "frequently" or "always" found a single solution, 32 percent stated they "rarely" or "never" saw a single solution, and 24 percent answered "sometimes" (Baum 1983). Baum's research also reveals that a number of planners believe that the political processes of decision making distract attention away from reasonable or optimal solutions. He concludes that there "is a common hostility of many planners toward politics, which they believe interferes with their planning" (Baum 1983).

Yet many of the planners that Baum surveyed accepted and even welcomed politics. I particularly liked the following three comments:

• "The type of project I work on is so complex that it is really a decision tree. Normally we are not even smart enough to see where the project is going to lead us. The way you pose the problem influences the outcome. It is not an optimization process, but really a suboptimization process."

• "When I first got out of planning school, I would have said [that I found a single unique solution] frequently or always. The longer I work, the lower my rating is. The older and wiser you get, the grayer things get. If you asked me several years ago, I would have said frequently. If you ask me several years from now, I may say rarely."

• "I do not think planners should ever back a public official into a position where he has only one choice. Sometimes planners decide to play God and say this is it. They have got to come up with options for a man who has got to make decisions."

Even when presented with several options, however, politicians are not nearly as quick to embrace change as some planners would like. Political courage and leadership is a lost art in many communities. Politicians are learning that it is safer to find a parade and get out in front of it than it is to build a following.

As a side note, I have found that it's not just politicians that are slow to embrace change. Many planners report that the real opposition to their initiatives are other department heads. Many planners note that they have great latitude within their own departments, but in other departments they find well-entrenched bureaucracies that are incredibly resistant to new ideas and to change. Typical is the complaint of Corinne Gibb, former planning director of the city of Detroit, that one of the major problems she had to deal with was "how to overcome the turf problem of a great many agencies, each independent of the other, each going its own way and each with divisions of bureaucrats going their own way" (Shirvani 1985).

With respect to my political experiences, I have been heartened by the success that comes about when multiple choices have been presented to elected officials. This approach facilitates negotiation and compromise, helps the participants to reach a consensus, and leads to a sense of individual ownership of the final product. Achieving change depends on hard work and political savvy. And I continue to be influenced by Paul Davidoff's counsel that "the realism of the possibility of change is less important than the continued effort to act to create such a possibility" (Davidoff 1974).

BEING SENSITIVE AND SCANNING THE POLITICAL ENVIRONMENT

Being sensitive to the political environment requires that planners become more systematic in their efforts to include political factors in the planning process. In a paper on "Political Feasibility and Policy Analysis," Arnold Meltsner proposed that political problems should be analyzed in terms of the *actors* who are concerned about the problem, their *beliefs* and *motivations*, the *resources* that the actors can use, their *effectiveness*, and finally the *sites* where and when decisions will be made (Meltsner 1972). Carl Patton, AICP, and David Sawicki, AICP, have suggested that this type of information might be compiled as: 1) checklists so that central actors and decision sites are considered; 2) decision trees so that the interrelation of actors, decision sites, and sequence of events is revealed; and 3) scorecards or impact tables so that the relative importance of issues to actors and the preferences of actors for various alternatives can be specified (Patton and Sawicki 1986).

In order to develop an appreciation for the Meltsner approach it is necessary to understand his terminology and to apply the concept to a real world situation. Actors, as used by Meltsner, are the various individuals, groups, or entities that will or might be affected by the problem and its solution. The first step in the political scanning process is to prepare a list of actors and assess each one's level of interest and potential for involvement. As alternatives are developed it is important to constantly refer back to this list to differentiate between those that are likely to support the alternative and those who might oppose it. The list of actors should be updated as needed. It is not static because some alternatives might affect actors that were not considered to be impacted when the problem was first analyzed. Also, actors are capable of involving other unaffected actors in the process as they network and try to broaden their base of support.

The next step involves identifying and then developing a better understanding of the beliefs and motivations of the various actors. This is usually not a difficult assignment. Most actors take great pride in expressing and sharing their beliefs with the world. Some actors such as associations and business organizations will have written statements or position papers that articulate their points of view. For some actors, it may be necessary to check old newspapers, interview acquaintances and colleagues, or even talk directly with them. I have found that the news media is frequently an excellent source for this type of information.

A critically important aspect of this part of the process is to identify the core values of each actor, and the intensity of these beliefs. Obviously it is difficult to mediate and resolve conflicts without this kind of information. But with knowledge of the fundamental objectives of each actor it is often possible to develop a proposal that accommodates their essential needs while only requiring them to make compromises in less significant or unimportant areas. It is important to understand that almost all actors have some positions or objectives that are nonnegotiable. If you want to be effective you better know what they are.

The next step in Meltsner's scanning process is to evaluate each actor's resources. These resources can be financial or technical, or can be intangibles like power, prestige, friendships, and influence. Technical knowledge, expertise, and professional representation can be purchased with financial resources, as can publicity and media exposure. Friendships and access to power are more difficult to achieve and may require lengthy cultivation. The ability to obtain legal representation in order to use the court system is another resource to be considered.

Resources are not of much value unless the actors use them to get results. Critical to the scanning process is the assessment of the effectiveness of all significant actors. What are their track records? Are they whiners or winners? Do they know how to mobilize and deploy their resources so as to influence decision making? Do they have credibility and respect? Are they likely to make a difference in the political process?

Lastly, you should diagram the formal and informal decision-making process, identifying the key sites or decision points and their anticipated order of progression. Typical sites are various meetings, formal public hearings, official elections, and even newspaper editorials. Some authorities have the tendency to make decisions before the formal date of action. If so, this should be reflected in the diagram. Other key things to look for are veto sites and the gatekeepers who control or have superior influence at each site.

Most of the information needed to prepare a quick, simple scan is readily available. It can often be obtained from the first-hand knowledge of the staff involved in the process or from limited research of common materials found in most public libraries. Once planners come to understand the importance of this scanning activity, they find it easy to accumulate political information and store it for future reference.

As planners become more comfortable with, and appreciative of, the value of scanning the political environment, they become more sophisticated in their analysis and devote an increased proportion of staff time to this activity. Many planning directors report that scanning consumes a significant amount of their own time and accounts for a significant portion of the many meetings they attend. Unfortunately, most planning departments do not undertake even a minimal scan of their political environment. It's as if they don't want to give themselves an unfair advantage in the decision-making process. It may also be that some planners intuitively sense the political hopelessness of their work and don't want to be influenced or discouraged by reality. Obviously, if you don't care if you win then you don't need to know the rules of the game.

MUSH BRAINS, DOUBLE DOMES, CRACKPOTS,
AND GOO GOOS

When I was growing up there was a popular television game show called "Who Do You Trust?" It seemed that high school English teachers always took delight in informing their students that this was not correct grammar, and that the title should be "Whom Do You Trust?" With respect to customer service the question should really be, "Whom do you trust and does whom trust you?"

Many planners are naturally suspicious of politicians. In that sense planners are not unlike the vast majority of the American public. The 1990s will not be a good time to be a politician. The growing national interest in limiting the number of terms that public officials may hold is the voters' way of saying "to hell with all you politicians."

Local politicians are not always respected by planning bureaucrats. One planning director told me that he learned very early in his career not to look up to politicians or pigeons. Another commented that while politics may not be the world's oldest profession, it produces the same results. There are three reasons why an untrusting planner may have doubts about elected officials: they are beholden to special interest groups and can't be objective; they are not as technically competent as the planner and therefore not as qualified to make decisions; and they have poor judgment for even wanting to hold public office in the first place. There you have it. Politicians are the three horsemen of the public apocalypse—evil of intent, incompetent, and foolish.

I am not exaggerating the bias that many planners hold toward elected officials. One of my favorite illustrations was provided by Rexford Tugwell, the first chairman of the New York City Planning Commission after it was formed in the 1930s. Tugwell was an incredibly ineffective planner. Despite an impressive intellect, Tugwell lacked the political skill and tact necessary to direct a successful planning program. With his arrogant and self-righteous manner, he accomplished the rare feat of alienating politicians, bureaucrats, businessmen, civic groups, and the general public alike. "Tugwell's excursions into public housing, zoning, and master planning," according to planning historian Jon Peterson, "would be marked by frustration and defeat" (Peterson 1985). Tugwell's personal view of the New York city council was summarized in the following comment from the diary he wrote shortly after his resignation: "[They] can be counted on to do their best to prove that Hitler is right;

that legislators are corrupt, always anxious to be subservient to any special interest, always ready to act against the public interest" (Peterson 1985).

Of course, the elected officials in New York were equally disturbed with Tugwell. Successful politicians fully understand the art of negotiation and compromise. Tugwell, like too many planners, was insensitive to the political climate, out of touch with political reality, and unwilling to compromise his positions.

Robert Moses provides a stunning contrast to Tugwell. Moses held a number of positions in New York City and, in the words of Donald Krueckeberg, AICP, "became known in New York and among planners the country over as 'the man who gets things done'" (Wilson 1983). For a full and critical description of the many accomplishments of Moses, read *The Power Broker* by Robert Caro. Moses knew how to use the political system to deliver results, not insults.

Alfred E. Smith was one of New York's most effective reform governors. Governor Smith wasn't interested in rhetoric, he wanted action and results. But he had little patience with professional reformers who could not function within the political framework. He found that the laws and proposals of such idealists never became reality. As a result, positive incremental reforms were delayed and the citizens became the real losers. "Mush brains," "double domes," "crackpots," and "goo goos" were what he called the noncompromising reformists (Caro 1975). (Note: If you thought the provocative terms in the heading for this section were referring to politicians, it ought to be an indication of the bias that the profession has against elected officials.)

While many planners have a natural tendency to think the worst of public officials, these suspicions are often mutual. Anthony Catanese argues that many politicians sense that planners are prejudiced against them. These politicians then adopt a defensive posture that "often means an automatic cataloging of recommendations from planners as being impractical, unrealistic, and irrelevant" (Catanese 1974). For a more thorough understanding of the natural conflict between planners and politicians, read Catanese's books on *Planners and Local Politics* and *The Politics of Planning and Development*.

BUILDING TRUSTING RELATIONSHIPS

If planners are going to be effective, they must gain the trust of public officials, of course. As you might have guessed, I do have some advice on how to build a positive, trusting, and mutually beneficial relationship with elected officials.

The first step is to show appreciation and respect for our democratic representative form of government. Planners must readily accept that they have only an advisory role in the political decision-making process. Ultimate authority resides with elected officials and their electorate.

The second step is to recognize that elected officials are the most important customers that planners have. Politicians should receive priority consideration and special treatment from the planning staff. This is true even for planners working under the city manager form of government. However, it goes without saying that the nature of the relationship that is to exist between the staff and elected officials should be dictated by the city manager and the planning director. Individual planners should not take it upon themselves to develop personal or working relationships with the manager or elected officials without the approval of the department's director.

Planners also need to be aware of the positive feelings and motivations that most politicians bring to their job. The feelings of Donna Sprull, former zoning commissioner and current mayor of Addison, Texas, are representative of many elected officials. "I've come to like politics a lot more than I thought I would," Sprull says. "You do it because of the benefits to your community, and then you find that there's something beyond that. You do it because of the love you have of the satisfaction and the personal challenge that comes from accomplishing things" (Hitt 1990).

People seek public office, says Sally Shipman, former member of the Austin, Texas, city council, because they have ideas and want to have influence, not because they want to implement the planner's vision. Her major complaint is that government bureaucrats have their own limited agendas and are unaware of those of elected officials. "Politicians don't want blind support," she says, "they simply want fair and objective consideration and treatment for their ideas and proposals and they want help in implementing them." She warns planners to be honest and brave enough to share both good and bad news. A politician appreciates being protected from a bad idea, according to Shipman, but only when he or she believes the staff has made a good faith effort to make the idea work and has the official's best interest at heart.

Knowing how far to take this support is another key to gaining trust. Planners can be political in either a positive or negative way, says Susan

Brody. Blind obedience, in her view, is bad politics and will usually be disastrous for everyone. Good politics means being honest and candid with the officials. This means working behind the scenes, educating them, and challenging them to do better. Floyd Lapp, the director of the transportation division of the New York City Department of City Planning, says planners can merely give the politicians what they want, or they can inspire and motivate them to achieve greater accomplishments.

In a presentation given at the 1989 annual conference of the Association of Collegiate Schools of Planning (ACSP), Norm Krumholz offered the following advice to planners on how to effectively argue with their mayors:

> This takes considerable tact. One must choose one's words with care, but one must really argue, not merely defer. The terms and words of such arguments must be respectful and of course allow for future agreement. If other agencies and directors support the mayor's views (and they will), one's criticisms of their position must be gentle, revealing and technical. The objective is to give the mayor an opportunity to see differing technical (not political) viewpoints, resolve disagreements among competent old friends and perhaps change his mind.

I would modify Krumholz's guidance only by suggesting that planners can dispense political advice as well as technical information. Planners are often the eyes and ears of the public official, and may possess valuable political insights. James Bellus, AICP, former director of planning and economic development for the city of St. Paul, Minnesota, notes, "The planning director has the responsibility for listening to all the different forces that are raising issues and identifying concerns that need to be dealt with. The planning director is really in between in many ways. The citizens and the special interest groups are on the one hand, and the elected officials—the planning director's bosses—on the other hand" (Shirvani 1985).

I would go one step further and suggest that planners are more than just caught in between the citizens and the elected officials, they have the opportunity to be the go-betweens for the two parties—to provide some of the communication (both directions) and the working linkage that will increase the political effectiveness of the elected officials. Ron Short, the planning director for the city of Phoenix, notes: "The director is a convener who helps the citizens come together, bringing their thoughts out and helping to focus many citizens' thoughts; provides them the technical information, the background data to bring these particular ideas together; and acts as an adviser to these citizens, the planning commission, and the governing body, bringing everything and everyone together to set forth a clear agenda for the future" (Shirvani 1985).

WHAT CAN PLANNERS DO FOR ELECTED OFFICIALS?

Earlier, it was suggested that one of the steps planners should take in overcoming the natural suspicions of elected officials is to treat them as valuable, high-priority customers. Steven Cohen, associate dean of the School of International and Public Affairs at Columbia University, advises public sector employees to develop marketable services and programs that generate political support. Success, in his experience, depends on the organization's ability to "perform some task valued by those who distribute resources" (Cohen 1988).

Many planners at my workshops have been puzzled by this advice. While they acknowledge the value of treating public officials as customers, they just don't know how to do it. One planner I particularly remember said, "I can't think of anything special I could do for my mayor or city council. They don't even know I exist." Another similar comment was, "I don't have much that would be of any use or value to an elected official."

Let's look at what planners can do to make themselves more valuable to elected officials:
- assist in finding or articulating a vision for the community;
- assist in developing an action or implementation program for a proposed project or service;
- provide information on the mechanics of how things really work within the city hall bureaucracy and the various people you need to know to get things done;
- provide position papers on important political issues;
- draft campaign literature and advertisements;
- attend fund-raising events and make financial contributions;
- provide them with specialized education and training by in-house staff or sponsor attendance at workshops and conferences.
- help their constituents navigate city hall to get a problem solved;
- ghost write letters for them in response to communications from constituents;
- listen to them, serve as a sounding board, and provide both a

professional and a candid personal assessment of their ideas and proposals;

- help them to develop a legislative agenda and work program;
- make them aware of meetings of various commissions and organizations where participation or visibility would be to their political advantage;
- provide public opinion sampling or polling on issues;
- help get publicity and recognition for their involvement in significant projects;
- nominate them for awards;
- arrange speaking engagements and assist in preparing speeches;
- provide "spin-doctoring" assistance to minimize political damage from failed projects or other mistakes;
- fill in for them at speaking engagements or ceremonial functions;
- provide training in conflict resolution, mediation, and facilitation techniques and skills;
- Take heat for risky proposals that the politician wants to "run up the flagpole"; and
- challenge them to reach their fullest political potential.

This last opportunity is particularly exciting to me. In three of the cities I have worked in, I was able to provide some small measure of advice and guidance to planning commissioners who went on to become not just elected officials, but mayors. And they all became outstanding mayors that provided strong leadership in their respective communities.

HOW TO SERVE UNETHICAL POLITICIANS

Some of you are probably troubled by the advice to treat elected officials like valued customers. The first question I always get on this subject is, "What if the politician is unethical?" My quick answer has been to heed the advice of Anthony Catanese and Allan Jacobs, who maintain that planners should always keep their bags packed. I then try to convince the questioner that most planners can't be effective in an unethical, or in an untrusting, political environment. Sy Schulman, president of the Westchester County Association in New York, recently wrote me with the following observations based on his many years of experience:

In *The Prince of 1513*, Machiavelli advises: "The prince ought always to take counsel but only when he wishes, not when others wish. . . ." I have known lots of princes—even a princess or two—and fully subscribe to the view that it is their interest that must be served. With some princes that is the only interest; others recognize that the ultimate interest being served is that of the community, however that is perceived. Happy is the planner whose prince is a decent, sensitive, honorable person solely (or mostly) devoted to community rather than personal interests. If that is very far from the truth or the reality, then no amount of, nor any kind of, planning will have any measurable impact. In fact, you will be lucky to be allowed to do any planning, considering that your prince is not really receptive. As Machiavelli suggests, "a prince who is not wise himself cannot be well advised."

In my experience, it is almost impossible to be an effective planner when you cannot respect or trust the officials you are supposed to be serving. Planners who believe they can turn a corrupt politician into a public-spirited community leader also believe that the kiss of a princess can turn a frog into a prince. Recent scientific studies have found very few examples of frogs turning into princes. What is far more likely to happen, such as in the movie *The Princess Bride*, is that the frog will turn into a huge rat.

The best way to serve an unethical politician is to be ethical yourself, a "sort of strengthening of the client," says Krumholz. Even if your values don't rub off on the politician, they might curb his unethical practices.

I once had the misfortune of working for an unethical, and stupid, mayor. He asked me to approve a building permit that was in violation of the zoning ordinance. I declined, and the mayor exclaimed that he would get a new planning director that would do what he was told. The city manager, however, defended me. After several more illegal and unethical requests were rejected or ignored, the mayor quit asking. But while I could protect him from his lack of ethics, I could not cure his stupidity. One of my favorite stories is about the time he publicly criticized the city manager for asking for a new position when the city council had imposed a hiring freeze. When the manager hesitantly replied that he was not seeking any new people, the mayor boldly pointed out the agenda item request for a word processor.

Keeping your bags packed is advice easy to give but hard to abide by. I have always followed this philosophy in my career, and have benefited personally and professionally. But my advice probably will not do much to calm the fears of those who can't risk unemployment. Fear has a powerful influence on people's lives. If it makes you more sensitive it is a positive force; if it corrodes your behavior and leads you into unethical or illegal acts it is a negative factor. I can't emphasize enough that in my experience and the experience of scores of practitioners that I have interviewed, most fears are blown way out of proportion. The risks of unethical practice greatly exceed the risks of ethical practice. One planner told me, "I thought if I did the right thing I would be fired. I was wrong. The council respects me more than ever and I don't even give it a second thought anymore." Another planner said, "the risks are greatly exaggerated. Some people will try to bluff you, but if you are right and stand your ground things will be okay."

IDEAL PLANNER —
BAGS PACKED, READY TO GO...

While the risks may be exaggerated, planning and government service is not as stable a profession as it once was. Robert Youngman, an experienced planner from Mason City, Iowa, with master's degrees in urban planning and public administration, lost a job after nine years because of a 10-percent budget cut. In a letter to *Planning* magazine, Youngman warns, "Planning is a high-risk profession. Graduate schools should better prepare their students for that reality." He adds, "I had no job offers in planning and was forced to make a career change to support my family" (Youngman 1991).

In Chapter 1, I mentioned that Uri Avin, the planning director of Howard County, Maryland, was fired by the newly elected county executive. Robert Marriott, president of the Maryland chapter of APA, observed that Avin suffered a fate common to many planning directors caught up in the process of adopting a general plan. Avin was the focus of controversy, and his plan led to the defeat of the former county executive (Gallagher 1991). The fear of being the center of controversy is often one of the reasons planners give for hiring consultants to manage certain kinds of projects. But planners can't insulate themselves from all risks. And I did not interview a single planner that advocated unethical or illegal behavior in order to keep a job. Always be true to yourself and, oh yes, keep your bags packed, because sometimes it will be necessary for you to leave.

DO YOU NEED A HEARING AID OR DO YOU JUST NEED TO GET RID OF YOUR PLANNING COMMISSION?

The basic premise behind planning commissions can be traced to the good government movement at the beginning of the 20th Century, which was born in direct response to the emergence of the big city political machines, the spoils system of rewarding political supporters, and the extensive graft and corruption that was present in many local governments. Some of the positive reforms that can be traced to the good government movement are the machine ballot, the merit system, competitive bidding, and auditing and budgeting requirements. Another important reform was the creation of boards and commissions to oversee specialized government functions and to insulate employees from political influence. In particular, it was thought that independent planning commissions were needed: if elected officials couldn't be trusted with the present, then they could hardly be trusted with the future.

Unfortunately, by separating planning from implementation, most commissions and the studies and plans they produced had only marginal, if any, influence on decision making in local government. Over the years, most planners have come to understand that planning must be a function of both the administrative and legislative branches of local government. This requires treating each branch as a customer. Planners don't need protection from decision makers, they need access.

While planning commissions have clearly outlived their original intended purpose, in some communities they are able to make limited contributions to customer service. When the membership of a commission is representative of the general population, it provides an excellent source of public input into the planning process. Unfortunately, in far too many communities, commissions are and have been dominated by the development profession, a fact that has contributed to the lack of meaningful public participation and involvement in planning and zoning decisions.

Today, there is much greater awareness of the need for balanced representation on boards and commissions, but the selection process is still dominated by political considerations. Elected officials can no longer promise jobs or contracts to their supporters, but they can promise appointments to boards and commissions. When a citizen recently asked one city manager what he had to do to become a planning commissioner, the manager suggested he run someone's political campaign. This answer was not flippant, but rather reflected political reality.

Several years ago I helped a major regional council of governments set up a series of training workshops for planning commissioners. I proposed that the COG use attendance at these workshops to certify eligibility for membership on the planning commissions of its member cities. Local governments would be asked to limit their selections of commissioners to individuals that had either completed the training program or would agree to do so within nine months. I was not surprised when the COG rejected this proposal because it involved an element of political risk.

The unwillingness of local governments to require commissioners to commit to continuing education reflects the lack of respect that many elected officials have for the technical nature of the planning function in local government. It is also an indication that a great many elected officials do not really want informed public participation.

But times are changing and an increasing number of public officials are trying to include more of the community in their work. These officials are not expecting their commissions to do more. Instead, they are bypassing them and going directly to the people. Too many planning commissions are a needless intermediary between the general public and the decision makers. Elected officials and the planning staff don't need a commission to function as a hearing aid. They need direct access and communication. If your commission can be reformed to help fulfill this function, then do so. If reform is not possible, then get rid of it.

SHIFTING FROM REPRESENTATIVE TO PARTICIPATORY AND COLLABORATIVE DEMOCRACY

Costis Toregas, president of Public Technology, Inc. (PTI), contends that "a truly 'customer' orientation, as is the rage now in the private sector, has in fact been recognized in democracy as an institution for many years." The problem is that as cities have grown in size many local government institutions have not been able to figure out how to continue to be responsive to the electorate. "As cities and counties grow larger," says Toregas, "as organizational structure gets more complex, and as budgets are strained, one might see a growing rift between the governed and those who control the apparatus of governance. Arithmetic alone plays some vicious games with the ability of anyone to understand, let alone react to the needs of a community. When you have thousands of residents, all with differing needs, cultural backgrounds, and expectations, it is not easy to hear and 'represent' their needs" (Toregas 1989).

The best and simplest advice that can be given for resolving the above dilemma is to share power. Robert Lineberry and Ira Sharkansky, respected academics in the field of political science, report there is a debate between political theorists concerning whether elected officials should play the role of trustee or delegate. "The trustee role," they write, "emphasizes the representative's obligation to vote according to conscience and best judgment, regardless of whether his or her vote happens to follow constituents' preferences. The delegate role obligates the representative to vote according to the perception of constituents' sentiments, regardless of personal views" (Lineberry and Sharkansky 1978).

Lineberry and Sharkansky found in their research that most elected officials overwhelmingly support the trustee role over the delegate role. I have observed the same preference in the cities where I've practiced. Most elected officials value their own opinions over those of their constituents or staff. When there is no community consensus, or a lack of information, or public apathy, then elected officials can freely exercise their independent judgment without fear of condemnation or political reprisals. However, when there is community consensus and participation, elected officials no longer have the same latitude. Now, there may well be a political price to pay.

Often, there's a correlation between the length of stay in office and a politician's insensitivity to the people in the community—apathy and lethargy lie at one end of the spectrum, arrogance and corruption at the other. "If you're in the same office too long," says Addison, Texas, mayor Donna Sprull, "you begin thinking about taking shortcuts that probably shouldn't be taken" (Hitt 1990). In several cities with long-time mayors that I studied, I was shocked at how the political establishment had become estranged or divorced from constituents—the people on the other side of the castle moat. I found these communities overmanaged and underled.

One striking example is provided by Kathy Whitmire, who recently lost her bid for a sixth two-year term as Mayor of Houston. Despite her long tenure, Whitmire's views on many issues were often in conflict with prevailing public opinion.

For example, Houston voters had rejected rail transit in 1974 and again in 1983. A comprehensive multimodal transportation improvement program was approved by the voters in 1988, but it did not emphasize the rail concept. In fact, the ballot did not even include the word "rail." Despite the fact that polls showed the public did not support a rail program, Whitmire maintained that if the issue were put to a vote, rail proponents could have persuaded voters to support it. Her statement showed a surprising disregard for public opinion and excessive faith in the power of money and promotion. There is a big difference between rallying divergent constituencies around a program and persuading voters to accept a top-down decision. The time to convince the public of the rightness of a decision is while it is being made, not after people have been forced to fight a lengthy battle just to gain access to the decision-making process.

The lack of adequate Hispanic representation on the Houston city council is further evidence of the failure of responsive local political leadership in that city. Hispanics make up a quarter of the population in Houston, yet only one of the city council's 15 members is Hispanic. Lawsuits have been threatened if the city does not pursue voluntary redistricting. In 1981 in Beaumont, Texas, a city of 100,000 located about 50 miles east of Houston, the African-American community made a similar request for more representation. In that case, the first-term mayor of Beaumont worked with the city council to voluntarily redistrict the city within a year of the request. It was a productive process that resulted in proportional representation for the black community and a strengthened relationship between elected officials and the general public.

Perhaps Whitmire's greatest failure in leadership was her vigorous opposition to city planning and to zoning regulations. The American Planning Association had scheduled its 1988 annual conference for Houston, but moved it to San Antonio because of Whitmire's vocal rejection of city planning. Houston has long been able to function without zoning because of deed restrictions and other regulations, but its failure to plan for the future has left it with a vast array of urban problems and a declining quality of life. Public opinion surveys have consistently shown for many years that the majority of Houston residents want more planning and zoning regulations. But it was not until 1991 when Whitmire was forced by the growing political popularity of councilmember and planning advocate James Greenwood, that Donna Kristaponis was hired as the city's first planning director.

As urban issues become more technical, complex, and politically divisive, there is growing willingness on the part of elected officials to share their decision-making authority with the community and technical experts. Furthermore, as elected officials become more aware of their own limits and learn that most of the significant urban issues of the day require multijurisdictional solutions, they become more aware of the need to involve others in developing and implementing solutions.

Fred Bair, Jr., in his classic book, *Planning Cities*, wrote, "There is considerable evidence that those civilizations have advanced most rapidly in which planning has been most effective as a guide to action. It is also notable that the empires which fell apart most rapidly were those in which the power to plan (to direct what to do) was concentrated in the hands of the few. In such regimes, discipline was the chief virtue demanded of the people, and the ability of the common man to think and act for himself or his group atrophied. . . .The strength of our democracy lies in the sharing of knowledge and in the sharing of decisions as to how to use it" (Bair, Jr. 1970).

A 1989 article in *Business Month* magazine on the best-managed big cities in America noted that many of the best run cities "have strong traditions of citizen participation and open government" (Peirce and Guskind 1989). These top cities, the article says, have leaders that practice the fine art of power sharing and who are adept at "detecting new concerns of the voters and sensing shifts in the public mood that may require adjustments of government priorities."

The $64 question that has been debated in this country since its origins is, should the burden of solving public problems rest most directly on citizens or on government? Thomas Jefferson, when pondering whether it was preferable to give energy to the government or information to the people, concluded that the latter "is the most certain, and the most legitimate engine of government." Henry Cisneros, the former four-term mayor of San Antonio, and John Parr, president of the National Civic League, offer a similar view: "Solutions to the problems we face as a society can be found, in part, in the rediscovery of an activist model of citizenship. In particular this model includes an understanding and acceptance by individuals of their stake in the community and responsibility to participate in problem solving" (Cisneros and Parr 1991).

The basic premise of government at all levels is changing because the electorate is changing. Increasingly, voters are looking for partnerships, not leadership. Jonathan Howes, the mayor of Chapel Hill, North Carolina, warns his colleagues that, "In city politics, the demographic changes now on the horizon pose political threats to current officeholders who fail to perceive the changes going on around them. An electorate that is older, more ethnically diverse, and increasingly active will inevitably challenge those in power and force changes in behavior or changes among those who hold office" (Howes 1991).

Anthony Downs, a senior fellow at the Brookings Institution, contends that the very structure of democracy operates against the exercise of strong leadership from the top. "If there is to be effective leadership," he says, "it must come from the bottom or from nonelected officials mustering popular support" (Downs 1991).

James Kunde, executive director of the Public Service Institute, says, "In the last several years political scientists who study local leadership . . . have found that the 'facilitative leader' has surpassed the 'executive leader' in terms of being able to get things done. Mayors like George Voinovich of Cleveland, Bob Bolen of Fort Worth and Henry Cisneros of San Antonio are frequently cited as models" (Kunde 1990).

Kunde's favorable opinion of Voinovich, now governor of Ohio, is buttressed by his support for citizen involvement in the development of

Cleveland's "Civic Vision"—a 10-year plan for charting the city's course. An assessment of the plan by *Nation's Cities Weekly* says "the decision to give citizens such an important vote in planning for the city's future stemmed from the feeling among city officials, including Voinovich, 'that a long-range development plan requires the understanding, support and participation of the people'" (National League of Cities 1984). This is what Paul Davidoff was talking about when he suggested, "If the planning process is to encourage democratic urban government then it must operate as to include rather than exclude citizens from participating in the process" (Davidoff 1965).

When Cisneros spoke at the annual conference of APA's Texas chapter in 1990, he acknowledged that "this country is shifting from a representative democracy to a participatory democracy." Says O. Wendell White, veteran city manager for Charlotte, North Carolina, "If you get things out in the middle of the street where everyone can see them, you'll do much better. If you operate in a dark alley you can get beat up pretty bad" (Barnes and Orlebeke 1991).

Efforts to solve community problems seldom fail because reasonable solutions are not available, adds Susan Carpenter, director of the Program for Community Problem Solving in Washington, D.C. In her experience, failure results when "key parties are not included in the decision making" (Carpenter 1989). Several city mayors quoted in recent issues of *Nation's Cities Weekly* follow this same reasoning. Current Cleveland mayor Michael White contends that, if he is to be effective, "people must believe the government is fair, and that the mayor is trying to go the extra mile to include everyone in decision making." Mayor Maynard Jackson of Atlanta says, "I believe in the politics of inclusion . . . not trying to move anyone away from the table of decision making but trying to put up additional chairs." An obvious exception to the generalization that tenure leads to insensitivity is William Hudnut III, the long-time mayor of Indianapolis. In his experience, the mayor must have a consensus-building management style, not authoritarian. "You have to be participatory," says Hudnut, and "the mayor is an agent of reconciliation."

Efforts by local government to empower people, according to Henry Cisneros and John Parr, should be accompanied by: 1) the provision of forums for public debate and discussion of issues (as well as access to officials); and 2) outreach on the successes of government, to increase voter confidence in the ability of public institutions to solve society's problems—offsetting the well-known failures of government with successes will go far toward turning the tide of civic disengagement (Cisneros and Parr 1991).

An outstanding example of this empowering type of leadership is Daniel Kemmis, mayor of Missoula, Montana. In his extraordinary book, *Community and the Politics of Place*, Kemmis argues that the true frontier spirit was not rugged individualism, but cooperation. Early pioneers, says Kemmis, ventured into a wilderness that defeated them until they learned to take care of each other. Cooperation was the key to survival then and now, but it is not possible, he says, until "people learn to listen to each other, build trust among each other, build patterns of working relationships which enable them to discover and build upon common ground." He adds, "the actual practice of finding solutions that people can live with usually reaches beyond compromise to something more like neighborliness—to finding within shared space the possibilities for a shared inhabitation" (Kemmis 1990).

Political pragmatism, not idealism, lies at the heart of Kemmis's leadership philosophy. In 1989, a group advocating the Down Home Project came before the Missoula city council to request community development block grant funds to construct a solar greenhouse. It was explained that this project would provide both work and food for a variety of constituencies, including developmentally disabled, elderly, and unemployed people. But because the project included a laundromat that would be attached to the greenhouse and would provide backup heat while contributing toward operating expenses, it was opposed by local laundromat owners. The greenhouse was to be located in the northern part of the city where there were no competing laundromats, but to the business community it was a matter of principle. They were opposed to public funds being used to support a project that would be in competition with the private sector.

The applicants for the project asked Kemmis to mediate the dispute. A joint meeting was held, and both sides presented their cases. One of the most vocal laundromat owners then asked the mayor for his views. Kemmis noted that "his tone made it clear that he expected, now that the opposing ideologies had been laid on the table, that it was time for someone 'in government' to choose between them." Rather than give his views, though, the mayor asked the applicant to respond again now that he had heard the opponents' views. The applicants talked about the need for the project, but acknowledged the reasonableness of the opponents' argument. The opponents stated they too had mixed emotions. They liked much of the project, but also feared the unfair competitive advantage it created. After more discussion, the applicant stated that even though he thought he had enough votes on the council to get the project approved, he could not in good conscience go forward with it. The laundromat owners were taken aback, and they then started discussing in earnest what changes might be made so they could support the project.

The point, says Kemmis, is that "once the parties themselves get the idea that they are responsible for coming up with the answer, rather than simply turning it over to a third party, they are very likely to begin to think and behave differently. In this instance, the major shouldering of responsibility was done by the Down Home Project. Rather than leave it to the city council to decide whether the arguments about unfair competition were sound or not, these people rather courageously took that responsibility themselves. There seems to be something inherently mutual about the taking of responsibility.

"As people learn to relate in this way to each other," Kemmis continues, "they discover in their patterns of relationship a new competence, an unexpected capacity to get things done. It is not getting things done by using bureaucracies or other instrumentalities of 'the government' but getting things done through the power of citizenship" (Kemmis 1990).

Robert Hawkins, chair of the U.S. Advisory Commission on Intergovernmental Relations and president of the Institute for Contemporary Studies in San Francisco, contends that two kinds of social responsibility are required for citizenship: "(1) a willingness by persons and communities to accept responsibility for their choices and (2) a willingness to act responsibly toward other persons and communities" (Hawkins 1991). He argues that balkanization can be prevented by creative education and public participation in municipal life, and by a renewal of the concept of local self-government in which citizens recognize their city as a community of communities, not as an interest-group battlefield.

The concept of sharing power is important not just for elected officials but for bureaucrats as well. Earlier in this book you learned about the efforts of William Gomes to develop and enforce a controversial sign ordinance in Littleton, New Hampshire. Gomes's efforts resulted in failure, but even worse he got the wrong lesson from his defeat. In writing in *Planning* magazine, he warned planners to "beware of the town meeting or any system that encourages zoning by popular vote" (Gomes 1991). Gomes is killing the messenger with this kind of advice. The ordinances he developed during his three years as planning director for Littleton may have been technically correct, but they clearly did not have the necessary support from the community.

There are four basic scenarios that can be followed when attempting to develop a new sign code. They are:

1. The planning director could use his or her education and expertise to develop a draft sign ordinance and present it at the required mandatory public hearing;

2. The planning director could consult with developers, real estate interests, representatives from the business community, and the general public and then prepare a draft ordinance for presentation at the required public hearing;

3. A task force consisting of developers, real estate interests, businesspeople, and general community residents could be appointed to develop the draft ordinance with staff assistance;

4. An ad hoc task force could be created with several members of the planning commission and city council, representatives from the real estate profession and the business community, and interested people from the community at large with technical assistance being provided by staff.

It appears that Gomes followed the first scenario in developing the draft sign ordinance that was presented and rejected at the annual town meeting. As he repeated the same scenario for other proposed ordinances, he became increasingly isolated and increasingly ineffective. In assessing his lack of success, he blamed the public, the very people he was trying to serve.

While I sympathize with anyone who deals with regulatory issues, the simple fact is that Gomes followed a staff-driven process that is not responsive to customer needs. Anyone who is an advocate for the first scenario needs to pull over to the side of the road and have a reality checkup.

I recommend using scenarios three and four, which are both customer-driven processes. With scenario three, the individuals and interest groups that have a stake in the conflict have a chance to work together with staff assistance to reach a consensus. When a solution is reached that reflects the common views of the various participants, the proposal can be forwarded to the planning commission and then to the city council for action.

Scenario four is even more attractive. It has all of the benefits of collaborative problem-solving found in scenario three, plus the added advantage of giving the ultimate decision makers the opportunity to participate in and to develop ownership of the agreed upon solution. Staff planners may prefer a staff-directed process, but it does not provide for customer satisfaction or citizen accountability. Christopher T. Gates, vice-president of the National Civic League in Denver offers the following advice to staff: "At first it is natural for public servants to see cooperation with community groups as a threat and to be less than thrilled at the notion of sharing turf; however, as time goes by, both government and community leaders are realizing that government alone cannot be held responsible for the well being of the community. The community itself needs to take responsibility."

All across the country, there is growing interest on the part of elected officials and citizens in the use of mediation, facilitation, and conflict resolution techniques that will make it possible for communities to work together. One of the best examples I have heard about is Leadership Santa Barbara in California. This program uses an ongoing educational forum to unite existing and aspiring community leaders from all segments of the surrounding county in a neutral, nonadversarial learning environment. Its primary emphasis is for participants to make decisions based on their own experiences.

In 1990, the National League of Cities received a grant from the National Institute for Dispute Resolution to train a corps of elected officials in mediation and facilitation skills and to make them available as council-mentors to provide advice and technical assistance to their colleagues around the country (Kunde 1990). The National League of Cities also houses the Program for Community Problem Solving in its Washington, D.C. headquarters. The program, a joint venture of many organizations, is designed to offer technical assistance and training for local government officials in developing and managing collaborative approaches to contentious issues.

For planners and educators that are interested in learning more about conflict resolution techniques, I recommend reading *The Planner as Dispute Resolver*, published by the National Institute of Dispute Resolution. This book, which was written by three of the profession's most respected educators—Bruce Dotson, David Godschalk, AICP, and Jerome Kaufman—promotes negotiation-based conflict management and is an outstanding text to rely upon for teaching mediation skills to planners.

TIPS FOR CONSENSUS BUILDING

Susan Carpenter recently authored a report on "Solving Community Problems By Consensus" for the International City Management Association. The following is a summary of the lessons she has learned from successful consensus-building programs across the country:

• *Take time to plan.* The temptation to get on with a program is strong, but bringing parties together without thinking through a constructive program can create far more problems than it solves.

• *Make participation inclusive.* Broader participation produces a broader range of solutions and promotes implementation.

• *Choose constructive participants.* After identifying all parties, work with each group to select a representative who is both knowledgeable and able to get along with the other participants.

• *Involve key groups in decisions about process and solutions.* Building ownership in the process is a key to reaching agreements.

• *Make clear what outcomes are expected and how they will be used.* Participants in a program need to know how the results of their efforts will be used.

• *Be realistic about the amount of time required.* Building consensus in a community takes time—time to plan, to convene, to gather and access information, and to develop and select options.

• *Pay attention to relationships as the program proceeds.* Parties need a climate of trust and mutual respect to share information and develop options. Ground rules can be used to define expected behaviors.

• *Work with a common definition of the problem.* Different definitions suggest different solutions. Developing a common definition is an important step in the process.

• *Focus on interests, not positions.* Interests, unlike positions, are seldom mutually exclusive, and on the basis of interests, parties can create solutions that satisfy their needs while avoiding the trap of advocating for their positions.

• *Maintain contact with constituency groups and the public.* The product of a consensus program is worthless if constituency groups or the public reject it.

• *Work with the media.* Treat the media as a partner in a consensus program.

• *Adapt the process to the community culture.* Programs that are structured with the help of interested parties are more likely to reflect the community culture, and, therefore, are more likely to be effective than efforts that exactly replicate a program in another community (Carpenter 1989).

I have made every possible mistake in my involvement in various consensus-building and community problem-solving activities. Susan Carpenter's ICMA report and the Program for Community Problem Solving are important resources for local governments. They have made me more effective as a planner. The most significant mistakes I have made over the years in working with problem-solving groups were failing to require participants to always treat each other in a courteous, respectful manner and assuming that the participants were maintaining contact with the groups they were supposedly representing. This latter situation has been particularly damaging. I worked nearly a year once to reach a consensus on a new zoning ordinance only to find out that most of the representatives from the development industry had not been meeting with their constituents, so there was no support for the ordinance from some of those who were going to be most affected by it. It took six more months and some very difficult negotiating to save the project.

In *Getting to Yes*, Harvard professors and best-selling authors Roger Fisher and William Ury show how to become a better communicator, negotiator, persuader, process facilitator, and conflict resolver (Fisher and Ury 1981). In other words, their book teaches planners how to do their jobs better. *Getting to Yes* is based on the concept of "principled negotiation" developed at the Harvard Negotiation Project. It means deciding issues on their merits rather than through a haggling process. It enables you to be fair while protecting you against those who would take advantage of your fairness.

Principled negotiation is based on the four following ideas: separate the people from the problem; focus on interests, not positions; invent options for mutual gain; and insist on objective criteria. Fisher and Ury remind us that negotiators are human beings with emotions, deeply held values, and different backgrounds. They contend that the ongoing relationship is far more important than the outcome of any particular negotiation, and so recommend building a working relationship before the negotiation begins. By separating the people from the problem, it is possible to maintain a working relationship good enough to produce an acceptable agreement if one is possible.

The authors point out that interests are what define the problem, and any solution depends on understanding your adversary's interest. Behind opposing positions lie compatible ones. You should note all interests as they are revealed. People listen better if they feel that you have understood them.

The third principle, inventing options for mutual gain, should have special appeal to planners. The traditional planning process is ideally suited for developing alternative options and for creating solutions based on shared interests and mutual gains.

In one of the book's most important chapters, Fisher and Ury show how to develop objective criteria and successfully use them in the negotiation process. They believe you should be open to reason, and yield to principle, not to pressure. *Getting to Yes* doesn't teach you how to get your way. Rather, it is based on the premise that the first thing you are trying to win is a better way to negotiate. Some of you will probably find yourselves saying, "Now I know what I've been doing and why it sometimes works."

THE ETHICS OF CUSTOMER SERVICE

"Moonlighting" is not just the name of a popular television show. It has also been the source of an ethics controversy within the planning profession. Several years ago, two other planning directors and I, with the approval of our city managers, formed a business group and began consulting to local governments in our spare time. We submitted a proposal to rewrite a small community's zoning and platting regulations and to integrate them into a unified development code. Our proposal was accepted over that of two private consulting firms. In selecting us, the city manager noted that for the same cost the city was getting individuals with far more experience in drafting and implementing development regulations than were offered by either of the other firms. Furthermore, unlike the consultants, one of our planners had previously written a unified development code and since we were using our homes as offices we would have a lower overhead and be able to devote more total person-hours to the project.

Shortly after we began to work on the project, one of the consulting firms filed an ethics complaint against two of us. The complaint alleged that we had a full-time responsibility to our primary employers (the cities where we were employed as planning directors) and that the public interest was being violated by our moonlighting. Furthermore, it was argued that we had an unfair cost advantage over the consulting firms that had offices and support staff.

The reviewer assigned by the American Planning Association to study the alleged violations was sympathetic with the accusers. He believed that a planning director should work only on behalf of the city for which he is employed. The only exception that he believed to be proper was for part-time teaching at local universities.

But upon review of the AICP code of ethics, it was discovered that there was no prohibition against a planning director or other city staff member having a second source of employment, including moonlighting for another nonconflicting jurisdiction. Immediately, an effort was initiated to amend the code to prohibit moonlighting by government planners. After significant debate, it was agreed that an advisory opinion would be issued that would recognize outside employment with the explicit approval of the employer. The lengthy advisory opinion that resulted attempts to discourage moonlighting and states: "Both the planner requesting, and the authority giving, approval for outside employment should consider that the main justification for approval is a demand for whatever special professional knowledge and experience the planner has that is not otherwise readily available" (Singer 1988).

Get real! The primary reason most planners seek a second job is the same reason as most other people with two jobs—a desire to make more money. Based on the advisory, it could be argued that most planners with two jobs are probably in violation of the code of ethics.

Why was this advisory ruling prepared? Who is it intended to protect? I believe it was designed to protect consultants from competition. I certainly do not think it was developed in order to protect the community or individuals that are trying to hire the best people they can. If enforced, it would make it difficult for planners to supplement their incomes and continue to earn a living in their chosen profession.

I actually encourage my employees to moonlight. Most of the cities I have worked for do not adequately pay their planners, and if planners can't supplement their incomes they'll job hop or even change professions. Furthermore, secondary jobs often provide learning and maturing experiences that make staff even more valuable to their primary employer. Of course, there can be abuses and it is the manager's job to protect the interests of the employer.

Forgotten in the conflict over moonlighting is the concept of customer service and who should determine customer satisfaction. As you might guess, I believe that this is a function of the marketplace and the customer. When the code of ethics discourages competition and makes it difficult for customers to select the service providers they want, and when planners are financially penalized because someone in the American Planning Association has different values than they do, then it is wrong. Ethics should not be a weapon to enforce personal preferences, but rather should be designed to promote customer service and satisfaction.

I am concerned and skeptical about the value of either APA's Statement of Ethical Principles for Planning or the AICP Code of Ethics and Professional Practice as presently constituted. Let's start with APA's statement, which consists of 13 principles. Most of my concerns are directed toward the first four principles, which are summarized below and accompanied by my own brief comments and some quotes from other respected planners.

I. *Serve the public interest.* The term public interest is layered with hidden meanings and mythologies. I would prefer a more substantive statement that addresses the need for planners to be committed to doing effective planning—planning that makes a real difference in peoples' lives. Similarly, Mel Levin argues, "Deciding exactly what is meant by the phrase 'public interest' can result in vastly different interpretations according to class, party, neighborhood, ethnic group, or era. It is axiomatic that at least a plausible case can be made for almost every conceivable action or inaction. Indeed, planners, and most particularly planning consultants, have done exactly that—however much hindsight suggests they may have been made in error" (Levin 1987).

William Lucy, AICP, associate professor of planning at the University of Virginia, acknowledges that "the most prominent opinion among political theorists seems to be that 'the public interest' is a phantom, unless the phrase means only an accumulation of individual wants, the merits of which others have no right to judge" (Lucy 1988b). Lucy, however, in his book *Close to Power*, writes that this is not his view of the public interest. He suggests that "representative democracy is the best available means of pursuing public interest on behalf of the entire polity" (Lucy 1988a).

Years ago, Theodore Hollander, the dean of planning at the City University of New York, pointed out that he knew "of no professional practitioner, even those with highly developed codes of professional conduct—law, accounting, medicine—where the 'credo' of public service takes precedence over a client's interests" (Hollander 1970). And he expressed a doubt that we can expect a "greater good" from individual planners. He argued that clients need more than a credo and advocated increasing the power of the underrepresented in the planning process.

The power and importance of the role of bargaining in determining what constitutes the public interest in the political process was emphasized by William and Margaret Wheaton, AICP, who offered the following thoughts in a paper on "Identifying the Public Interest": "Different people and groups which have different concepts of the public interest must somehow find a common ground by bargaining. . . . Only in the haggling of the market, the adjudication by the courts, the enactments of legislative bodies, and the administrative acts of legitimate authority, can we discover what that balance between conflicting ends and the means to achieve those ends may be" (Wheaton 1970).

II. *Support citizen participation in planning.* This is a valid principle, yet according to surveys by Howell Baum, a majority of planners believe that decisions should be made on the basis of planners' rational analysis (Baum 1986). Most planners tend to give only lip service to the notion of citizen participation. I would prefer a code that promotes a full commitment to empowering citizens so they can not only participate, but also take the responsibility and authority for planning that affects their well-being. APA does advocate "forums for meaningful participation and expression," but nothing is said about the need for decisions to be controlled by our customers. Why not?

III. *Recognize the comprehensive and long-range nature of planning decisions.* This is not the problem. The problem is that the typical planner doesn't understand the need to balance and to integrate the comprehensive, long-range responsibilities of planning with the short-range, incremental action strategies that are needed to produce results. Effective planning depends on linking today's decisions to a vision of the future. The key to making vision relevant is connecting it to the present, making it possible to make decisions today on current problems with an awareness of their impact on the future.

The APA guidelines for this statement note that "the planner and official must continuously gather and consider all facts . . . and explicitly evaluate all consequences before making a recommendation or decision." Yet the public is fed up with planning bureaucracies that do nothing but collect data and study it. People want solutions to their problems and they want a planning process that gives them timely results. Timeliness is valued by our customers, but not given much weight by APA. Again, I would call for increased effectiveness to be our major objective, which also means less comprehensiveness and quicker response time.

How ironic that the neglect of the short-range aspects of planning is the real threat to long-range planning. When we value one over the other, the profession and our customers suffer.

IV. *Expand choice and opportunity for all persons.* Oh yes, and they lived happily ever after. If there is anything we agree upon today in local government, it is that resources are limited. Priorities have to be established and choices made. There is competition between interests and conflict between ends and means. Some people will win while some will lose—that is the nature of our competitive society.

The APA guidelines indicate that planners and public planning officials have "a special responsibility to plan *for* the needs of the disadvantaged people, and urge changing policies, institutions and decisions that restrict their opportunities and choices." I have never been excited about planning *for* people, and prefer planning with people and helping them to plan for themselves. I even believe that disadvantaged people are capable of planning for themselves. Given the option, I prefer serving individuals rather than groups or classes of people, and I don't want to be limited as to whom I can serve. Robert Einsweiler, AICP, former national APA president and a professor at the Humphrey Institute at the University of Minnesota, has also expressed disagreement with APA's attempt "to require *all* planners to be bound by the reformists' agenda, to be *advocates* for the poor."

Herbert Smith, AICP, in his new book, *Planning America's Communities*, also opposes requiring *all* planners to be advocates for the poor. "The general electorate does not share this view," he says. "Therefore, many elected officials resent being positioned on an issue that lacks political support. This does not mean planners should have no concern for the poor; rather, the profession should not impose a requirement that sets the planner at odds with duly elected or appointed officials. This is a democracy. They are elected to represent the public interest. No other profession has hung such a millstone around the neck of its members; neither can we and survive" (Smith 1991).

The twelfth principle in APA's statement is "maintain public confidence." The guidelines state that a "public planning official must conduct himself/herself publicly so as to maintain public confidence in the public planning body, the official's unit of government, and the official's performance of the public trust." Apparently, the authors of this principle don't know that the general public currently doesn't have much confidence in our commissions and government units. At a minimum this statement should be revised to read "establish and *promote* public confidence." If this principle could be accepted, then we could go to work on revising the first four principles so that planners could be challenged to increase their effectiveness without violating the statement of ethical principles.

The AICP Code of Ethics and Professional Conduct has much of the same vague and simplistic language that is found in the APA statement. Again, it is pointed out that the "planning profession has a special responsibility to serve the public interest." Planners are also to "have special concern for the long-range consequences of present actions," to "give citizens the opportunity to have meaningful impact on the development of plans and programs," and to "expand choice and opportunity for all persons. . . ." My major objection to the AICP code concerns its numerous and frequent references to the public interest. The code says that planners must accept the decisions of a client unless they are "illegal or inconsistent with the planner's primary obligation to the public interest." This imposes a standard that requires the planner to be judge, jury, and executioner in situations with unclear outcomes. Peter Marcuse, AICP, in a 1976 article entitled "Professional Ethics and Beyond: Values in Planning" argued, "In most cases, even the rules for telling right from wrong are not clear. Obligations to clients conflict with obligations to the public; following professionally accepted standards of conduct produces results repugnant to most laymen; professional integrity and democratic decision making seem to conflict; the bounds of professional concern are hazy" (Marcuse 1976).

Yet into this nightmare of ethical confusion and conflict comes another AICP advisory ruling that pompously states: "A code of ethics should not be a what-can-I-get-away-with-code. It should not be tortured into loopholes and technicalities that would allow a person to be formally correct while ethically wrong. The AICP Code looks for more than the minimum threshold of enforceable acceptability. It sets aspirational standards that require conscious striving to attain" (Singer 1988).

Heck, what it really sets is aspirational gobbledygook, based on outdated and indefinable notions of the public interest, that violate the basic tenets of both customer service and democracy. I question whether planning can be relevant or effective when its professional code of ethics is based on such a mythological foundation. Until it is amended I can only say that I am frequently in violation of the code and proud of it. I can't think of what is more unethical than collecting a salary while failing to deliver satisfying services to your customers. Too bad the code of ethics doesn't recognize this kind of violation.

IS THE CUSTOMER ALWAYS RIGHT?

There is a sign that is frequently seen in many businesses: "The two rules for success: Rule #1, the customer is always right. Rule #2, if the customer is wrong, see rule #1." This sign is as correct as it is witty. Unless clients are legally incapable of making decisions, planners should trust and respect them. Of course, unethical or illegal behavior should not be condoned. If a client's actions violate your personal standards, you should seek to serve other clients. In my opinion, it is not ethical for planners to undermine their clients while in service to them.

Professional planners should be service providers, not guerrilla decision makers. The reluctance of many planners to trust people was recently demonstrated by the draft Policy Implementation Principle (PIP) on "the making of land use decisions by initiative and referendum," which was prepared in 1989/1990 for review and adoption by the American Planning Association. The following are the first two paragraphs and final paragraph of the position paper which was developed to oppose the use of initiatives or referendums for land use decisions of any kind.

> Citizens in sunbelt states have increasingly sought to take land use decision making, both planning and regulations, from their elected and appointed officials by citizen initiative and referendum. The reasons are varied: outrage over particularly sensitive decisions, frustration over rampant and seemingly unplanned development, or anger at seemingly unresponsive officials over the inability of communities to provide the necessary infrastructure to support new development. In addition, in some cases, professional planners and planning institutions have been accused of being unprepared and unwilling to exert the requisite leadership to present citizens with reasonable alternatives.
>
> Whatever the cause, planning and zoning by popular vote is fraught with peril for the wise use of land and for sound planning. The initiative process in particular is devoid of the planning process of even the most rudimentary

"REMEMBER THE CUSTOMER IS
ALWAYS RIGHT!"

sort as plans are amended and land rezoned without any guarantee of hearings or other deliberations. The process becomes, in the words of one jurist, a Gallup Poll. The referendum, which at least has the benefit of whatever planning process and hearing went into the measure subject to voter approval, is less pernicious to sound land use, though it has the capacity for ignoring altogether the logical results of sound planning. . . .

It is therefore consistent with past APA policy and sound planning practice and principles that APA object to the use of initiative or referendum as a method of making land use decisions. Mindful that this position may seem self-serving, it is important to remember that elected officials make the decisions. The "proper" approach to changing their decisions is in the courts or through the electoral process (Callies and Curtin 1990).

When I chanced upon this position paper, I was shocked and angry. I was not alone, obviously, because the PIP was eventually rejected at the 1991 APA national conference in New Orleans. Adoption of this PIP would have placed the American Planning Association on record as being opposed to one of the most effective citizen participation methods and one of the most basic safeguards in our democratic form of government.

Rather than using initiatives and referendums, the authors of the proposed PIP would have the voters replace the elected officials whose decisions or lack of action they do not agree with. But it is widely accepted that incumbents have significant advantages, such as media exposure, that make them difficult to unseat.

I would also question the desirability of recalling or electing representatives on the basis of a single issue. The city council of Plano, Texas, recently passed an ordinance allowing the advertising signs of real estate and home builders to be placed in the street right-of-way throughout the city. This ordinance was subsequently repealed in a record turnout by the voters of Plano. The people's wishes were served, on an issue that certainly is not significant enough to have council members unseated.

Though it was rejected, I could not keep from being concerned about the broad support that the PIP received from the leadership of APA. On one hand, it seems planners want some citizen participation, but on the other hand the use of initiatives and referendums is obviously going too far. The proposed PIP contended that "the initiative process in particular is devoid of the planning process of even the most rudimentary sort" while the referendum has the "capacity for ignoring altogether the logical results of sound planning." I wonder why planners continue to argue for processes and procedures while our customers want results. How logical can planning be when it doesn't reflect the preferences and political realities of the community? How could planners support a PIP which would isolate and protect planners and public officials from their constituents?

John Herbers, contributing editor of *Governing*, recently commented that "while much of the world is moving toward democracy, the United

States seems to be going in the opposite direction." He contends that "elected officials, to put it bluntly, are becoming impatient with public participation in the process of making policy decisions. After an initial airing of issues, officials at the state and local levels increasingly go behind closed doors to make up their minds, unfettered by dialogue with the public" (Herbers 1990).

The Kettering Foundation report on *The Public's Role in the Policy Process* contends that officials only pay lip service to extensive public participation and actually try to restrict it. The report notes that the tradition of this country is one of "deliberative democracy," which requires policy makers and the public to "engage in a continuous dialogue where the public not only comes to understand policy issues, but informs policy makers of their value on what policy directions are important to them" (Herbers 1990). The current approach, says the report, is strict representative government in which the public official decides what is best with little input from the public. This practice, it concludes, has led to obvious abuses.

Reform is needed. In *Common Wealth: A Return to Citizen Politics*, Harry Boyte contends that "political life is more democratic and more effective when it is grounded in face-to-face relationships among citizens—rather than one-directional communications from experts or elites, when it involves far more than the act of voting, and when particular issues or campaigns become occasions for education in the political arts of judgment, imagination, evaluation and the use of power" (Boyte 1989).

The proposed PIP I have been discussing would have put APA on record against using referendums on "land-use decisions of any kind," apparently such as bond issues involving land acquisition and other important land-use decisions concerning airports, parks, schools, utilities, and transportation facilities. The complete list would be quite impressive.

Some want to have their cake and eat it too. Stuart Meck, immediate past president of the American Planning Association, is not troubled by exposing broad land-use policy issues to referendum or initiative. But he opposes using these procedures on decisions that seek to rezone individual parcels of land. He argues that "voter-approved zoning belittles, indeed, eviscerates the role of planning in the land-use decision-making process . . ." (Meck 1990). Meck has the laudable goal of depoliticizing the zoning system, but his views of zoning just don't measure up to political reality. Most planners might not know what "eviscerates" means (they can guess and get pretty close), but they do know that most zoning decisions are not the result of objective, technical choices made in reliance upon a comprehensive plan. When, at a 1990 multistate planning conference in Louisville, I asked for a show of hands from planners whose local zoning decisions were based on a comprehensive plan, there was no response.

The simple reality of planning and zoning is that most decisions are political and, as such, the public should have the right to override bad decisions. Even in the rare situations where zoning decisions are linked to planning, the system can be abused and safeguards are needed. For instance, though Florida is clearly in the forefront of the movement to require consistency between planning and zoning, a May 1990 article in the *Christian Science Monitor* attributes the increasing number of elected officials under indictment in Dade County to the taking of money for zoning decisions. The article reported that "plans can always be changed and exceptions made to the color coded maps" (Ingwerson 1990).

Limiting what citizens may vote on is no better than making decisions for them. Either you believe in initiatives and referendums or you don't. For those such as myself who do believe, there should be a commitment to expanding the possibilities for deciding issues by citizen vote.

Susan Carpenter, in a report published by the International City Management Association, concluded that "the complexity of today's community issues and the number and diversity of people who expect to participate in making decisions makes it difficult for a community to solve problems using only traditional ways of doing business." She adds, "the days when a handful of people, often from one sector of the community, could determine and implement a solution are gone." Her conclusion is, "as the number of people who expect to have a role in making a decision grows and the complexity of issues increases, so must the range of tools for making decisions" (Herbers 1990).

What about the legal aspects of initiative and referendum? According to Robert Freilich AICP, Hulen professor of law at the University of Missouri-Kansas City, referendums and initiatives fulfill fundamental needs, complement the legislative process, and are "an indispensable companion in an effective governmental system." He argues, "there are not persuasive public policy reasons or legal issues which justify preventing the electorate from holding an ultimate control over land-use policy" (Freilich 1989).

The Supreme Court, in *City of Eastlake v. Forest City Enterprises, Inc.,* 426

US 668 (1976), upheld the use of referendum powers for zoning issues. The court concluded that the referendum is "a means for direct political participation, allowing the people the final decision, amounting to a veto power, over enactment of legislative bodies. The practice is designed to give citizens a voice on questions of public policy." Citing Justice Black's opinion in *James v. Valtierra*, 402 US at 143 (1971), Chief Justice Burger explained that the referendum procedure "ensures that all the people of a community will have a voice in a decision which may lead to large expenditures of local government funds for increased public services." It is interesting to note that APA was on the losing side of this issue.

Initiatives and referendums are good not just for democracy but for planning too. In a letter to the *Journal of the American Planning Association*, Nico Calavita, from San Diego State University, says, "In San Diego, initiatives—whether they have been passed, defeated, or threatened— have led to the affirmation of planning principles, or have spurred the city council into drafting and passing increasingly tougher growth management or environmental protection legislation" (Calavita 1990).

It should be pointed out that initiative and referendum procedures do not transfer absolute authority to the voters. They are only part of our system's checks and balances. If voters act in an arbitrary or discriminatory manner, their actions are subject to the same judicial review and constitutional limitations that govern any legislative act. "The electorate may make mistakes, but the system is designed to let those mistakes be worked out," says Philip Seib, a Southern Methodist University professor and political columnist for the *Dallas Morning News*. "That process includes testing whatever the voters want, then perhaps holding more elections and sometimes finally involving the courts. But the sequence takes time . . ." (Seib 1991).

Thus we have our answer to the question, "Is the customer always right?" Of course not, but bad decisions and mistakes are the customer's right. I am reminded of the story of a widow who was preparing for her husband's funeral just before Christmas. She enlisted a vocalist from her church to perform several of her husband's favorite songs: *Amazing Grace, The Old Rugged Cross,* and *Jingle Bells.* The singer was taken aback by the nature of the last song, but it was Christmastime. Who was he to question the widow's request? He sang all the songs at the service, finishing with a peppy rendition of *Jingle Bells.* Afterwards, the widow approached him and asked if she had requested *Jingle Bells.* When the singer acknowledged that, indeed, she had, the widow replied, "You'll have to forgive me. I was so upset at the time that I obviously misspoke. I really meant for you to sing *Golden Bells*."

Customers make mistakes, and it is the planner's job to understand exactly what they mean and to help them clarify their views, but not to deny them the right to make choices. Planners who choose sides, prejudge the electorate, or find them guilty in advance of the facts are advocating changing the fundamental structure of this country's political system. They are singing a tune their customers do not want to hear.

DISCRIMINATION: MITIGATION OR MIGRATION?

Connie Cooper, AICP, my good friend and the president of the American Planning Association (1991–92), favors the concept of empowerment. But her commitment is with some reservation, as is revealed by the following discourse in a letter to me: "I am an advocate of your position that the public is the client and we must empower them to increase their effectiveness. But, placing rezoning issues on the ballot to be voted up or down, is that making our client a more effective force within local government? I wonder what the success rate of rezoning elections on subsidized housing, group homes and day care facilities within our traditional residential neighborhoods would be?"

I sympathize with Cooper and the other planners that remain troubled by the notion of trusting voters, especially in areas where the NIMBY syndrome is prevalent. But in my experience, communication and education are the best ways to assist people in making choices. Planners should treat initiatives as opportunities to communicate with their clients. Regardless, I believe that elected officials are just as apt to deny a request for a day care center, halfway house, or landfill as are the voters. (In fact, the refusal of elected officials to even deal with these kinds of tough political choices has led to the coining of the term NIMEY, which stands for Not In My Election Year. What the heck.) Discrimination is discrimination no matter who does it, and hopefully the courts will protect us from such injustice regardless of the source.

Planners who are opposed to the use of initiative and referendum are, in essence, advocating the disempowerment of the voters and setting in motion a powerful force for negative change. If people can't vote with ballots they will vote with their feet. When people decide they don't have access to power or control over their lives, many will find other ways to protest and to express themselves. Migration is the ultimate expression of dissatisfaction with one's surroundings. In Eastern Europe, the Iron

Curtain kept people from voting with their feet. No such barriers exist in the cities of America, and it's the people with energy, ambition, and self-reliance that are more likely to express themselves and move. People cannot be denied their basic rights to directly influence or determine the important political decisions that affect the quality of their lives.

INCENTIVES VERSUS MANDATES

Many of my colleagues are persistent advocates of "forcing citizens" to do the right thing. Their reasoning is that if people won't voluntarily put the needs of the community before their own selfish interests, then ordinances and police powers should be used to achieve public interest objectives. But my contrary view is that public leaders should first attempt to induce their citizens into accepting regulations, even "undesirable" ones, by offering various forms of mitigation or compensation.

Mitigation is not a new idea to environmental planners, but it historically has not been a popular idea with many local governments. After all, why pay for something that you have the legal right to force people to do without compensation? Gradually, though, communities are learning that there is always a price to pay when some individuals are required to sacrifice for the betterment of others. Sometimes it's a political price, while other times it's increased migration. I contend that mitigation is better than migration, and besides, it's the fair and wise thing to do for all interests.

Mitigation benefits the community because it encourages neighborhood stability while still meeting the special needs that must be accommodated. Communities that recognize the importance of neighborhood stability are usually the leading proponents of mitigation and compensation for affected property owners.

The city of Minneapolis is in the forefront of the movement that emphasizes neighborhoods as the key to a city's future. Its vision statement says, "Minneapolis will be a city of complementary, collaborating, diverse and well-integrated neighborhoods; a city in which all citizens, property owners and employees are positively involved and embrace a sense of community." In developing Minneapolis's Twenty-Year Revitalization Plan, various committees developed a series of intervention strategies designed to maintain those neighborhoods which were presently healthy, stabilize those in danger of decline, and revitalize those that had already experienced severe problems. Central to these strategies was the supposition that the agencies responsible for the provision of public services needed "to find new ways of doing business."

Richard Heath, director of the Minneapolis planning department, reports that his staff has a new way of responding to the siting issues associated with locally unwanted land uses (LULUs). The key is the city's new policy that states, "Incentives and rewards should be provided to neighborhoods to accept their fair share of special facilities like group homes and to give special recognition and consideration to neighborhoods with a current overburden in serving city-wide recipients and interests." And, unlike most other cities, Minneapolis has significant financial incentives to offer its neighborhoods through its $400 million revitalization plan. (Papatola 1990).

An increasing number of cities are learning how to use incentives to accomplish community objectives without leaving scars. In Fort Worth, for example, the operator of a landfill that is used by both public and private sector contractors asked the city to extend its operating permit for an additional five years. There was significant public opposition, but the board of adjustment approved the short-term extension. During the remaining years of service, the operators met with city staff members, neighborhood representatives, and nearby property owners to determine if there were any conditions that would allow for the continuation of the landfill in the future. While the discussions were taking place, the operators made a number of improvements to the facility that made it less harmful to the surrounding area.

As a result of the discussions, an agreement was reached to allow the landfill to continue for an additional five years. In return, the owners agreed to eventually close the facility, dedicate the land to the city, and provide funds to reclaim the site and develop it for a neighborhood park. Furthermore, they agreed to donate $100,000 to the neighborhood association for local improvement projects and another $100,000 to a nearby private school to serve as seed money for a gymnasium fund.

The surrounding community was now willing to endure the facility because it had received compensation to offset the negative impacts of the landfill. The residents in the area decided that the long-term benefits exceeded the short-term consequences.

It is difficult to understand why there is not more support for using incentives to deal with LULUs. Most local governments do not even consider the possibility, and prefer instead to use brute legislative force. I

have found that win-win solutions are almost always politically preferable to zero-sum outcomes.

POLITICS AND COMPREHENSIVE PLANNING

The comprehensive plan can be generally defined as a document that
establishes policies for the future of a community. The major impediment to effective and successful comprehensive planning is that it is
difficult, if not impossible, to predict the future with much accuracy. If
you look at most forecasts by trained futurists, you will find that they
quickly become meaningless. This is because most futurists use existing
facts and straight-line extrapolations that become increasingly inaccur-
ate with the passage of time. The future is not simply an extension of the
past or present with only slightly changed conditions. The future is not
always neat and clean, but instead often messy and chaotic. How would
you like to be a transportation planner in West Berlin who didn't take
into account the street pattern of East Berlin because you "assumed"
there would always be a wall dividing the cities?

In Sir Isaac Newton's era the universe was thought of as a kind of
magnificent clock, the very soul of rationality. When physicists began to
express doubts, Albert Einstein declared, "I refuse to believe that God
plays dice with the universe." Yet with the advent of quantum physics,
the cosmos has revealed itself to be more like a floating crap game.
Events at the micro level are irredeemably infested with randomness.
Thus rationality is really order without predictability, which is perhaps
better known as "chaos." So what does this have to do with city
planning? T. J. Cartwright, associate professor of Environmental Studies
at York University, contends that the chaos theory promises to have
profound implications for what planners do and how they do it. "The
world may be both easier and more difficult to understand than we tend
to believe," he says, "that noisy and untidy cities may not be as
dysfunctional as we often assume, and that the need for planning that is
incremental and adaptive in nature may be more urgent than we tend to
think" (Cartwright 1991).

The following is a summary of some of the most important points that
Cartwright made in his recent *JAPA* article, entitled "Planning and
Chaos Theory":

• "No matter how much data we gather, no matter how global and
complete our models, no matter how rigorously we test them—even so,

according to chaos theory, prediction may in some cases be beyond our grasp."

• "What chaos theory suggests is that planning based on prediction is not merely impractical in some cases; it is logically impossible."

• "We must get used to working . . . with an 'ensemble of forecasts' . . . If the best we can do is make 'approximate predictions,' then we should be trying to make 'parallel' predictions of similar or 'surrounding' events."

• ". . . chaotic systems are predictable on only an incremental or local basis . . . on an incremental or local basis the effects of feedback from one time period into the next are often perfectly clear. This is a powerful argument for planning strategies that are incremental rather than comprehensive in scope and that rely on a capacity for adaptation rather than on blueprints of results."

• Planning for chaotic systems may be more successful when it is viewed as a succession of judicious 'nudges' rather than as a step-by-step recipe. For in chaotic systems, relatively small changes in inputs can have a dramatic effect on system behavior" (Cartwright 1991).

Several years ago I had the experience of hearing Roger Staubach, former quarterback of the Dallas Cowboys, tell a story that advocates the contingency approach. It's about a boy who had been riding the bench on his high school football team for a whole season. Late in the fourth quarter of the last game of the year, the team's star quarterback is injured and has to leave the game. Looking down the bench the coach sees the untried player, calls him over, and explains the situation and his coaching strategy. This game will decide the city championship. The score is tied with two minutes to go, and his team has the football on their own 30-yard line. The coach tells the boy that, under the circumstances, he has decided to play for a tie and to share the city title. He instructs his new quarterback to run a quarterback sneak on each of the next three plays and then on the fourth play to punt the ball.

The dejected boy goes into the game and proceeds to follow the coach's instructions. On first down he runs a quarterback sneak and, catching the other team by surprise, gains 20 yards. He repeats the play and gains another 20 yards. His third play is another quarterback sneak, on which he runs to the five yard line before being tackled.

Some of you may be able to guess what's going to happen. Sure enough, on his fourth play, the quarterback drops back into punt formation and boots the ball out of the endzone. As he is running off the field, the coach runs up to him, grabs him by the shoulder pads, and screams, "What the hell was going through your mind when you punted that ball?" The player looks him in the eye and replies, "I was just thinking, boy do we have a dumb coach!"

Effective planners must have a kaleidoscopic and contingent view of many possible futures. Using a living, evolving plan, and depending on the flow of the situation, decision makers can quickly react as unforeseen events unfold. It is necessary to constantly ask, "What would happen if . . . ?" The contingency approach contradicts the tendency of too many planners to seek the one best solution or the one best future. An excellent example of using multiple visions can be found in the Strategic Comprehensive Plan for Arlington, Texas, which received a national award from the American Planning Association in 1988. The following is a brief excerpt from the introduction of the Arlington plan:

> Making predictions about future events has long been a focus of planning because it enables cities to take action in the present to accommodate future growth. However, making such predictions in volatile high growth areas is difficult. Past plans for Arlington have demonstrated how difficult such projections are to make. Arlington's past projections of population growth have been anywhere from 10 to 50 percent off.
>
> The approach that this Comprehensive Plan has taken towards growth is not to rely on one best guess analysis of local, regional, and national trends as past plans have. Instead, three strategic scenarios are proposed. This approach adds flexibility in the sense that it is more elastic and resilient than traditional time line forecasts (i.e. by 1995 Arlington will have a population of XXXXX). It is, therefore, more responsive to changing economic conditions.
>
> Examination of future growth decisions for Arlington in light of these scenarios provides a better understanding of the rewards and pitfalls of development. Strategies can be initially adopted to anticipate possible pitfalls and take advantage of possible rewards. These strategies can then be periodically reviewed in light of changing economic conditions, and appropriate action can be taken (Arlington 1987).

It is obvious to most observers that traditional comprehensive planning is a failure. At best, comprehensive plans reflect only crude good faith attempts at comprehensiveness. True comprehensiveness is neither feasible nor desirable, as evidenced by any systematic review of existing comprehensive plans. Furthermore, most attempts at comprehensiveness have only served to weaken the effectiveness of planners by lengthening the planning process, complicating the issues, and producing thick planning documents that overpower and intimidate the potential user.

One of the few positive legacies of traditional comprehensive planning is that it attempts to view the planning jurisdiction as a systematic phenomenon with fundamental interrelated linkages of a physical, social, and economic nature. The real validity for the concept of comprehensiveness lies in the growing recognition that most of the significant issues facing urban America require multidisciplinary and multijurisdictional team-developed solutions. This means there is a growing and important role for planners to act both as specialists and as general strategists that span boundaries between political jurisdictions, special interest groups, and the general public. The concept of boundary spanning was discussed by Jerome Kaufman in "Teaching Students about Strategizing, Boundary Spanning and Ethics" (Kaufman 1987). The role of the boundary spanner is to reduce the distance and facilitate involvement between the various participants in the planning and decision-making process through negotiation, conflict resolution, and consensus building. The planner's specialized training and experience provides an important generalist overview of the various functional components and critical interrelationships in the urban system. With proper training, a planner is qualified to identify and solicit the involvement of the individuals and groups for the satisfactory solution of the most significant planning issues and problems.

Comprehensiveness, on the other hand, in terms of geography or information, is easily an impediment to effective planning. Problems need to be broken down into actionable components. Efforts and resources must be concentrated and focused. Physical size usually correlates directly with time and resources.

Daniel Kemmis points out that "any kind of active citizenship where different interests are directly engaged in working out their problems and possibilities among themselves, is going to work better in small than in large political entities" (Kemmis 1990). And I agree with Paul Davidoff, who argued that instead of overemphasizing comprehensive planning, planners should seek to produce a plurality of plans, each with its own clients (Davidoff 1965).

What is also of critical importance is how quickly planners act to meet the needs of their clients. Timeliness is clearly more valuable than comprehensiveness in many situations, yet timely responsiveness is often a moving target to clients. Banking has been transformed from bankers' hours to 24-hour service. Photos are processed in one hour instead of one week. Pizzas are ready in five minutes for lunch at Pizza Hut and delivered in 30 minutes or less by Domino's. From eyeglass service to mail delivery, speed is valued.

Planners can noticeably improve service by shortening the lag-time between the observed demand and the actual delivery. The space shuttle *Columbia* was able to rendezvous and snare the 11-ton Long Duration Exposure Facility by flying upside down and easing the shuttle in closer, a few inches each second. Flight controllers called it using "creeping speed." Creeping speed is appropriate for a highly dangerous space rendezvous but not for planning. The goal of effective planners should be to be immediately available, not tomorrow, not next week, and not only when there is a staff person free to work on it. Clients want immediate service with zero-based waiting time, not promises of a better tomorrow. Customers will not wait for planners that cannot function in real-time.

Can comprehensive planning be linked to the concepts of customer service, effectiveness, and political satisfaction? This raises the fundamental question of "Who are the primary customers for comprehensive planning and what are their needs and expectations?"

It was T. J. Kent's opinion that while there are many clients for what he calls the general plan (including the chief executive, planning commission, city departments, the general public, the development community, the courts, and other governmental jurisdictions), the primary client is the local legislative body. Kent in his 1964 book, *The Urban General Plan*, argued, "If a conflict should arise between the different needs to be accommodated, it should be resolved in favor of the needs of the municipal legislative body." Kent identified the following legislative needs that general plans should provide for:

• *Policy determination.* The general plan is first and foremost an instrument through which the city council considers, debates and finally agrees upon a coherent, unified set of general, long-range policies for the physical development of a community. The general plan should be designed, therefore, to facilitate the work of the council as they attempt to focus their attention on the community's major development problems and opportunities. It is essential that the plan be prepared in a manner that enables the members of the council to be familiar with it and at ease with it.

• *Policy effectuation:* The general plan should enable the council to make weekly decisions on specific projects, policies and laws on the basis of a clearly stated, unified set of general, long-range development policies. Policy effectuation leads to day-to-day decisions on specific proposals and issues requiring definite and immediate action. The existence of an adopted general plan is without meaning or significance unless it is actually used by the city council.

• *Communication.* The plan should present a clear picture of the city council's long-range, general policies on community development to all other persons concerned with development. It persuades private developers, suggests development projects to them, and enables them to anticipate decisions of the council. The success of the communication depends upon the free, widespread distribution of the plan. It should be written and designed in a manner that will be both understandable and interesting to the average citizen. While the general plan must be suited primarily to the needs of the city council, it also must be suited to the needs of those to whom the council must communicate its policies. A plan that has no meaning for the citizens or is in conflict with their views will not receive public support.

• *Conveyance of advice.* The general plan enables the city council to receive staff advice in a coherent, unified form, rather than on a piecemeal, expediency basis. Staff advice includes initiating and advocating proposals. The advisory use of the general plan is most apparent in the background and statistical material on geography, population, the local economy, existing land use, and physical conditions. It is up to the city council to accept, modify, or reject the recommendations it receives from its advisors.

• *Education.* The general plan helps to educate the council and everyone who is involved with it or who reads it as to the conditions, problems, and opportunities of their community. It arouses the interest of people, awakens them to the possibilities of the future, offers them factual information on the present status of the city and probable future trends, informs them about the operations of their local government in matters of physical development and stimulates them to be critical of city-planning ideas. Council members are the major recipients of the education impact of the plan. The publication and wide distribution of the plan-document is the culmination of the educational use (Kent 1964).

In my experience in both preparing and reviewing comprehensive plans, few if any of them were able to do a very good job of meeting the legislative needs that were identified by Kent. The first impediment to the production of satisfying plans is the size and complexity of most comprehensive plan documents. Many comprehensive plans are published in multiple volumes, in large three-ring notebooks, or as oversized coffee-table books. And most come with a stiff price tag. However, a few plans are published as newspaper supplements or in a poster format with the plan on one side of the document and text on the reverse side.

Customer satisfaction demands that planners downsize their plans, studies and reports, and convert them into more user-friendly and user-inviting publications. The planners' mission is not to show people how hard they have worked in collecting data or how technically sophisticated they are in analyzing it; their job is to give customers the essential information that they need to make decisions and solve problems. Filtered essential information is what people really want from the vast amount of information available today. It's clear that there is real value in the person that can take a broad stream of raw data and refine it into knowledge that can be acted upon. Furthermore, because different clients need different types of information—and in different styles or formats—it is important to customize documents to meet their individual needs.

Fred Bair, Jr., observed over 20 years ago that "planning is poorly designed for its purpose—guiding action by nonplanners—because it is designed for the wrong purpose—preparation of a comprehensive plan for physical development which makes sense to the planner" (Bair 1970). Most users want and need less information than planners feel comfortable delivering. This is especially true of consulting planners. One consultant complained to me that competitors would gain an advantage if he tried to reduce the size or complexity of his products. But the need of the client should prevail. The secret is to pack more perceived value into a smaller space and to make the client aware of the real value of the final product. Plans that are too big to be carried around will be left behind; portable ones will be used.

If you do the shopping or laundry in your family, you probably know that some powdered soap boxes have undergone a significant transformation in recent years. Those gigantic boxes of laundry soap that we used to haul home have been downsized. But this doesn't just mean that soap now comes in smaller boxes. What it also means is that it now takes less soap to do the same job. In the past, soap companies ascertained that consumers believed the amount of soap had something to do with its cleaning ability and value. Thus, the manufacturers fluffed up their product by adding a filler like sodium carbonate to make consumers think they were getting a bigger, more effective product, and more for their money.

Marketers are now learning that consumers want value and prefer purchasing soap in smaller boxes if they can wash the same amount of laundry as before. Now there is fierce competition to determine who can pack the most punch into the smallest box. Does this situation herald a new age of smallness or is it an aberration? Look around and judge for yourself. The compact disk is smaller than the old phonograph records, yet it provides a much better reproduction of sound. The 5.25-inch floppy disk has been surpassed by the superior 3.5-inch disk. Portable personal computers are not as capable as an office PC, but people will pay more for portability. There is no reason why the same principle should not apply to comprehensive planning.

Planners should be challenged to evaluate their past performance in producing comprehensive plans. Some of you may well be satisfied with your accomplishments, but many, if not most, of you will recognize that you failed to produce truly customer-satisfying comprehensive plans.

I believe that you cannot produce effective plans unless you understand the unique perspectives and needs of the local legislative body. Elected officials value their right and ability to exercise independent judgment, particularly with respect to land speculation and the development process. One of the few remaining opportunities that politicians still have to reward special interest supporters is zoning. This keen interest in zoning is one of the major reasons traditional comprehensive planning is so ineffective. Planning injects stability and predictability into the development process, discourages speculation, and makes it much more difficult to manipulate zoning. Under the circumstances, comprehensive planning is a threat to the power and authority of many politicians. Some local government officials so cherish their freedom to respond to requests for land-use decisions that in the experience of my good friend and consulting planner George Raymond, AICP, "they would rather not give their communities the advantage of guided growth in accordance with a carefully developed plan" (Raymond 1978).

Planners have two diametrically opposed options to choose from when developing comprehensive plans. The first option is to develop a flexible general plan. These plans protect the power of the elected official and only provide general "guidance" to the land-use decision-making process. Such plans promote flexibility in the development process and allow growth and development to be heavily influenced, if not determined, by speculative market forces and political factors.

The second option is for planners to support legislation for mandatory planning that would specify the elements of a comprehensive plan and require that all land-use decisions be consistent with that plan. While this approach would weaken the zoning authority of the elected officials, it would provide a valuable service to the development community and the general public. In my experience with land-use regulations, most developers value certainty over the opportunity to manipulate the development process. As citizens continue to become more effective in the politics of zoning, developers become very interested in protecting their existing development opportunities and in keeping the rules from being changed in the middle of the game. Also, elected officials still have the ultimate authority when adopting the plan. This provides them with clear opportunities to be of service to special interests. What negates the political value of this form of planning to the elected official is that the plan is adopted long before there is a market for development and before many individual developers are ready to initiate their projects. Developers, politicians, and comedians instinctively know that timing is everything, and flexibility in implementing a plan maximizes the power of politicians by extending the period of their authority over the development process.

But there are also political benefits to be gained from the linkage of mandatory planning to regulatory decisions. One is that it strengthens the public's faith in planning, local government, and public officials. While politicians lose flexibility, they also are able to promote their own vision of the public interest and of a better tomorrow. Consistency and linkage leads to coordination, cooperation, and economic efficiency— and to measurable progress toward targeted goals and objectives. Order and predictability also lead to stability in the development process and minimize zoning controversies. Once it becomes clear that the plan is credible and useful, the public becomes much more interested in participating and influencing the final product.

One note of caution is in order. Mandatory planning and consistency requirements are not the cure-all for what ails comprehensive planning. Linda Dalton, who teaches in the city and regional planning department at California Polytechnic State University in San Luis Obispo, found in a recent survey of 270 cities and 39 counties in California that two-thirds of all general plan amendments that private parties initiated were approved by the local legislative body. She concludes that planners accept these policy modifications as being reflective of ". . . the circular motion of policy implementation, which allows for continuing adjustment over time" (Dalton 1989).

In my opinion, effective comprehensive planning depends on developing downsized plans that reflect the shared values and approximate vision of the community, and that are flexible and accommodate the unexpected. In such an environment, good planning is good politics and vice versa. A harmonious community working together to achieve a common approximate vision is a powerful force for economic development. A thriving local economy means an expanding pie and growing development opportunities for speculators, investors, and residents alike. Planners are capable of developing and delivering effective comprehensive planning when they understand the needs of their customers and the opportunities that are present in the local marketplace. For too long our customers have been telling most of us that traditional comprehensive planning is a lemon of a product and that they want something that is new and improved. Let's listen to our customers and try to do a better job of serving them.

REFERENCES

Altshuler, A. 1965. *The City Planning Process: A Political Analysis.* Ithaca, New York: Cornell University Press.

Arlington Planning Department. 1987. *Arlington Comprehensive Plan.* City of Arlington, Texas.

Banfield, E. 1973. "Ends and Means in Planning." *A Reader in Planning Theory.* New York: Pergamon.

Bassin, A. 1990. "Does Capitalist Planning Need Some Glasnost?" *Journal of the American Planning Association* Vol. 56, No. 2.

Bair, F. 1970. *Planning Cities.* Chicago: American Planning Association.

Barnes, W. and C. Orlebeke. 1991. "Scanning the Horizon: Local Response." *Nation's Cities Weekly* Vol. 14, No. 11.

Baum, H. 1983. *Planners and Public Expectations.* Cambridge, Massachusetts: Schenkman Publishing Company.

Baum, H. 1986. "Politics in Planners' Practices" *Strategic Perspectives on Planning Practice.* Lexington, Massachusetts: Lexington Books.

Baum, H. 1990. "Caring for Ourselves as a Community of Planners." *Journal of the American Planning Association* Vol. 56, No. 1.

Beauregard, R. 1987. "Process and Object in Planning." *Proceedings of the 1987 Conference on Planning and Design in Urban and Regional Planning.* New York: American Society of Mechanical Engineers.

Beauregard, R. 1990. "Bringing the City Back In." *Journal of the American Planning Association* Vol. 56, No. 2.

Benveniste, G. 1989. *Mastering the Politics of Planning.* San Francisco: Jossey-Bass Publishers.

Boyte, H. 1989. *Common Wealth: A Return to Citizen Politics.* New York: Free Press.

Burchell, R. 1988. "Planning, Power and Politics." *Society* Vol. 26, No. 1.

Calavita, N. 1990. "Citizen Initiative and Referendum on Land Use Decisions: Two Views." *Journal of the American Planning Association* Vol. 56, No. 4.

Callies, D., and D. Curtin. 1990. "On the Making of Land Use Decisions through Citizen Initiative and Referendum." *Journal of the American Planning Association* Vol. 56, No. 2.

Caro, R. 1975. *The Power Broker: Robert Moses and the Fall of New York.* New York: Vintage Books.

Carpenter, S. 1989. "Solving Community Problems by Consensus." *MIS Reports* Vol. 21, No. 10.

Cartwright, T. 1987. "The Lost Art of Planning." *Long Range Planning* Vol. 20, No. 2.

Cartwright, T. 1991. "Planning and Chaos Theory." *Journal of the American Planning Association* Vol. 57, No. 1.

Catanese, A. 1974. *Planners and Local Politics.* Beverly Hills, California: Sage Publications.

Catanese, A. 1984. *The Politics of Planning and Development.* Beverly Hills, California: Sage Publications.

Cisneros, H., and J. Parr 1991. "Reinvigorating Democratic Values: Challenge and Necessity." *Public Management* Vol. 73, No. 2.

Cohen, S. 1988. *The Effective Public Manager.* San Francisco: Jossey-Bass Publishers.

Dalton, L. 1989. "The Limits of Regulation." *Journal of the American Planning Association* Vol. 55, No. 2.

Davidoff, P. 1965. "Advocacy and Pluralism in Planning." *Journal of the American Institute of Certified Planners* Vol. 31, No. 5.

Davidoff, P., and M. Davidoff. 1974. "Commentary." *Journal of the American Institute of Planners* Vol. 40, No. 1.

Downs, A. 1991. "Obstacles in the Future of U.S. Cities." *Journal of the American Planning Association* Vol. 57, No. 1.

Eplan, L. 1978. "Atlanta: Planning, Budgeting and Neighborhoods." *Personality, Politics, and Planning.* Beverly Hills, California: Sage Publications.

Fagin, H. 1970. "Advancing the 'State of the Art'." *Urban Planning In Transition.* New York: Grossman Publishers.

Fisher, R., and W. Ury. 1981. *Getting to Yes.* New York: Penguin Books.

Forester, J. 1982. "Planning in the Face of Power." *Journal of the American Planning Association:* Winter 1982.

Freilich, R. 1989. "Removing Artificial Barriers to Public Participation in Land Use Policy: Effective Zoning and Planning Initiatives and Referenda." *Proceeding of the 1989 Institute on Planning, Zoning and Eminent Domain.* New York: Matthew Bender.

Friedmann, J. 1973. *Retracking America: A Theory of Transactive Planning.* Garden City, New York: Anchor Press/Doubleday.

Gallagher, M. 1991. "Maryland County Fires Director." *Planning* Vol. 57, No. 2.

Gomes, W. 1991. "The Unhappy Saga of a Small Town Planner." *Planning* Vol. 57, No. 5.

Hawkins, R. 1991. "Diversity and Municipal Openness." *Nation's Cities Weekly* Vol. 14, No. 14.

Herbers, J. 1990. "They're Taking the Public Out of Public Policy Making." Vol. 3, No. 5.

Hitt, D. 1990. "Bright Lights, Little City." *Dallas Times Herald,* December 30.

Hoch, C. 1984. "Doing Good and Being Right." *Journal of the American Planning Association* Vol. 50, No. 3.

Hoch, C. 1988a. "Conflict at Large: A National Survey of Planners and Political Conflict." *Journal of Planning Education and Research* Vol. 8, No. 1.

Hoch, C. 1988b. "A Pragmatic Inquiry." *Society* Vol. 26, No. 1.

Hoch, C. 1990. "Planners and Political Conflict." *The Western Planner* Vol. 11, No. 6.

Hollander, T. 1970. "How Encompassing Can the Profession Be?" *Urban Planning in Transition.* New York: Grossman Publishers.

Howes, J. 1991. "Futures Forum: Governance in the Nineties." *Nation's Cities Weekly* Vol. 14, No. 6.

Ingwerson, M. 1990. "Indictments Seize Dade County." *Christian Science Monitor* May 4.

Kaufman, J. 1978. "The Planner as Interventionist in Public Policy Issues." *Planning Theory in the 1980s.* New Brunswick, New Jersey: Center for Urban Policy Research.

Kaufman, J. 1987. "Teaching Students about Strategizing, Boundary Spanning and Ethics." *Journal of Planning Education and Research* Vol. 6, No. 2.

Kemmis, D. 1990. *Community and the Politics of Place.* Norman, Oklahoma: University of Oklahoma Press.

Kent, Jr., T. 1964. *The Urban General Plan.* San Francisco: Chandler Publishing Company.

Knack, R. 1986. "Woman's Work." *Planning,* Vol. 52, No. 10.

Krumholz, N. 1978. "Make No Big Plans . . . Planning in Cleveland in the 1970's." *Planning Theory in the 1980s.* New Brunswick, New Jersey: Center for Urban Policy Research.

Krumholz, N., and J. Forester. 1990. *Making Equity Planning Work.* Philadelphia: Temple University Press.

Kunde, J. 1990. "No. 1 Problem 'Getting along with each other'." *Nation's Cities Weekly* Vol. 13, No. 49.

Leubsdorf, C. 1990. "Cavazos Resigns Top Education Job." *Dallas Morning News,* December 13.

Levin, M. 1987. *Planning in Government.* Chicago: Planners Press.

Lewis, S. 1991. "Another Side of the Story." *Planning* Vol. 57, No. 5.

Lineberry, R., and I. Sharkansky. 1978. *Urban Politics and Public Policy.* New York: Harper and Row Publishing.

Long, N. 1972. *The Unwalled City.* New York: Basic Books.

Lorentzen, P. 1986. "Leadership: Changing Contexts, Flexible Concepts." *The Bureaucrat,* Fall.

Lucy, W. 1988a. *Close to Power.* Chicago: Planners Press.

Lucy, W. 1988b. "APA's Ethical Principles Include Simplistic Planning Theories." *Journal of the American Planning Association* Vol. 54, No. 2.

Marcuse, P. 1976. "Professional Ethics and Beyond: Values in Planning." *Journal of the American Institute of Planners,* July.

Meck, S. 1990. "Citizen Initiative and Referendum of Land Use Decisions." *Journal of the American Planning Association* Vol. 56, No. 4.

Meltsner, A. 1972. "Political Feasibility and Policy Analysis." *Public Administration Review* Vol. 32, No. 6.

Murray, C. 1988. *In Pursuit of Happiness and Good Government.* New York: Simon and Schuster.

National League of Cities, 1984. "Cleveland Residents Share in Shaping Future." *Nation's Cities Weekly,* November 14.

Papatola, D. 1990. "In Minneapolis, Neighborhoods Know Best." *Planning* Vol. 55, No. 10.

Patton, C., and D. Sawicki. 1986. *Basic Methods of Policy Analysis and Planning.* Englewood Cliffs, New Jersey: Prentice-Hall.

Peattie, L. 1978. "Politics, Planning, and Categories—Bridging the Gap," in R. Burchell and G. Sternlieb, eds., *Planning Theory in the 1980s:* A Search for Future Directions. New Brunswick, New Jersey: Center for Urban Policy Research.

Peirce, N., and R. Guskind. 1989. "Hot Managers, Sizzling Cities." *Business Month,* June.

Perloff, H. 1980. *Planning the Post-Industrial City.* Chicago: Planners Press.

Peterson, J. 1985. "The Nation's First Comprehensive City Plan." *Journal of the American Planning Association* Vol. 51, No. 2.

Potapchuk, W. 1991. "New Approaches to Citizen Participation." *Planning in Virginia.* Richmond, Virginia: Virginia Chapter of the American Planning Association.

Raymond, G. 1978. "The Role of the Physical Urban Planner," in R. Burchell and G. Sternlieb, eds., *Planning Theory in the 1980s:* A Search for Future Directions. Center for Urban Policy Research.

Rondinelli, D. 1973. "Urban Planning As Policy Analysis: Management of Urban Change." *Journal of the American Institute of Planners,* January.

Seib, P. 1991. "City Council is no credit to Dallas." *The Dallas Morning News,* February 13.

Shirvani, H. 1985. "Insider's View on Planning Practice." *Journal of the American Planning Association* Vol. 51, No. 4.

Singer, S. 1988. "APA News." *Planning* Vol. 54, No. 9.

Spaid, D. 1978. "Professionalism and Timing of Planning." *Personality, Politics and Planning.* Beverly Hills, California: Sage Publications.

Toregas, C. 1989. "Electronic Democracy: Some Definitions and a Battle Cry." *Public Management* Vol. 71, No. 11.

Vasu, M. 1979. *Politics and Planning: A National Study of American Planners.* Charlotte: University of North Carolina Press.

Walker, R. 1941. *The Planning Function in Urban Government.* Chicago: The University of Chicago Press.

Wheaton, W. and M. Wheaton. 1970.

"Identifying the Public Interest: Values and Goals." *Urban Planning in Transition*. New York: Grossman Publishers.

Will, G. 1983. *Statecraft as Soulcraft*. New York: Simon and Schuster.

Wilson, W. 1983. "Moles and Skylarks."

Introduction to Planning History in the United States. New Brunswick, New Jersey: Center for Urban Policy Research.

Youngman, R. 1991. "Another Story that Should Be Told." *Planning* Vol. 57, No. 2.

3

Linking Privatization Decisions to Customer Service

WHAT IS PRIVATIZATION AND WHY IS IT POPULAR?

The basic premise of privatization is quite appealing. Services are contracted out or transferred from the public sector to the private sector in order to save money and increase efficiency. Many people believe that because of the profit motive in the private sector and the cumbersome bureaucracy of the public sector, the private sector is therefore inherently more efficient. John Naisbitt, best known for his book *Megatrends*, reported in 1986 that "privatization—the private delivery of public services—is sweeping the country" (Naisbitt 1985). I have found that it's sweeping the country alright, but it's using a small broom. Privatization is an idea that has been much discussed but in actual practice has had only a limited impact on *most* local government operations. Yet many local governments are dabbling with privatization, and I believe it will become increasingly important as people become more knowledgeable and comfortable with the concept.

A 1987 report on *Privatization in America*, sponsored by Touche Ross, the International City Management Association, and the Privatization Council, indicated that local governments were spending $1 billion dollars for contracted services and would "be spending nearly $3 billion in public-private partnerships on public works improvements in the next three years" (Hecimovich 1987). A 1988 survey by the ICMA revealed that eight percent of local governments provided some limited contracting (Rogers 1989). Most of the contracting was focused in key public works and transportation areas. Typical examples include contracting for the management of transit operations and for maintenance or new construction work on streets, highways and water utilities. Other, but less common examples, were contracting for legal services, refuse collection, golf course management, data processing services, airport operations, management of zoos, fleet maintenance, and accounting and payroll services. Privatization can involve an entire department or be limited to a particular service. One city has a contract with a local Jiffy Lube operator to change the oil in all city automobiles. Jiffy Lube was able to service the city's vehicles at approximately one-third of the city's service center costs and in less time.

Privatization is not an unknown concept to city planners. It is very common for local governments, especially those in small towns, to hire private sector consultants in lieu of hiring additional staff. The general public, however, knows little about the issue of privatization. Residents just want their governments to get things done without raising taxes or service fees. Local governments are under increasing pressure to reconsider their basic approach to service delivery. *Insight* magazine reports that some studies show that "private firms can deliver public services from 20 to 75 percent more cheaply than cities" (Lochhead 1988). Joseph Bast, president of the Heartland Institute in Chicago, states that "most of the credible empirical research on privatization stretching over 20 years shows substantial savings to the public, generally in the range of 30 to 50 percent" (Bast 1991).

Faced with rebellious taxpayers and a serious decline in federal grants and other forms of revenue sharing, local governments are finding it increasingly difficult to fund existing city services and to satisfy their citizenry. In 1990, federal government funding accounted for only 6.4 percent of city revenues, compared to 17.7 percent in 1980 (Conte 1991). Other reasons for the growing interest in privatization are that it provides a way to solve labor problems, makes it possible to share development risks, and permits faster implementation for some projects. Under the circumstances, transferring public services to the private sector can be an appealing opportunity for both the public and private sectors.

Adam Smith, in *The Wealth of Nations,* suggested there were limits to what governments could do. Recent election results clearly show there are certainly limits to the kind and amount of taxes that local governments can propose. A December 1990 *Wall Street Journal* editorial contends that the opportunity and time for adjustment in the public sector is at hand. The American private enterprise system, it says, spent the 1980s adjusting to the realities of the competitive world. The manufacturing industries and white-collar businesses were "restructured" to reach some sustainable level and leanness of operation. The editorial argues that the time is now right for the rational pruning of the nation's governments at all levels: "The public . . . sees what the politicians implausibly deny: that government at all levels has breached the limits on what services it can be relied on to provide well. This is hardly a matter of ideology anymore. The physical evidence, the wreckage, is all around us to testify that the public sector is collapsing under the weight of its own bloated responsibilities. . . . The private economy rationalized itself. Now is the time for the public economy to do the same. It might start by jettisoning operations that could better be done by spinoff enterprises" (Bartley 1990a).

With steadily growing interest and support from both the public and private sectors, the basic concept of privatization is slowly but profoundly altering the field and practice of public administration. City managers and public officials are increasingly being challenged to come up with imaginative and entrepreneurial ways to operate local government. The fundamental premise on which most local government services are based is no longer sacrosanct. Dan Miller, the publisher of *City and State,* notes that many local officials are asking, "Where is it written that I *must* provide all the services tomorrow that I provided yesterday?" (Miller 1990). A steadily growing number of public administrators and local governments are demonstrating a willingness to reconsider their traditional role as the actual service provider. Instead, they are ensuring that services are provided in the simplest, most efficient, economical, and satisfying manner possible—without regard to source. In this new role, "local governments may act more as brokers and overseers than as service delivery agents" (McCloud 1990). It is the support for privatization, says Mark Menchik, a senior analyst for the Advisory Commission on Intergovernmental Relations, "that is forcing governments to reconsider the nature of the service, the rationale for providing it, and the means by which it is provided" (Darr 1987).

Since the early 1900s, the public mood has swung back and forth with respect to what sector should deliver public services. Private transit, fire protection, and garbage collection services were commonplace at the turn of the century. Over time, under the reform and good government movement, local governments became more professionalized and citizens supported the transfer of such services to the public sector. This pendulum is now swinging back to the private sector. There is a simple explanation for this, says Dr. A. Lee Fritschler, director of the Center for Public Policy Education at the Brookings Institution in Washington, D.C.: "When the marketplace doesn't work well, we let government do it. And when government doesn't work well, we go back to the private sector" (Naisbitt 1985).

In 1986, Ecorse, Michigan, a community of 11,000 near Detroit, was in default on a large debt and in violation of a court order to balance its budget. A judge decided that government in this instance was not working well and placed the community in receivership. He gave a municipal bond expert authority to operate the city without political interference. In four years, the expert privatized almost all municipal services. The public work force was cut nearly in half, private firms we're hired to handle most services, and taxes were frozen. According to Larry Salisbury, former mayor of Ecorse, "It was painful, but we're getting our money's worth now" (Bartley 1990b).

Privatization is increasingly being viewed in nonideological terms as simply a way to make scarce public resources go further. The old advertising adage, "try it, you'll like it," is proving to be true. A recent survey by the Mercer Group, a consulting firm based in Atlanta, found that 97 percent of the cities that had tried privatization were pleased with the results (Bartley 1991). The Mercer Group noted that *all* of the survey respondents reported saving money while 45 percent indicated that the quality of services had significantly improved as a direct result of privatization.

PRIVATIZATION CAVEATS

There are limits to privatization. Ronald Moe, a specialist with the Congressional Research Service of the Library of Congress, explains: "The current challenge facing privatization advocates as well as public management leadership is to incorporate a number of factors, economic, legal, managerial and political, into a criteria for determining which public functions are appropriate for assignment to the private sector for performance and which functions are best assigned to officers and employees of the government. . . . The limits may involve judgment calls, but there are boundaries and the crossing of these boundaries is not without its cost" (Moe 1987).

First, it should be recognized that there are functions which can and should only be provided by government. But in the instances where public services can properly be provided by the private sector, the role of government should be to pave the way for privatization.

Ted Kolderie, director of the Public Services Redesign Project at the Humphrey Institute at the University of Minnesota, cautions privatization advocates about what he calls "creaming" (Kolderie 1986). He uses this term to describe situations in which contractors serve only the easiest and most profitable customers while ignoring difficult or unprofitable markets. Of course, the public sector itself can also be guilty of creaming or cherry-picking. I have observed any number of planning agencies that were concentrating their activities in regulatory areas that were producing substantial processing and permitting fees while ignoring basic planning services, particularly in inner-city areas. Also, to the extent that bureaucrats are their own best customers, you can argue that this is ultimate creaming.

Local governments need to be aware of the potential for abuse when they consider privatizing a service. The way to guard against abuse is to include measurable performance standards and criteria in service contracts and to consistently monitor and evaluate the contractor's performance. HUD's 1989 homeless-housing program learned this lesson the hard way. The stated goal of this laudable program was to increase the supply of affordable housing for homeless and low-income families while filling some of HUD's inventory of repossessed homes with responsible occupants. HUD proposed to lease up to 10 percent of the department's foreclosed homes across the country for $1 a year to tax-exempt groups such as churches and local housing authorities. These nonprofit groups would match homes with qualified homeless families (*Federal Register* 1990).

HUD believed that privatization of the administration and operation of the homeless-housing program would produce faster results and not require any additional staffing. But rather than being the new start that Jack Kemp envisioned, the program was riddled with the same vague rules and lax monitoring that led to abuses under former HUD Secretary Samuel Pierce, Jr. The rules defining homelessness were so poorly written that, if taken literally, they could even apply to traveling salespeople. Anna Kondratas, assistant secretary for community planning and development at HUD, acknowledged that the definition of homelessness was "vaguely written," but she also argued, "there is a presumption of poverty in the definition of homelessness that any responsible man interpreting the law would apply" (Jones and Welchlin 1990). Apparently HUD has yet to learn that there are sometimes irresponsible people involved in their programs.

The results of HUD's homeless-housing program have been mixed. HUD's staff admits they were unable to adequately monitor this program in some areas because of its popularity and rapid growth. The *Fort Worth Star-Telegram* ran an investigative story in late 1990 that detailed serious abuses in the program that a regional HUD official aptly described as "obscene" (Jones and Welchlin 1990). The abuse included: HUD homeless-housing program sponsors living in the houses themselves and placing relatives, friends, and fellow church members in such homes; people with upper middle-class incomes, late-model automobiles, and voluminous furnishings paying nominal rent for luxury homes; opportunities for sponsors to behave like real estate speculators; and, cases of homes being used for office purposes.

The newspaper pointed out that the intent of the program is good and proper, but locally it was clearly undermined by conflict-of-interest abuses, cronyism, and venal, hypocritical exploitation.

In San Antonio, however, the program was well administered by the local housing authority. Nonprofit organizations in the Phoenix area banded together under a single administrative entity, with each taking responsibility for one home. Andy Heald, from HUD's Region 8 office, tells me that he makes yearly monitoring visits to all properties in his region because he is concerned about the vagueness of the rules and wants to prevent or limit abuses of the program. In Oklahoma, state authorities placed a maximum limit of $55,000 on the value of any house which could be used in the program.

Some of the abuses in the Dallas-Fort Worth area took place because there were no limits on the value of houses which could be included in the program. Many friends and relatives of program sponsors were placed in homes valued at over $90,000. The opportunity to live cheaply in a luxury home was very tempting. One sponsor tried to obtain a home located on a five-acre tract with a swimming pool and a stable. When asked by a reporter to justify this action, the sponsor explained that the house could be appropriate for a homeless family with many kids, or for some bank president that lost his job on a bank takeover.

Almost any government function that can be privatized can also be abused. In recent years, local governments have attempted to shift responsibility for financing public works from the taxpaying base at large toward the developers and users who will be directly benefiting from the capital outlays. User-based financing is considered to be a more equitable way to pay for new growth and development. It also has privatization potential.

One popular method of public finance is to create a special assessment district. With the agreement of the property owners, a taxing district is created and extra fees are levied to pay for the cost of special capital projects like water, sewer, and street improvements. Special assessment districts can also be used by private developers to finance the costs of converting raw land into developable tracts.

This financing method has been very popular in Colorado where, unfortunately, it has also been seriously abused. These problems resulted from the fact that the boards of the taxing authorities usually consisted of developers and their employees. Tax-free municipal bonds were sold, capital improvements were provided, and each board set the tax rate that was to be charged to property owners. However, the temptation was great to keep the tax rate low so that district developers would have an advantage in attracting residents to the area.

The rules governing special assessment districts in Colorado are especially lax. It was easy for developers to get approval for their districts from rubber-stamping county commissioners who had no oversight interest or responsibility. Bond underwriters who typically made one percent of each deal were eager to peddle these high interest bonds to an uninformed public. One special district was able to issue $25 million in debt for a district with a total assessed value of $17,000 (Zolkos 1991).

The districts appeared to be successful for the first years of operation. They used capitalized interest to cover initial interest payments until there was tax growth from new development. If the area boomed and new homes and commercial or industrial development were added to the tax base, the district prospered. If development was slow or failed to equal overoptimistic growth forecasts, there was real "trouble in River City."

The Colorado Centre Metropolitan District is a case in point. When this district defaulted on its bonds in 1989, the annual property tax for an $85,000 house rose from less than $100 a year to $12,000. The board of the district had kept taxes artificially low by relying on capitalized interest and bond reserve funds. Bonded indebtedness for each of the 148 homes in the district now amounts to $210,000. In a story on abuses in the municipal bond market, the *Wall Street Journal* stated that the problems in Colorado were familiar to followers of the S & L crisis: lax regulation, greedy investors, outrageous appraisals, and outright fraud (Charlier 1990).

About 20 percent of the homes in the Colorado Centre Metropolitan District have been abandoned. It appears that all the homes will ultimately have to be sold at a tax sale to satisfy the district's debts. It is now harder for local governments in Colorado to float traditional municipal bonds, and many municipalities are having to pay higher interest rates on the bonds they are able to sell. In the February 25, 1991, issue of *City and State*, it was estimated that 41 special-district debt issues in Colorado were in default (Zolkos 1991).

There are valuable lessons to be learned from the HUD homeless-housing program and the abuse of special assessment districts in Colorado. When privatization involves the use of public resources or when it significantly affects the public health, safety and welfare, government must recognize and accept its critical responsibilities. This involves developing clear rules, regulations, performance standards, and safeguards, and systematically monitoring and evaluating the program or service. Privatization is not an opportunity or excuse for government to neglect or abandon its responsibilities to the public. Privatization only changes the nature of the public manager's duties and responsibilities. The bottom line is that neither the state nor the marketplace can produce beneficial results when left unchecked.

Richard Leone, chairman of the Port Authority of New York and New Jersey and a critic of privatization, concedes that "privatization has its virtues, but only when competition and fairness are assured" (Leone 1990). Healthy competition between the public and private sector depends on a level playing field. If one sector has an unfair advantage, then true competition is unlikely and incentives are created for unethical or corrupt behavior. A vivid example comes from Texas, where state law allows private attorneys to add a 15-percent penalty for collecting delinquent property taxes for local governments. The same law also prohibits the public sector from adding this 15-percent penalty if a government uses its own in-house legal staff. The incentive that local governments have to privatize the collecting of delinquent taxes is due solely to state law and has resulted in the appearance of questionable relationships between state legislators and the private collection firms that don't want the law changed. One collection firm has contributed hundreds of thousands of dollars in campaign contributions, helping to secure local collection contracts. Many bills have been introduced in the legislature to enable local governments to collect the 15-percent penalty while using in-house staff. None, however, has made it out of committee and onto the house floor for a vote. In late December of 1990, an elected official was even indicted for accepting and failing to report a gift from one of the state's largest tax collection firms. Regardless of the legal outcome of this indictment, the real lesson is that privatized services that are sheltered or protected from competitive forces can easily lead to the appearance of political favoritism. The sad part of this story is that the images of the state and local governments and the collecting firms have been needlessly damaged by this legislatively mandated advantage to the private sector. Privatization should be legitimized, not subsidized. When services are protected from competition everyone loses, especially the consumer.

I want to emphasize that just because something has been transferred to the private sector doesn't mean that people will forgive the public sector for any subsequent failures. For instance, one city had contracted with a respected nonprofit group to operate its animal control facility in order to save thousands of dollars annually. But when a local animal rights group exposed the facility for inhumane treatment of the animals, it was the city staff and elected officials that took the heat from the public, not the nonprofit contractor. The city had been so excited about the prospect of saving money that it had not provided for any treatment standards or for any monitoring of the animal shelter operations. Privatization does not excuse the public sector from its responsibilities to the public.

Nor is privatization the simple quick-fix solution it is often envisioned to be by anti-government types that want to restrain tax expenditures and reduce the size of government. Some conservative critics of government even oppose certain aspects of privatization because they might make government more effective and lead to increased support for public services. For example, Stuart Butler, head of domestic policy studies at the Heritage Foundation in Washington, D.C., issues the following warning to conservatives: "Moving the supply (producer) function out of government may replace a muted bureaucratic pressure for bigger programs with a well-financed, private-sector campaign. This significant drawback means that contracting should be viewed with caution as a means of privatization. Contracting can lead to more efficient government, but it does not guarantee smaller government" (Butler 1985).

While I obviously don't share Butler's fear of privatization as an agent of more efficient and effective government, I do realize that there are significant dangers. Will there be adequate competition after the service has been privatized? If anything goes wrong with the contractor, will the loss or interruption of service be a severe problem? Can the required level of quality of service be assured? Will the contracting of a particular service cause any negative impacts on any other public service? Will privatization result in higher levels of customer satisfaction? These are all questions the public sector will have to ask itself before deciding to privatize.

MAXIMIZING EFFECTIVENESS AND CUSTOMER SATISFACTION

It has been suggested that local government simply needs to become more businesslike to become more effective. But Peter Drucker in his 1973 book, *Management: Tasks, Responsibilities, Practices,* stressed that this is the wrong diagnosis and thus the wrong prescription for the ills of service institutions. What characterizes a business, says Drucker, is control by performance and results, while "businesslike" to the service institution means control of costs. The service institution, he says, lacks effectiveness, not efficiency (Drucker 1973).

In the absence of competition and alternatives, there is limited control on costs and almost no incentive for performance. Most local governments have what is basically a long-term, noncompetitive, sole-source contract with the general public. Institutions from which the customer cannot escape, says Drucker, are paid for good intentions and for "programs," not for satisfying their constituents.

It appears that pay for performance and for improved effectiveness is a critical aspect of customer service. If true, and I believe it is, this represents a serious problem for most local government. In the traditional local government budget, department head compensation is usually based on the number of employees, the size of the budget, and the scope of functions for each department. Under this system, managers are rewarded for adding employees and increasing their budgets. This adversely affects the way that resources are allocated and insulates the department from the marketplace. In the public sector, bureaucrats maximize budgets because it leads to greater salaries, prestige, and power. Naturally, department heads can be expected to oppose any privatization that reduces their staffs and budgets.

The typical planning department budget consists primarily of funds from the city's general revenue stream. In most sunbelt cities, this revenue comes principally from local property taxes. Each year the department is given a budget allocation. It is common to find across-the-board increases or decreases for all departments. Funding seldom, if ever, is tied to some performance. Yet it is clear that employees should be paid for what they earn, not for what they need or believe they deserve. They must be paid for satisfying customers.

Changes in the local government budget system are already taking place, and the rate of change can be accelerated by injecting competition into the public sector. In my opinion, competition is the essential benefit from privatization.

A recent Harvard Kennedy School study also concluded that the real issue in privatization is not public sector versus private sector management practices, but rather the need for competition (Gomez-Ibanez 1990a). It was noted that studies comparing private and public monopolies in areas such as water and electricity services found little difference in long-run costs. In essence, a monopoly is a monopoly regardless of source. John D. Donohue, a leading scholar in this field, argues "it is competition, not ownership, that leads to reduced infrastructure costs."

COMPETITIVE PRIVATIZATION

Under the guidance of former city manager Marvin Andrews, the city of Phoenix became a leader in alternative service delivery. Andrews reported in 1986, "Phoenix officials feel very strongly that they have an obligation to provide needed municipal services to citizens in the most economical, yet effective, manner" (Andrews 1986). City government in Phoenix is now forced to compete with private business. Each department is driven by the marketplace to reduce costs while maintaining and even improving services.

Ronald Jensen, the public works director for the city of Phoenix, has become a leading advocate for what he calls the "concept of public/

private competition and cooperation" (Jensen 1990). Jensen reports that where services can be provided by either the public or private sectors, a competitive bidding process can be very effective in determining who should be doing the work. According to Jensen, a privatization decision is not a static situation. "It may change with time, it may be politics, it may be resources, it may be weight scales, it may be a number of things, but you look at that continuously," he says. (Jensen 1989).

In Phoenix, the privatization process works as follows: when city officials determine that a particular service is eligible for privatization, they initiate a competition and the appropriate city department is permitted to bid on providing the service in direct competition with private sector firms. The technical evaluation process used is impartial. This process, according to Andrews, "puts many departments in a very competitive climate. They know that if they cannot perform and function efficiently, they may lose their operation to the private sector" (Andrews 1986).

In the experience of Phoenix officials, the process has worked well in both directions. The continued ability and interest of city departments to regain a lost service puts pressure on the private sector contractor to continue to be efficient and competitive. For example, the Phoenix sanitation department was able to regain a contract it had lost five years earlier to serve almost half of the city of Phoenix by studying and improving upon the operating system of the private contractor. The department was able to win the competition only after its managers and employees learned to cooperate. The sanitation department was able to lower costs and improve efficiency by using larger trucks equipped with mechanical arms to pick up garbage bins from the sidewalk. Larger trucks meant fewer trips to the landfill and the mechanical arm made it possible for the trucks to be operated by a single driver.

By only privatizing half of the services for the city originally, Phoenix was able to maintain its in-house capability to compete with the private sector contractor. If local governments lose that capability, the ability to continue the service in the event of contractor default is lost. Maintaining in-house capability is also important because it allows the manager to adequately evaluate the quality of the services being delivered by the private sector contractor.

Impressive results from privatization have been achieved in many jurisdictions and at every level of government. In 1985, the Minnesota Department of Administration persuaded the state legislature to let state agencies buy a wide range of products and services from the private sector—if they could be purchased at a lower cost. Sandra Hale, the commissioner of the Minnesota Department of Administration, said some people in her department feared that their central purchasing system and other management support functions would not be competitive with the private sector, and they would lose business, budget allocations, and positions. Instead, Hale reports that her department is doing 50 percent more business, charging an average of two percent less than five years ago. In addition the department realized $3.4 million in profits for fiscal year 1990. That's right, profits. "We've dropped some services, such as computer systems and programming, that we simply couldn't provide as cheaply as private vendors," explains Hale. "We've added other services, like management consulting, where we found that we could beat the private vendors. Being competitive is constantly on your minds. . . ." (Hale 1990).

Arthur A. "Don" Mendonsa, AICP, the city manager of Savannah, Georgia, reports his city uses cost-effective engineering studies to determine the best method of delivering services. When Savannah annexed a 25-square-mile area, the city staff analyzed service delivery alternatives for fire protection, and found that it would be more cost-effective to contract with the area's existing volunteer and paid fire fighters than for the city to establish its own service in the area. Mendonsa contends that the quality of service in the newly annexed area is similar to that in the rest of the city (Darr 1987).

In St. Louis and San Antonio, the public transit systems used comparisons with the private sector to convince labor unions to scale down wage and benefits demands. Under the threat of privatization, both management and labor must be sensitive to the image they have with local taxpayers.

An international example of privatization comes from Great Britain. The British Transportation Act of 1985 produced the following three significant changes: government controls over entry into the local bus industry were relaxed to promote increased competition; publicly owned and operated local bus companies were privatized into separate for-profit corporations; and local authorities were authorized to subsidize additional services where warranted by social concerns (Gomez-Ibanez 1990b).

Jose Gomez-Ibanez a professor at Harvard's Kennedy School of Government, studied and evaluated the impact of the British Transportation Act and reached the following conclusions:

- The biggest winners from the act are British taxpayers who have seen government expenditures for local transportation cut about 25 percent in the first two years of operation.

• Labor probably lost but the record is ambiguous. Basic wage rates were protected and much of the attrition was accomplished voluntarily through retirement or departures tied to large severance payments.

• Privatization and competition reduced costs, improved productivity and encouraged the development of market-oriented services. Competition clearly brought major service innovation.

• Innovations in the design of subsidized services by public authorities were stimulated by better information about the costs of individual bus service gained through the contracting process (Gomez-Ibanez, 1990b).

A final example of the benefits of privatization is a personal one. In the mid-1980s, the Arlington, Texas, park and recreation department issued a request for proposals to prepare a park and open space master plan. The Arlington Planning Department that I managed submitted a proposal that had some innovative elements and was competitive with the proposals that had been submitted by several consulting firms. Unfortunately, our planning department was small and inexperienced in park planning. The park department wanted a more experienced staff and hired an outside consultant. However, the department liked some of our ideas for obtaining public involvement and participation in the planning process and incorporated them into the final service contract. The planning process that was used and the final planning product that was produced were superior to what would have resulted without the competition. This plan went on to win the 1988 project planning award from the Texas chapter of the American Planning Association.

The lesson to be learned from these examples of privatization is that no sector has a monopoly on efficiency, productivity, and effectiveness. The most important thing the public can do is to unleash a self-perpetuating, external force for change that is free from the control of those who have been in charge. That force is fueled by competition and market-based pricing.

How can anyone in the public sector argue against having a better idea of what services should cost and what kinds of productivity improvements could be achieved if these services were provided by the private sector? This kind of information is needed before local government can look critically at itself. "The managerial attention that is given to a function put under the microscope of cost comparison," says Mike

Lemyre in an article in *The Privatization Review*, "increases its effectiveness and quality" (Lemyre, 1989).

One of my concerns about privatization is that most, if not all, of the literature on the topic seems to emphasize cost comparisons as the primary criteria for selecting the mode of service delivery. Usually considerations of effectiveness are neglected. A 1987 privatization survey of municipalities mentioned at the beginning of this chapter revealed that only one of the responding cities indicated that "better service" was the reason for deciding to contract out a particular service (David 1988). The number one reason given for considering privatization was cost savings. Yet I will remind you that Peter Drucker contends that the reason for the decline in the service industry is because managers emphasize efficiency rather than effectiveness. Nothing is less productive than to make more efficient something that should not be done anyway. In essence, this is what Thomas Peters and Robert Waterman, Jr., were saying in their classic book, *In Search of Excellence*. They concluded that excellent companies more often "tend to be driven by close-to-the-customer attributes than by either technology or costs" (Peters 1982).

Peters and Waterman found that excellent companies really are close to their customers. These companies are not low-cost producers, but rather the ones that exhibit a concomitant to customer orientation and satisfaction. They focus on generating revenue through fulfilling customer needs and expectations. Satisfied customers produce more than satisfactory profits. It is competition that has led the private sector to understand this, and it can have the same influence on the public sector.

Any product or service provider with a captive clientele and funding that is guaranteed is going to be resistant to change. Without competition, it is doubtful whether local governments will be willing to pay the price to institute the reforms that are needed to consistently satisfy their customers. Most customers want choice while bureaucrats and elected officials fear and argue against it. A typical defense is that choice will victimize lower income groups and minorities.

The debate on choice is particularly heated in the field of public education. Many educators believe that giving parents the choice of which school their kids will attend is the key ingredient to increasing the performance of our schools. Critics say that, at best, choice would hurt the poor and resegregate the schools. At worst, it would doom public education. But I don't believe the critics and neither do parents. A Gallup

Poll published in September 1990 indicated that 65 percent of American public-school parents favor choosing their children's schools. Furthermore, young, southern, nonwhite city dwellers of modest means were the most likely to favor choice, an argument that the disadvantaged have just as much, or more, to gain from choice.

People want choices in almost all areas of their lives. A survey conducted in 1990 by the *Wall Street Journal* and NBC News found that one-third of the respondents said most of the time they prefer businesses that charge higher prices but provide better service. Does this survey have any application to the public sector? I think the answer is yes. Regardless of the source of the service, people want to be treated like valued customers. They want someone to listen to them, to care about them, and to take personal responsibility for helping them. In other words, treat your customers like you want to be treated when you are a customer.

PRIVATIZATION CASE STUDY

There is growing interest on the part of local governments to privatize municipal airport facilities and operations. Airport sales have been contemplated in Atlanta, Los Angeles, Philadelphia and Albany, New York. Cash-strapped cities are intrigued by the potential of placing airports on their tax rolls. The following is a case study of the airport privatization issue in Arlington, Texas. Information for this study has been provided by Arlington's Office of the City Manager.

The Arlington Municipal Airport encompasses approximately 350 acres, of which 210 acres are developed. It consists of a single north-south runway 4,000 feet long and 100 feet wide, a terminal building housing the airport administrative offices and lease tenants, approximately 96 hangar and 90 tie-down spaces owned and leased by the city, and approximately 66 hangar spaces owned and leased by fixed-base operators. The fuel operation, which consists of aviation and jet fuel, is operated by the city.

The city leases approximately 54 acres to Bell Helicopter for hangar and test facilities, and has ground leases with four other fixed-base operators. These leases allow the construction and lease of hangar spaces, aircraft sales, aircraft repair and service, private flight schools, and lease of office space. The city also leases office space to approximately five tenants in the airport terminal building.

There are approximately 250 aircraft based at the Municipal Airport, with a waiting list of approximately 210 persons desiring hangar space. The majority of the based aircraft are single engine with a smaller number being twin-engine aircraft. There are no jet aircraft based at the airport, nor are there any facilities available to house jet aircraft at the present.

The airport is owned and operated by the City of Arlington. The airport staff consists of an airport supervisor, a service coordinator, a senior clerk, eight service attendants, and two part-time security guards. The airport staff is responsible for hangar and tie-down rental, land and building leases, fueling operations, ground and building maintenance, and enforcement of FAA and city rules and regulations.

In 1985, because of the city council's growing interest and concern with several issues relevant to the expansion of the municipal airport, William Kirchhoff, city manager at the time, appointed an eight-member committee to study the airport privatization issue. This committee consisted of the deputy city manager, a councilman, the city attorney, the director of internal audit, the director of transportation, the director of finance, the director of planning, and the director of support services. A technical assessment of the privatization potential was prepared by the director of internal audit with the assistance of the research operations manager and an industrial engineer.

The initial staff research concluded that contracting airport services to a fixed-base operator would be somewhat less costly than continuing to have the city operate the facility. However, there were other significant costs, such as the maintenance of the runway, which the city would still have to be responsible for because the fixed-based operators were not willing to accept this responsibility due to the high risk and high cost of insurance.

The city attorney advised the city that it was legally permissible to enter into contracts with the private sector to provide services at the airport. However, it was noted that the city would be required to repay any FAA grant monies that had been received in the past if the city relinquished control of the airport to a private individual. Furthermore, any future FAA funding would be jeopardized if the city did not retain control of the airport.

Research performed by the research operations manager and the internal audit department indicated that the number of qualified fixed-base operators was limited. However, the surveys of other municipal airports revealed that most of the services contracted out were contracted to several small fixed-base operators instead of one or two large fixed-base operators. It was believed that such an approach would probably provide the city with a greater opportunity to attract qualified, competent fixed-base operators.

Staff research and analysis produced the following summary of the advantages and disadvantages of the privatization of the Arlington Municipal Airport:

Advantages:

• Direct cost and overhead could be reduced by contracting out high-cost services.

• Working capital required for capital improvements would be provided by fixed-base operators. Thus the City's investment would be reduced significantly for future capital improvements.

• Expansion of the airport could be achieved with a limited investment of working capital by the City.

• Revenues and expenditures could be projected with a reasonable amount of accuracy and consistency on an annual basis.

• The profit factor would motivate fixed-base operators to actively pursue tenants and airport customers.

• Resources currently being allocated to the airport could be channelled to areas where the demand for services is higher.

• Tax revenues would increase for real and personal property owned by fixed-base operators.

• City management could devote more time to planning and monitoring the airport's development.

• Fixed-base operators would specialize in airport operations. Thus the quality and level of service should improve and increase.

• Ownership of leasehold improvements would transfer to the City at the end of the lease term. Thus the City would obtain assets without any major capital investment or the cost of long-term debt financing.

• The City could lease city-owned facilities at the airport and reduce the cost currently associated with the maintenance and upkeep of these facilities.

Disadvantages:

• Increased activity at the airport could result in citizen complaints and possible litigation.

• The City could lose some control over the airport.

• The airport would require close monitoring by management to ensure the quality of service at the airport.

• Displaced employees would have to be absorbed into other City operations or laid off.

• Service interruptions may occur if the fixed-base operator(s) default on their contractual agreements.

• The City could incur operating expenses to continue services in the event of contractor default or bankruptcy.

• The City could be involved in costly and lengthy litigation in the event of contractor default or bankruptcy.

• Long-range planning might be difficult to achieve because of contract obligations.

• The City would be required to continue maintenance of the runways and other airport facilities due to the high risk and insurance cost associated with the airport operation.

• The availability of FAA grant monies would be lost if the City relinquished control of the airport to a private contractor.

The results of the study and the following four alternatives were presented to the city council:

Alternative 1: The City would continue to staff and operate the Municipal Airport with the same level of services being offered to airport customers. The existing runway would not be expanded. Accordingly, no major airfield improvements or expansion would be made under this alternative.

Alternative 2: The City would continue to staff and operate the Municipal Airport, extend the existing runway from 4,000 feet to 5,000 feet and install an instrument landing system. In addition, 160 hangars and 100 tie-down spaces would be constructed. An airport master plan would be developed to monitor and direct the expansion and development of the Municipal Airport. An airport manager with a professional background in aviation would be hired to oversee the airport operation and supervise the expansion and development of the Municipal Airport.

Alternative 3: The City would develop an RFP and solicit qualified professional fixed-base operators to take over the operation of the Municipal Airport. The City would retain control of the airport by hiring a professional airport manager to negotiate contracts for airport services and to monitor the quality of service being performed by fixed-base operators. The City would extend the existing runway from 4,000 feet to 5,000 feet and install an instrument landing system.

Construction of capital improvements such as hangars, tie-down areas, fueling facilities, restaurants, and other improvements necessary to develop a first-class airport would be funded by private fixed-base operators with the approval of the City Council. A master plan would be developed to monitor and provide guidance for expansion and development of the Municipal Airport. Consideration should be given to establishing an airport board to advise and provide input to the City Council and City management regarding expansion and development of the Municipal Airport.

Alternative 4:   The City could discontinue operation of the Municipal Airport and sell the airport property. The estimated value of the airport property was approximately $100 million. The downside to this option was the possibility of litigation by tenants holding long-term leases and objections from the residential property owners surrounding the airport property.

The eight-member airport privatization committee presented the following recommendations to the city council:

- City should continue to own, manage, and operate the Airport;
- City should hire an airport manager who also has experience in promoting aviation related economic development;
- City should use the airport as an economic development tool to attract corporate relocations either to the airport or in the City of Arlington;
- City should use the private sector to develop a marketing plan to sell the benefits of the airport to corporations and their pilots. The city must also allocate money to implement the marketing effort;
- City would then pursue the utilization of the private sector to complement or replace city sponsored development of the remaining airport acreage, consistent with the objectives of the marketing and master plans;
- When determining if the city or the private sector should do the development, factors related to the type of development, the return on investment, and the degree of risk should be evaluated; and,
- Proceed with the master plan/noise abatement and airport improvements as funds become available.

The committee recommended against full privatization because the operating proposals that had been submitted by the private sector would have been more costly to the city. In addition, the city staff had a good track record in managing and operating the airport and the private firms had demonstrated only marginal expertise in running the airport beyond the city's current capabilities. Concerns about various legal liabilities also contributed to the committee's position. After reviewing the report and the committee's recommendations, the city council adopted Alternative 3. In taking this action, the city council stated that its decision "builds on the city's strength in managing and operating an airport while incorporating the private sector's strengths in marketing and in developing the remaining property."

REFERENCES

Andrews, M. 1986. "Municipal Productivity Improvements Are a Way of Life in Phoenix." *National Civic Review* Vol. 75, No. 3.

Bartley, R. 1990a. "Golden Opportunity." *The Wall Street Journal* December 5, 1990.

Bartley, R. 1990b. "The Public Fat Cats." *The Wall Street Journal* December 28, 1990.

Bartley, R. 1991. "Public Going Private." *The Wall Street Journal* May 1, 1991.

Bast, J. 1991. "Privatization Works" *City and State* Vol. 8, No. 4.

Butler, S. 1985. *Privatizing Federal Spending, A Strategy to Eliminate the Deficit.* Washington, D.C.: The Heritage Foundation.

Charlier, M. 1990. "Many Tax-Free Bonds Are Going Into Default In Colorado Land Bust." *The Wall Street Journal* December 12.

Conte, Christopher 1991. "Labor Letter". *The Wall Street Journal* February 5, 1991.

Darr, T. 1987. "Pondering Privatization May Be Good for Your Government." November 1987.

David, I. 1988. "Privatization in America." *The Municipal Year Book: 1988.* Washington, DC: International City Management Association.

Drucker, P. 1973. *Management: Tasks, Responsibilities, Practices.* New York: Harper and Row.

Gomez-Ibanez, J. 1990a. "Privatization—Promise and Pitfall." *The Public's Capital* Vol. 2, No. 1.

Gomez-Ibanez, J. 1990b. "Privatizing and Deregulating Local Public Services." *Journal of the American Planning Association* Vol. 56, No. 1.

Hale, S. 1990. "A Commitment to Competition Presents Ethical Dilemmas." *Governing* Vol. 4, No. 3.

Hecimovich, J. 1987. "Emphasis on Privatization Becoming More Evident." *Public Investment* December 1987.

Jensen, R. 1989. "Municipal Service Contracting." *The Privatization Review* Vol. 4, No. 4.

Jensen, R. 1990. "New Theory is Win-Win." *Nation's Cities Weekly* Vol. 13, No. 45.

Federal Register. 1990. "Single Family Property Disposition Homeless Initiative: Interim Roles." January 11.

Jones, S. and B. Welchlin. 1990. "Home, Sweet Deal." *Fort Worth Star-Telegram* December 2, 1990.

Kolderie, T. 1986. "Two Different Concepts of Privatization." *Public Administration Review* Vol. 4, No. 3.

Lemyre, M. 1989. "Contracting Out for Assets and Services: Implementing a Cost Comparison Program." *The Privatization Review* Vol. 4, No. 4.

Leone, R. 1990. "Privatization? A politician's promise too good to be true." *City and State* Vol. 7, No. 21.

Lochhead, C. 1988. "Cities Finding Public Services Better-Run by Private Firms." *Insight* February 22, 1988.

McCloud, T. 1990. "A Market Approach to Service Delivery." *Nation's Cities Weekly.* Vol. 13, No. 45.

Miller, D. 1990. "Re-evaluating local services." *City and State* Vol. 7, No. 21.

Moe, R. 1987. "Exploring the Limits of Privatization." *Public Administration Review* November/December 1987.

Naisbitt, J. 1985. *The Year Ahead 1986.* New York, NY: Warner Books.

Peters, T. and Waterman, R. 1982. *In Search of Excellence.* New York, NY: Harper and Row Publishers.

Rogers, M. 1989. "Municipal Service Contracting." *The Privatization Review* Vol. 4, No. 4.

Zolkos, R. 1991. "State's Troubles Jolt Districts." *City and State* Vol. 8, No. 4.

Listening To Your Customers

WHAT'S YOUR EXCUSE?

Are you listening? Your customers are continuously trying to communicate with you and others at city hall. Yet planners constantly complain that people don't care about or want to participate in city planning. The sad truth is, as mentioned elsewhere, that for too many planners the public is a nuisance to be endured and not a welcome partner in the planning process. "Planners in public agencies normally tend to have little contact with the citizens who are their agencies' constituents," says Howell Baum. "In part, this isolation represents a response to an abundance of demands for the completion of projects in limited time. In addition, however, most planners prefer to have limited contact with citizens. A majority of planners believe that citizens have only limited information to contribute to the planning process and regard work with citizens as generally unrewarding" (Baum 1983).

The reality is that citizen participation works, and if planners spent a fraction of the time listening to people that they do devising ways to exclude them they would be much more effective.

Good doctors don't prescribe medication for patients without first talking with them and giving them a checkup. Planners themselves need a healthy dose of listening and understanding. Los Angeles design critic Sam Hall Kaplan warns planners to "beware of paradigms; what works in one place will not necessarily work in another. To find out what might work, the planner must get out, walk the streets, ask what a particular neighborhood wants to be—which might be far different from what the 'experts' want it to be'' (Kaplan 1990). ''Feedback,'' not Wheaties, is the real breakfast of champions and a key to effectiveness in city planning. Nobody knows what your customers want better than they do so my advice is to listen to them and learn.

As a general rule, no one has more customer data than the local planning organization. The typical city planning department has file cabinets and computer storage disks jam-packed with demographic and socioeconomic information on the people that live and work in the community. Yes, planners do a superior job of collecting data, yet they tend to have a lousy performance record when it comes to understanding their customers. If you are interested in learning how to become a better listener, then the following information should be useful to you.

ONE-ON-ONE CONTACTS

One-on-one is a form of competition in basketball but it is also an important and preferred characteristic of superior customer service. Robert Spaulding, the planning director for the city of San Diego, likes to

CUSTOMER LISTENING DEVICE

ask people face-to-face about their experiences with his department. Talking to customers one-on-one, he says, makes it possible to obtain rich qualitative data. Spaulding advises managers to consider these questions when talking to customers: "Was there clear communication about expectations and assistance offered to meet those expectations? Were schedules being met? Was information flowing freely? Was responsibility for decisions clearly established and placed at appropriate levels in your organization so decisions could be made quickly? Did your 'customer' know who in your organization was *responsible* for this project? Were people's needs at your 'front door' or counter service area being satisfactorily addressed?" (Spaulding 1989).

In *The Service Advantage*, Karl Albrecht and Lawrence Bradford, management consultants specializing in the emerging field of service management, point out that the whole menu of human response is accessible in the one-on-one interview. They note that unlike a telephone call or written survey, the interview allows you to watch the respondent's reactions to your questions. You can see when the brow furrows and the face frowns. You can experience the intensity of the customer's feelings about the various service attributes that you are interested in, and you can access and understand their meaning in a way that pencil and paper surveys do not permit (Albrecht and Bradford 1990). Of course, another significant advantage of direct contact is that you come to see your customers as individuals who bring specific preferences and expectations to your department or organization.

The primary liabilities of relying on the face-to face interview are that there is a limit to the number of customers that you can interview and that you obviously need some way to verify what you do learn. It is potentially dangerous to generalize or extrapolate from the feelings and experiences of just a few customers. You will therefore need to supplement your personal interviews with quantitative surveys that systematically reach a broader world of customers.

Most of the planning directors that I interviewed shared Robert Spaulding's preference for face-to-face meetings with their important customers, but because of time demands they relied primarily on the telephone for most of their communications. There was almost universal awareness of the desirability and need for obtaining feedback from people with power and influence in the local community. Yet a surprisingly high percentage of planners indicated that they did not aggressively seek out these types of contacts. Fear of being accused of playing "politics," taking sides, or "selling out" were some of the reasons given for avoiding personal contacts. One director responded that if his planners were going to be objective and rational, then they had to minimize involvement with special interest groups. Fortunately, his was an atypical response.

Even when people want to listen to each other it's not always easy to do. In fact, it requires training to be a good listener. Too many people take listening ability for granted. Most planners know the importance of being able to speak well in public, so they work at it. They attend conferences and workshops and read materials on how to be better communicators. But I have yet to meet a planner that has attended a listening workshop and, yes, such programs are available and very popular with managers in the private sector.

What you learn at listening workshops is that one major reason people find it difficult to listen is that they can hear at a much faster rate than people can talk. As a result, the listener's mind starts to wander and engage itself with additional activity. The first step in becoming a better listener is to evaluate your present listening ability. I ask you to stop reading at this time and take the listening test shown as Figure 4-1 on the next page.

When I evaluated myself as a listener I was appalled by the results. The two biggest failures on my part were "spending time getting ready to talk instead of listening to every word" and "trying to do something else while listening." Unfortunately, I discovered that I had several other poor traits that also contributed to a less than satisfactory assessment of my listening abilities.

Below is a list of the characteristics of good listeners. This list should be copied and posted in a visible place to serve as a constant reminder on how to be a more effective listener. I have no idea where this list came from, so I can't give proper credit to its originator.

Research has revealed that good listeners:

• Defer their judgement—more controlled—listen for the customer's feelings and situation.

• Pay most attention to CONTENT—not to appearance, form, or other surface issues.

• Listen completely FIRST—try to get every nuance of meaning. Try to really understand. This enthrones people.

• Are more mature in their listening habits. They listen for the MAIN IDEA and disregard minor points.

Figure 4-1. Test Yourself as a Listener

Do You . . .

1. prejudge or tune out the other person at the beginning?
   _____ never   _____ sometimes   _____ often

2. mentally criticize grammar, appearance, or speaking style?
   _____ never   _____ sometimes   _____ often

3. spend the time getting ready to talk instead of listening to every word?
   _____ never   _____ sometimes   _____ often

4. try to take in EVERYTHING—try to reply to everything, expecially exaggerations and errors?
   _____ never   _____ sometimes   _____ often

5. fake or pretend attention?
   _____ never   _____ sometimes   _____ often

6. divide your attention or try to do something else while listening?
   _____ never   _____ sometimes   _____ often

7. give up too soon when you realize you have to work actively at understanding what the customer is trying to say?
   _____ never   _____ sometimes   _____ often

8. lose control of your emotions; sometimes lose your temper and lash back?
   _____ never   _____ sometimes   _____ often

9. give little, if any, verbal response?
   _____ never   _____ sometimes   _____ often

10. become impatient and want the speaker to "get on with it?"
    _____ never   _____ sometimes   _____ often

• Concentrate only on the main issues. They don't worry about replying to everything. Avoid sidetracking remarks, especially those that might be considered sarcastic.

• They are aware of their human tendency to fake and give themselves internal cues to listen.

• Do one thing at a time—they realize listening is a full time job. They maintain eye contact as much as possible.

• They listen CAREFULLY. They sort, give feedback, and ask for confirmation.

• They feel their honest anger but control it. They do not allow their emotional reactions to govern their behavior.

• Give affirmative and affirming statements. Invite additional comments.

- Maintain patience and concentration while listening.
- Ask good questions.

I would close this section by noting that even God wants us to be good listeners. God gave most people two ears and one mouth, and if they are used in that proportion we all will be better listeners and communicators.

SURVEYING YOUR CUSTOMERS

Conducting statistically valid surveys of your customers is an important way to obtain information about your clients. Surveys were popular in the 1970s due to the combined pressures of social change and federal mandates but, according to Gary Streib, in the School of Public Administration and Urban Studies at Georgia State University, interest waned in the 1980s as fiscal issues became the dominant concern (Streib 1990). In a *Management Information Service Report* prepared in 1987 by the International City Management Association, it was noted that timely information and feedback on the results of programs and services are needed by local governments. Yet the same report concludes that "few governments regularly obtain feedback on service quality and responsiveness. While many operating agencies track the amount of work done, they rarely monitor the quality and effectiveness of that work" (Hatry, Greiner, and Swanson 1987).

Streib contends that local governments should reconsider using surveys because they are such an effective means of communication in an era that is marked by a lack of citizen involvement. Here are a few of the benefits of surveys, identified by Kenneth Webb and Harry Hatry of the Urban Institute in 1973:

- Measuring satisfaction with the quality of specific services including identification of problem areas;
- Uncovering facts, such as the numbers and characteristics of users and nonusers of various services;
- Discovering the reasons that specific services are disliked or not used;
- Evaluating demands for new services; and
- Examining citizen opinions on various community issues, including feelings of alienation toward government officials (Webb and Hatry 1973).

A growing number of local governments are starting to use surveys.

For example, as part of a systematic effort to improve the overall efficiency and quality of services in the Community Development Department in Grand Prairie, Texas, former planning director Roger Hedrick initiated a quantitative and comprehensive service evaluation program. The program included a survey that solicited input from individuals who had used the services of one or more of the department's three divisions during the first six months of 1985.

Client-centered evaluations are particularly valuable, and a most effective use of citizen surveys according to the previously referenced *MIS Report*. Some of the specific benefits of client-centered surveys are:

• Client surveys can be more efficient than general citizen surveys for getting information from persons who have had experience with a given service, facility, or program. To pick up these individuals from a general survey would be very expensive:

• Because client surveys focus on only service users, they are likely to allow sample sizes large enough for meaningful examination of a variety of user subgroups:

• Surveys can be more detailed, allowing examination of more characteristics of a particular service and reasons why respondents rated a particular service attribute poorly. Thus client surveys can be useful to program managers in uncovering problems and deciding how to address identified problems (Hatry, Greiner, and Swanson 1987).

For the client-centered survey in Grand Prairie, a survey form was sent to nearly 200 individuals who had participated in the development of a sector plan, applied for a building permit, requested a zoning change, applied for plat approval, or had recently received any other planning service. These customers were asked to evaluate each of the divisions that had served them, and also to add personal comments.

The overall evaluation in Grand Prairie was generally favorable; however, a number of recurring criticisms regarding specific services and the efficiency of service delivery were received. In direct response to an analysis of the survey results, several actions were taken to improve customer service in that city.

Reducing processing time became the department's number-one priority. In particular, resources were committed to developing a comprehensive "fast track" system for building plans that meet specific criteria or for final plats that are in compliance with approved preliminary plats.

To ensure consistency for all regulations, each division was directed to develop a standard operations policy and to hold periodic staff meetings to address emerging concerns of ordinance interpretations on operations or management policies.

Standards for intradepartment communication were developed to eliminate either needless duplication or processing failures resulting from cases "falling through the cracks." Use of memorandums, "tickler" files, regular weekly meetings, and daily communications among individuals working on pending cases were mandated.

Staff members were instructed to commit themselves to working with applicants to find solutions to problems rather than simply identifying problems.

The service evaluation survey form was made a formal part of the application process by being attached to all zoning, subdivision, and building permit applications. This commitment to continuous monitoring of service levels was strengthened by adding the name and phone number of the director to encourage direct contact.

Besides initiating these general improvements, the director presented a series of written recommendations to each division head for review and implementation. The director's guiding memo on the subject stated that, "regardless of whether or not the recommendations are endorsed by practice, it is imperative that each division recognize the area of concern and implement whatever measures are necessary to insure service improvement over the next period of assessment."

Hedrick developed the Grand Prairie survey questionnaire on the basis of previous interviews with selected representative customers and focus groups. A focus group consists of eight to 12 volunteers selected from a customer population. Responding to a series of open-ended questions, these customers provided insight that was used as a guide in the design and development of questions for the more extensive survey.

It was important to Hedrick that the survey questionnaire cover the concerns that customers said they were interested in as well as what he and his staff wanted to know. In any report card, not all subjects are of equal value or have the same weight. In obtaining feedback, it is important for the service provider to learn which attributes are particularly valued by customers. The evaluation process should therefore involve customer ranking of the relative desirability and importance of each of the factors they value. The focus group helped Hedrick to develop the questions that his customers wanted to answer.

Planners that are interested in using focus groups might want to consider differentiating between major classes of customers. At a minimum, I would suggest having a series of separate focus groups for internal and external customers. Depending on the degree that your department segments its customers, additional focus groups may be desirable. In the private sector it is not uncommon for people to be paid a small fee for participating in a focus group. The location and time of day of the focus group interviews should be as convenient as possible for the volunteers.

There are private firms which offer support series for conducting focus group exercises. If your organization cannot afford to employ a specialist trained in the field, then the individuals responsible for the interviewing must educate themselves on the subject. *The Service Advantage*, by Albrecht and Bradford, is a good place for beginners to start.

Focus groups can be used for purposes other than evaluation of various products and services. In a *Planning* magazine feature on "New Angles on Citizen Participation," it was noted that focus groups can provide planners with information about places. Planners in Chicago used focus groups to help them prepare a new "framework plan" for the city's central area. Marcel Acosta, assistant commissioner for central area planning in Chicago, points out that "to some extent downtown is a product, and focus groups are a way of finding out how it can be improved" (Zotti 1991). In Chicago, Acosta and his staff used four focus groups comprised of twelve people to help them learn more about what people like about the downtown area. Selection of participants for the focus groups was handled by a hired local advertising agency.

The real value of the experience was that it provided a reality check for the planning staff. "We get very close to certain projects and we lose perspective," Acosta says, "The discussion made us more sensitive to downtown workers' needs." The total cost of the focus group program in Chicago was $10,000, which included the facilitator's and ad agency's fees, room rental, videotaping, and payment of $40 for each participant.

Another good job of surveying has been done by the Lafayette Areawide Planning Commission (LAPC) in Lafayette, Louisiana. In July of 1990, LAPC initiated a survey of 90 local elected and appointed public officials that were considered to be the primary clients of the commission. Twenty-eight percent replied, with the best response by far coming from the appointed officials. The questionnaire that was used asked these officials to evaluate LAPC's services, work program, and budget. They were also asked to give their opinions on possible changes in LAPC's funding sources and to identify "serious problems in their community." The results of the survey were used to develop LAPC's work program and budget for the next year and to focus the staff's planning services on prioritized problems.

The last example that I want to share with you comes from the city of Gillette, Wyoming. Director of community development, David Spencer, says the city has been surveying its citizens annually since 1975 in order to tap residents' opinions on a wide range of topics, including local services and facilities, city offices, local issues, quality of life, shopping patterns, demographics and housing data, and the public's priorities. The surveys are used by elected officials and the city staff in making management and budget decisions. The consistency in the type of questions asked each year allows for multiyear comparisons of responses.

Each year, 1,450 households in Gillette are mailed two survey questionnaires and a stamped return envelope. A random sampling is achieved by taking every third name from the city's residential utility billing list. For the year 1990, 642 surveys, from 486 households, were returned, equalling a 34 percent response rate. The responses were tabulated by computer, while written comments were compiled by hand and included in the appendix of the final report. The report states that the survey represents only a sample and acknowledges the existence of certain biases. The written analysis in the report suggests that the best use of the survey results is as a relative indicator of comparative performance with past years.

In addition, John Darrington, the city administrator of Gillette, has recently urged his employees to focus on the concept of customer service. Employees took a course in "Achieving Extraordinary Customer Relations." Darrington also arranged for an evaluation of city procedures and policies by outside consultants.

As part of his own service strategy, David Spencer developed his own "Customer Service Follow-Up" form (see Figure 4-2), and initiated a series of workshops with his staff. The workshops were designed to answer the following customer service questions: What is our business and who are our customers? What counts most to our customers? What can we do with our service that customers would really notice? How do our customers see us now?

In developing a customer orientation, these are the kinds of questions that planners must ask of themselves. For accurate answers, contact and communication with your customers is necessary. More details about the Gillette program are provided in the final chapter.

Figure 4-2. Customer Service Follow-Up Form—City of Gillette

Department #_____
Division   #_____

Instructions

Please ask the customer to rate the employee contact on a scale of 1-10, with 10 being the most positive rating. If the trait was not observed or not applicable, write N/A.

1. Greeted customer in a cheerful manner _____
2. Learned and used the customer's name _____
3. Demonstrated full attention and appropriate listening skills _____
4. Was polite during the transaction _____
5. Expressed concern over the matter, if a mistake was made took personal responsibility to see that it was corrected _____
6. Remained calm and receptive _____
7. Explained policies and rules to customer's satisfaction _____
8. Offered to explore options for solving the customer's problem _____
9. Before closing checked to see that all the customer's concerns had been addressed _____
10. Closed the contact on a positive note _____

TOTAL SCORE _____
Divide by Number Rated _____
Average Score _____

Source: Department of Community Development, City of Gillette, Wyoming

I can't end this section without mentioning the city of Dayton, Ohio. That city's 1990 *Program Strategies,* an impressive management and finance document, reflects the superior commitment that municipal government in Dayton has to citizen participation. As part of its annual budget and performance evaluation program, the city conducts an annual public opinion and evaluation survey of approximately 900 residents, as well as an annual neighborhood needs survey. More information about Dayton's programs can be obtained from George Farmer, secretary to the city plan board in Dayton.

ELECTRONIC LISTENING

Costis Toregas, president of Public Technology, Inc., points out that there is growing interest within local governments for the use of information and telecommunications (ITC) technologies to enhance, strengthen, and enable public officials to carry out the functions of governance. He reports that emerging technologies can provide "a connectivity 'network' that can cheaply create ears and eyes for us throughout the community, and develop a new system of representation and participation" (Toregas 1989). The following examples from Aurora, Colorado, Kansas City, Missouri, and Mercer Island, Washington, demonstrate the use of telecommunication technology.

Aurora's Computerized Council Request System

Since 1985, the City of Aurora, Colorado, has had a computerized request-for-information system for its city council. Each of the eleven members of the council has been loaned a personal computer for his or her home and a user-friendly electronic mail system for contacting city hall. As council members receive complaints or questions, they use their computers to seek responses from city hall. According to Christine MacMillan, assistant city manager in Aurora, every council member's request is considered a top priority by the city manager's staff and all departments are expected to provide quick and complete responses. Replies are sent back directly to the council member through the computer-linked system. MacMillan estimates that the city staff processes between 400 and 600 requests each year. Computerization also facilitates daily and monthly monitoring of the progress of responses to the requests.

MacMillan reports the system has produced the following benefits:

• The amount of staff time required to track items has been reduced considerably. The process is very much automated and, over the years, the on-time rate has increased to close to 100 percent.

• The city manager has usable data on performance as it pertains to staff responsiveness to requests from council.

• Requests entering the system aren't lost, as sometimes happens when they are verbally transmitted or passed along during a meeting on a scrap of paper.

• The council receives prompt replies to its questions. Council members may not always agree with the answers, but they do receive the prompt attention their inquiries deserve.

• The system enforces accountability on staff and provides an efficient way of generating answers.

• It provides reports to council members on where their requests are occurring.

• The system can be used at any time, thereby eliminating telephone tag or garbled phone messages (MacMillan 1990).

MacMillan notes that some council members still like to phone in and discuss their inquiries with a live person. In Aurora, the computerized system is intended to enhance communications, not to be a device to discourage interaction between staff and council. The interest in all forms of communication is important, says MacMillian, because "much of the council's opinion of staff's capabilities is formed by interactions such as responsiveness to requests."

City Hall in the Mall

A significant advance in local government's ability to communicate with its customers is the "City Hall in the Mall" demonstration project in Kansas City, Missouri. The basic concept is to use touch-screen computer technology to provide a wide range of information about local government to the general public 24 hours a day. Eventually, the system will be upgraded to allow users to request personalized information, and ultimately to conduct business with city hall.

At present, the system offers on-screen text, high-resolution computer graphics, video and audio outputs, and paper printout capability. The user can easily get such information as: dates, times, and places for council and commission meetings; availability of city jobs; names, phone numbers, and photos of city staff and local, state, and federal elected representatives; lists of current recreation programs and community events; and voter registration information, licensing procedures, and city services. According to Rich Lovett, the manager of the Information Services Division in Kansas City, users may also complete multiple-choice questionnaires and register their views about the system. During a typical 33-day period in the spring of 1990, Lovett reports, the city's two kiosks "recorded a combined 35,805 screen touches, or an average of 542 per kiosk per day. During that same period, users requested 2,538 printouts, viewed 1,993 videos, read 7,959 text files on screen, and responded to 2,677 survey questions" (Lovett 1989).

This demonstration project, which began in 1988, is sponsored by the city of Kansas City, the IBM Corporation, Public Technology, Inc. (an affiliate of the National League of Cities), and the International City Management Association. The following cities are also installing versions of the system: Albuquerque, New Mexico; Dallas, Texas; North County, North Carolina; Hillsborough County, Florida; Plano, Texas; and Mercer Island, Washington.

The Mercer Island experiment is unique in that the facility is located in a kiosk in a supermarket, which has shared in the cost of the project. Staff planner Gerald Bacon says that the system has not been tapped to its fullest potential yet, but he believes that eventually it will have a tremendous impact on increasing public interaction with local government.

LISTENING TO YOUR EMPLOYEES

The above heading may seem out of place in a section on listening to customers, but it isn't. Common sense should tell you that your employees are one of the most valuable sources of information about your customers. Every employee should be a market researcher. And by listening to employees, managers reinforce the importance of listening to customers.

One of the best locations for conducting research is at your office's reception desk. Sensitive and trained front-desk personnel can make casual inquiries and collect useful feedback from your customers: "Do you have all the information you need?" "Do you feel that the staff really helped you?" "Do you believe the staff is on your side in helping you?" "Was there anything that bothered you or disappointed you?" "Do you have any suggestions for improving our services?"

Collecting customer feedback is not some type of clandestine activity. Its purpose is not to undercut staff and create internal strife, but rather to be part of a comprehensive and systematic effort to deliver superior customer service. "When employees take customers under their wings and see that the customer's problem is solved," write Albrecht and Bradford, "you open the door to a good deal of important information about the buyer of your service or product" (Albrecht and Bradford 1990). This information can then be used to deliver better services and products.

Managers should regularly ask their employees what management can do to make them more effective. What kind of training, equipment, or improvements in the system or process are needed? Robert Spaulding, the planning director for the city of San Diego, says, "many of the frustrations shared by your customers will also be expressed by your staff—lack of clarity on responsibility for decisions; complicated and bureaucratic processes; poor organizational structure (who's in charge?); poorly trained, understaffed front door or reception/public service counter area" (Spaulding 1989).

It's very difficult for managers to listen to employees and customers when they stay in closed offices. By opening their doors, and making listening an active part of their jobs, managers reinforce the importance of this activity to all employees.

REFERENCES

Albrecht, K. and Bradford, L. 1990. *The Service Advantage*. Homewood, Illinois: Dow Jones Irwin.

Baum, H. 1983. *Planners and Public Expectations*. Cambridge, Mass.: Schenkman Publishing Company, Inc.

Gardner, J. 1990. *On Leadership*. New York, NY: Simon and Schuster.

Hatry, H., Greiner, J., and Swanson, M. 1987. "Monitoring the Quality of Local Government Services." *MIS Report* Vol. 19, No. 2.

Kaplan, S. 1990. "The Holy Grid: A Skeptic's View." *Planning* Vol. 56, No. 11.

Lovett, R. 1989. "City Hall in the Mall." *Public Management* Vol. 71, No. 11.

MacMillan, C. 1990. "Aurora's Computerized Council Request System." *Public Management* Vol. 72, No. 5.

Spaulding, R. 1989. "Toward Better Management of City Planning Departments." *City Planning and Management News* July - August.

Streib, G. 1990. "Dusting Off a Forgotten Management Tool: The Citizen Survey." *Public Management* Vol. 72, No. 7.

Toregas, C. 1989. "Electronic Democracy: Some Definitions and a Battle Cry." *Public Management* Vol. 71, No. 11.

Webb, K., and H. Hatry. 1973. *Obtaining Citizen Feedback: The Application of Citizen Surveys to Local Government*. Washington, D.C.: The Urban Institute.

Zotti, E. 1991. "New Angles on Citizen Participation." *Planning*. Vol. 57, No. 1.

5

Customer-Satisfying Citizen Participation Programs

One of the best ways to communicate with citizens is to involve them in goals programs. The following examples, from Fort Worth, Dallas, Phoenix, and Savannah, are noteworthy for their success in helping citizens develop their own visions for their communities.

The section on Goals for Dallas was written expressly for this book by the program's executive director, John Lewis. The Phoenix Futures Forum's director, Rod Engelen, wrote his program's case history. And Arthur A. "Don" Mendonsa, city manager of Savannah, Georgia, contributed the chapter's final case study.

CITIZEN PARTICIPATION IN FORT WORTH

Fort Worth has a long history of solid city planning and citizen participation in the planning process. As early as 1908, city plans were commissioned and implemented for the development of parks and boulevards. In 1925, the importance of planning for a rapidly growing Fort Worth was acknowledged by the creation of a permanent five-member city plan commission.

This interest in planning continued, and in 1964, with the assistance of numerous city boards and other public entities, the city plan commission completed and adopted the long-range Comprehensive Plan for the Fort Worth 1980 Urban Area. The plan proposed, in broad strokes, a general pattern of residential, commercial, and industrial land use. It outlined a system of major streets, as well as the quantity and location of schools, parks, libraries, and fire stations. The city council adopted the plan by resolution in 1965, noting the need for the public to become acquainted with the plan, which would "achieve its maximum value only through its acceptance by all Fort Worth citizens." That same year, the city initiated a "Town Hall" neighborhood meeting program to promote and strengthen public/private communication, for which it later received an All-America City award.

But the city's planners were not satisfied with their accomplishments. During the mid-1960s, Paul Davidoff was urging planners to move from traditional comprehensive planning into developing a plurality of plans, each with its own client. He was also advising that the physical focus of comprehensive planning be expanded to take in nonphysical issues. Davidoff argued that "a system of plural city planning probably has a much greater chance for operational success where the focus is on live social and economic questions instead of rather esoteric issues relating to physical norms" (Davidoff 1965). He also suggested that planners should work closely with local groups so that their interests could be incorporated into the plans.

In 1969, local planners initiated the Sector Planning Program for Fort Worth. The focus of sector planning was citizen participation and self-determination. One of the important aspects of the program was the commitment to mini-plans for each sector of the city. Eleven separate sectors were originally delineated, each containing 30,000 to 50,000 residents and no more than 20 square miles in area. Each sector constituted a complete planning area, homogeneous, where possible, in terms of social and economic characteristics. Generally, sector boundaries followed rivers, railroads, and major streets, which tended to promote the homogeneity of development and people.

The city council appointed a Sector Strategy Committee of citizen leaders to assist the city plan commission and staff in the establishment of an overall, coordinating Sector Planning Council. The committee made the initial organizational arrangements, motivated residents to serve on individual sector councils, conducted a publicity campaign, and selected a temporary chairman and officers.

Since sector planning was new and untested in Fort Worth, the decision was made to begin the project in a relatively affluent area with few serious physical planning problems. It was recognized that the first sector plan would be a learning experience that would establish the model for the process. The area selected was near Texas Christian University, and its residents had a history of being active in civic activities. As anticipated, many of the residents were eager to participate, and it was a simple process to organize and involve them. For the first time, Fort Worth citizens were given the opportunity to identify problems, develop goals, and formulate implementation policies on a local basis.

In October 1969, the Sector One Planning Council completed its report on goals and policy guidelines for future development. Over the next eight years, this and other plans from each sector were presented to the city plan commission and then forwarded to the city council for review, adoption, and implementation. As each sector finished its plan, the city plan commission was responsible for integrating it into a unified comprehensive plan. The last of the 11 initial sector plans was completed in 1976.

The sector plans were basically traditional general plans. The rapport that developed between the planning staff and local residents, however, was far more than traditional. The program showed that citizens were willing to devote long hours to study, discussion, and debate, and were not apathetic when given an opportunity to participate in a meaningful planning process. A report prepared by the city noted that sector planning was more demanding of citizens in terms of time and effort, and more costly to the local government, requiring more than twice the usual staff for example. But the report concluded that the higher costs and increase in preparation time were justified by the positive citizen involvement. The Texas chapter of the American Planning Association recognized the significance of the program when it gave Fort Worth its 1978 merit award for outstanding contributions to the field of professional planning.

In 1980, the city council decided that the 11 sector plan should be updated. Since most of the sector councils disbanded after completing their plans, the first step was to reactivate and renew them. Second, in order to expand opportunities for citizen participation and to add a citywide perspective that was not previously available through sector planning, a Committee for the Future of Fort Worth was established as a subcommittee of the city plan commission. With more than 50 members, the committee was representative of many backgrounds, interests, and viewpoints. Many of the members of this "blue ribbon" committee were in leadership positions in various respected community organizations.

The committee was conceived as a new type of citizen advisory body to fulfill an overview function. It was not established to review and comment on the sector plans, nor did it have any prescriptive role toward the sector councils. Instead, the committee was responsible for developing citywide policies with respect to the year 2000 and disseminating this information to the sector councils.

In 1982, the committee's final report on The Future of Fort Worth was published and distributed. The recommended policy guidance was expressed in formal statements of goals. The work of the committee was unique in several respects. The substantive range of the agenda, combined with the diversity of backgrounds and viewpoints represented among the membership, served to ensure that the committee's recommendations reflected a credible consensus of use to the sector councils, city plan commission, and city council. The report emphasized that "the report is, above all, the product of the committee itself and not a staff document dressed up with a veneer of citizen participation."

One other important modification to the original sector planning process was added during the updating. Two of the sector councils initiated a series of public meetings on the basis of smaller sub-areas (one sector was divided into seven sub-areas) and created committees to assist the work of the sector councils. Separate plans were developed for each of these areas under the jurisdiction of local committees and consolidated into the final sector plan.

In mid-1983, the Rockwood Sector Plan, the last of the 11 plans, was completed and adopted by the city plan commission and city council. More than 60 persons residing, working, or owning property in the sector attended one or more meetings. Thirty-two persons participated in three or more meetings, and almost 350 were in attendance during the two-year process.

The impressive record of formal involvement represented only the organized part of the citizen participation process. The sector planners also acquired useful information and ideas in other more informal discussions with residents, business owners, employees and employers, developers, landowners, religious congregations, and neighborhood associations.

The Goals for East Fort Worth Process

As you have read, citizen participation and involvement in planning in Fort Worth has been an evolutionary experience, not cyclical. Citizen participation has not been a fad, nor has it been used as a sop to placate citizens or neighborhood groups. Goals for East Fort Worth is a continuation of this evolution and an advancement in citizen participation.

In the summer of 1988, Kay Granger, immediate past chairman and member of the Fort Worth Zoning Commission, heard John Lewis, director of Goals for Dallas—discussed later in this chapter—describe how the Dallas program had helped pull the community together from the shock, disillusionment, and loss of confidence that followed the assassination of President Kennedy. Granger was a leader in East Fort Worth, and knew that the area needed a boost in confidence. The 60-plus square mile area, including almost one-fourth of the city's population, had a reputation as a high crime area with poor living conditions. What was most disturbing to Granger was that East Fort Worth had a worse image among its residents than among the rest of the city. Furthermore she felt much of the negativity was unjustified.

Granger met with Lewis and became convinced that an areawide goals program would have a positive influence on the community. She developed a program proposal and presented it to the planning director. The director thought it was a good idea and agreed it should be a grass roots, citizen initiated effort with no direct involvement of the city staff. It was also agreed that the planning department would provide $25,000 for most of the operating expenses of the program. A nonprofit corporation was created and the proposal was presented to the city council. The council authorized the city to enter into a contract with Goals for East Forth Worth that provided $25,000 in return for developing a program and process that would achieve the following functions:

- foster public discussion and gather from a broad range of citizens their thoughts on what are the major issues facing this community and what are the positive qualities or attributes of this community;
- facilitate communication of this information to leadership groups and decision makers in the public, private and nonprofit sectors;
- bring together representatives of leadership groups in the public, private and nonprofit sectors to each discuss and share information about the major issues they are working on or are worrying about;
- facilitate communication of this information to the general public;
- enable citizens to work together to solve problems and to formulate, identify and achieve a consensus on critical goals and objectives for their community; and
- encourage and form committees, task forces and other groups of

interested citizens to conduct meetings, forums, workshops and seminars for the promotion and implementation of agreed upon plans, programs and goals.

The proposed goals program became involved in local politics when Kay Granger decided to seek a council seat. Granger was closely identified with the program, and she defended and promoted it throughout her campaign. She argued in defense of the need for the residents to develop common, shared goals. "If it doesn't get community support, I'd rather see it not even start," she said in a press conference, according to the March 2, 1989, *Fort Worth Star-Telegram.* "The only way it's going to work is if we have the community working behind it. Twenty people in a room deciding what needs to be done doesn't work."

Granger's opponent was a former city employee. Having been involved with goals programs during his tenure at city hall, he noted that they can "give a community a unity of purpose." However, he also warned that goals programs can create frustration because "they aren't something that will change things quickly" (Bernard 1989). City planners were not able to determine if the candidate was less than enthusiastic about the program because it was associated with his opponent or because he believed that the frustration from unfulfilled expectations can exceed the benefits of bringing people together in a common cause. But, as a former bureaucrat, he obviously knew the danger of raising the public's expectations and then not delivering results.

Granger was elected to the council and immediately invited Eugene McCray, a newly elected councilman from the east side, to assume a co-leadership role with the goals program. Together they became a powerful force, and worked tirelessly to involve the community in all aspects of the goals program.

To start the program, a 10-member representative steering committee was appointed. The committee met throughout the summer of 1989 to shape the process that was to be followed. The committee then selected 45 group meeting leaders and briefed them on how the program would work. A kickoff reception was held, and everyone in the community was invited. Over 300 citizens from East Fort Worth attended and were introduced to the idea of a goals program. The response was electrifying. Obviously it was both a good idea, and an idea whose time had come. The media coverage was excellent and word of the program quickly spread throughout the community.

The mechanics of the program were simple. Group meetings were held throughout East Fort Worth. Individuals, neighborhood associations, and businesses were given the opportunity to host or to attend a group meeting. To arrange a meeting, it was only necessary to call the goals office and provide the scheduling secretary with the date, time, and estimated number of people that would be attending. In three months, 54 group meetings were held with more than 1,000 participants.

One of the most unique and critically important aspects of Goals for East Fort Worth was the process that was followed at the group meetings. Each of the meetings was conducted by two volunteer leaders. All group leaders, 45 total, had been trained at a workshop on how to conduct the meetings, and were given a guidebook to help them through the goal-setting process.

After the program objectives were explained by the group leaders, individual participants were expected to: 1) identify the needs of East Fort Worth from their viewpoint; 2) discuss how they and their group are dealing with those needs or could deal with them; and, 3) suggest a maximum of five priorities at the community level to deal with these needs.

Now let's explain what was unique about the group meetings and what other planners can learn from them. First, the emphasis was on personal responsibility and accountability. Participants were given the chance to identify their most pressing concerns, but they also had to share with the group what they themselves had been doing to help make the situation better. As it turns out, most of the people had been doing something about their top concerns. Often, there were others in the group that had been working to improve a given situation. This open sharing provided encouragement to the group and led to future cooperative efforts.

The sharing process also personalized the issues, and got people excited about what others were already doing and about opportunities for further involvement. Participants learned that positive results could come from individual initiatives. When it came time to discuss priorities and implementation activities, the focus was on self-help and individual or group actions, not on government assistance.

Toward the end of each meeting, participants were charged with developing a list of specific suggestions for dealing with five needs that had been singled out for priority attention. They were asked to keep in mind seven qualities of a valuable goal:

A good goal is:

- **Community-wide.** Which goals deal with the needs of the greatest number of citizens, or call for a community-wide effort to meet the pressing needs of a particular group of citizens?

- **Achievable with Local Action.** Which goals can you visualize being achieved with local initiative?

- **Precise.** Which goals are stated in broad enough language to possibly gain a consensus of citizen support, yet worded precisely enough so that they are meaningful and their achievement can be recognized?

- **Understandable.** Which goals would most citizens understand as stated without further explanation?

- **Challenging.** Which goals would most likely motivate citizens to action? Goals that are too easy to achieve, or, on the other hand, too unrealistic, may call forth little motivation to achieve them.

- **A Commitment.** Which goals would you support with your vote, time, money, enthusiasm, or other contribution?

- **Important.** Which goals—whether they can be achieved in two years or twenty—are most important for the community to be working on now? Which goals, if achieved: Would contribute most to moving the community toward fulfilling its basic values? Would do most to facilitate the achievement of other goals?

It was explained to each group that if any of the five issues they selected were too narrow or too limited in support, their efforts would be wasted. Participants took this advice to heart, and the groups were never dominated by a special interest group or individuals with a small axe to grind.

The steering committee then reviewed 810 proposals that were developed by the various groups, and selected 84 to be grouped into six subject areas for review at the final goals-setting conference. Goals and suggestions were selected by the steering committee on the basis of the frequency in which they had been mentioned and the extent to which they satisfied the criteria for good goals. The subject areas in which the goals were grouped were public safety, government, development and promotion of the east side, recreation/human resources, housing, and education.

The final goals-setting conference was a day-long event for all group meeting participants. One hour was devoted to each subject area. Resource panels staffed with knowledgeable individuals and professionals answered questions while the delegates discussed and debated the issues and possible goals among themselves. At the conclusion of the hour, the delegates voted electronically and selected two goals for the subject area.

This process was repeated for each subject area. There was a break for lunch and a keynote speech by Ed Bass, a respected local developer, who detailed successes and disappointments in his family's development projects in downtown Fort Worth.

After the delegates had selected two goals for each of the six subject areas, they went through one more balloting process to select five top goals regardless of subject area. Because of a tie, the final list had a total of six goals (listed in the article that follows).

Assessment of Goals for East Fort Worth

I have my own opinions of the Goals for East Fort Worth program, but thought readers might prefer a more impartial evaluation first. The following appeared in the *Fort Worth Star–Telegram* on April 16, 1990, under the heading "Goals program shows strong leadership."

All of Fort Worth owes a deep debt of gratitude for the leadership demonstrated by the Goals for East Fort Worth campaign, which has set the standard—and the challenge—for a community's taking control of its own destiny.

Under the umbrella of the top six goals set by East Fort Worth residents for the improvement and enhancement of their part of the city, there is room to accommodate scores of more specific concerns.

Indeed, those top priorities can be viewed as the mechanisms for concerted, continuing community action to achieve most of the other 78 goals over which they were selected.

Creating a citizens' crime task force, for example, would provide a vehicle for continuing efforts to:

• Increase the number of police officers on patrol in the area, provide a new police substation there and achieve 100-percent participation in neighborhood associations and crime-watch programs.

• Provide dollar incentives for reporting criminal activity; stiffen criminal penalties; improve safety and security on buses and in subsidized housing; and make East Fort Worth the safest part of the city.

Forming an East Side Arts and Cultural District would do much to:

• Promote a sense of community among all the diverse ethnic groups and income levels in that part of the city.

- Promote a better overall perception of the quality of life and the cultural richness and variety of that part of the city.

Promoting and improving local business opportunities through tax incentives and local financing and recruitment of major employers and minority business embraces the primary concerns under the proposed development and promotion goals.

It speaks to the urgency of providing tax abatement in the enterprise zones to attract new business and industry.

It addresses the need to stimulate quality development and commerce along Loop 820, Interstate 30 and East Lancaster.

It embraces such suggestions as a marketing campaign for East Fort Worth, development of an East Fort Worth slogan and newsletter and more business support and awareness of community needs.

Modifying zoning ordinances to limit the number of multifamily developments and Monitoring zoning and development could have been combined into one goal to express residents' great concern with overconcentration of housing and its attendant social and economic consequences.

In addition to strictly zoning matters, those two goals establish a context for seeking block grants and tax incentives to improve housing; limiting the amount of subsidized housing in east Fort Worth; establishing a revolving-loan home ownership program and monitoring the enforcement of Section 8 standards.

Organizing and coordinating existing leadership groups is the key goal and the first step that must be taken in order to establish such other vital vehicles as the citizens crime task force, a housing and zoning committee, and a promotion and development committee.

The umbrella group that emerges under this goal also will need to spin off committees and subcommittees to address the specific education and human-services goals proposed by the hundreds of residents who attended the 54 neighborhood meetings that were held during the last six months. Among those are:

- More citizen representation in the establishment of the annual goals and mission of the Fort Worth Independent School District; transportation over hazardous roadways for elementary school-children who live within two miles of their schools; drug counselors in the schools; a latchkey program; reduced dropouts; and more adult community-service classes.
- A satellite health center; low-cost drug-treatment centers; more parks and recreation centers; a dance hall for teenagers; and a senior citizens center for far East Fort Worth.

Some of the goals generated by the 54 meetings held by various groups of East Fort Worth residents can be accomplished in a relatively short time.

Others are more long-range in nature. Some are timeless and more conceptual than concrete.

Perhaps the greatest achievement of the goals movement thus far is the bringing together of so many people from different perspectives to develop a comprehensive concept of East Fort Worth—what it is and what it could be.

The resultant process is a commendable achievement and worthy of emulation all around town. Other parts of the city should imitate the example of East Fort Worth, strengthening, solidifying and energizing the spirit of common purpose at the neighborhood level and providing a master strategy by which to unite the entire community in pursuit of a safer, healthier and more robust future (Denton 1990).

Personal Observations

The above editorial is well-earned praise for the Goals for East Fort Worth program, but the local newspaper is still caught up in the top-down approach to problem solving. For example, the goal of "creating a citizens' crime task force" was seen by the paper as a way of increasing the number of police officers or adding dollars to the city's budget for the public safety department.

When the proposed goals program was first brought to the attention of city staff, there was an initial negative reaction. Concern was expressed that this program would only result in more organized requests for funds, programs, and services for the east side. The program was eventually supported not only because it was a good idea, but because of the political influence and strength of its backers.

On the first anniversary of the goals program, an employee in the city manager's office commented that it had been a waste of time and effort. The city council, he noted, had not received any funding requests as a result of the program. But this person failed to understand that the goals program was not designed to tap city hall resources, rather to help people help themselves.

As this is being written, the residents of East Fort Worth are still *not* coming to city council meetings and making demands on the city's budget or on taxpayers. More importantly, they are not fighting and arguing among themselves. There are no longer any divisive issues being reported by the media. Residents are organized, focused, and learning how to work together. They are establishing a cultural museum that celebrates their rich heritage. They are raising funds and supporting revitalization efforts for Texas Wesleyan University—a key institution in the area. They are working with the police department on an innovative self-help Combat Crime Campaign (CCC), which has resulted in the creation of neighborhood crime-watch groups and an umbrella organization to coordinate their activities. A voice mail arrangement has been reached with the police department so that residents can get quick and simple reports on the type and location of criminal activity in East Fort Worth. A crime task force is publishing a monthly newsletter that reports on criminal activity and offers security tips. A security fair has been scheduled with the vendors of burglar bars, electronic alarms, door locks, and other safety devices.

A beautification task force has been created, and businesses and civic groups are being asked to adopt areas and to provide landscaping and maintenance services. A local church is providing breakfast to volunteers participating in neighborhood clean-up activities. Other task forces may arise as public participation continues to increase.

City hall may not know about Goals for East Fort Worth, but the program is incredibly successful and an outstanding example of what people can achieve when they decide to help themselves. It truly is neighbor helping neighbor.

GOALS FOR DALLAS
(By John Lewis)

Just as a business must listen to its customers to survive and grow, a city needs its customers—its citizens—to prosper and remain competitive with other cities. In 1963, Dallas lost most of its customers.

On November 22, President John F. Kennedy was killed in Dallas. Two days later his accused assassin was murdered on live national television. Dallas was branded a "City of Hate," and, to cope with their shame, citizens turned away from the affairs of the city to their own private concerns.

Compounding matters, the mayor of Dallas, Earle Cabell, resigned to run for Congress. The city council turned to Erik Jonsson, chairman of Texas Instruments, Inc. "We didn't know what to do. We thought Jonsson might," recalled one councilman. Jonsson was asked to fill the council seat vacated by Cabell. Then, as allowed in the city charter, council members elected him mayor. He went on to win elections on his own, served four consecutive terms, and is widely regarded as one of Dallas's greatest mayors.

One reason for Jonsson's success was that, in the wake of the Kennedy assassination, he paid attention to the citizens of Dallas. He feared that the spirit of the city had not only been broken, but was in danger of being extinguished. And without confidence and pride, he knew that citizens would not support the private and public investments necessary for Dallas to move forward. Broad citizen involvement, then, became a key element in lifting Dallas off its knees.

A second key element in Jonsson's approach was performance. "Some people said Dallas should hire an advertising firm to change its image," he said. "I always thought you change your image by what you do. So I made the decision that performance is what I should be judged on."

The ideas of performance and broad citizen participation came together in the Goals for Dallas program, which Mayor Jonsson proposed in 1964. He said that the goals program was the best way "to ensure accomplishments of the level and scope which we desire and of which we are capable."

In the following months, Jonsson shared the outline of the program with community leaders. Virtually every leader supported the plan and pledged to take an active role in its implementation.

Goals for Dallas formally began in late 1965, when Jonsson and 26 other Dallas leaders agreed to serve as an initial board of trustees. The program was incorporated as a Texas nonprofit organization. It survives today, guided by a 45-member board of trustees representing a cross section of community leaders. All trustees serve one-year terms, and each may be re-elected.

Principles

A number of principles have evolved over the years that have ensured the usefulness of the program to the Dallas community.

They are:

• Goals for Dallas is a neutral organization with no present agenda.

• Goals for Dallas is not a single-issue organization. All aspects of the community are open for consideration.

• Opinions of all segments of the citizenry are included in determining goals.

• The program primarily is a facilitating organization, not an implementing organization. Its basic aim is to provide a mechanism through which citizens can express their views regarding the type of community they desire.

• The success or failure of Goals for Dallas rests with volunteers. Only a small staff exists to provide support to volunteers.

• Goals for Dallas is not an all-things-for-all-people panacea. Rather, it offers a way for people to discuss their problems, their hopes, their aspirations—and a way to marshal action on a limited number of specific and achievable goals.

Phases and Process

There are three phases to Goals for Dallas: goals, plans, and results. Surveys and/or community meetings ensure that goals reflect the desires of citizens.

Achievement committees of trustees and others make certain that plans are in place for achieving goals. The board of trustees of the program is responsible for presenting goals and plans to implementing organizations, such as the City of Dallas and various chambers of commerce.

Completion of all three phases constitutes one cycle or round of Goals for Dallas. Three cycles have been completed to date: the first between 1965 and 1972, the second between 1976 and 1982, and the third between 1983 and 1987. The fourth round of Goals for Dallas is in its third phase—results.

The goals-setting method chosen for a particular cycle has varied, depending on the characteristics and needs of the community at the time.

For example, the third cycle of Goals for Dallas was designed to assist a proliferation of organizations in matching their activities to common goals. Over 300 meetings were held with 250 different organizations. In each meeting, community needs were identified, organizations' responses were discussed, and priorities for goals were established. Final goals were decided at a communitywide goals-setting conference.

This process had significant results. For instance, it was instrumental in coordinating and focusing historic preservation efforts. The Dallas Heritage Council—a federation of 24 organizations—responded to the overall goal of more historic preservation by developing nine more specific goals and plans for achieving them.

In another example, a church pastor in Dallas wrote to the Goals office: "Our congregation is embarking on a period of self-study, and this Goals for Dallas workshop has now become an extremely useful first step—since we had to look at the community as a whole. In addition, seven of the Lao people in our membership were full participants in the workshop. Five years ago, none of the Lao women could speak English. All seven of the Lao participants made good statements and engaged in the remaining discussions, and two of the goals sought by the Lao people were two of the final five we adopted. Though she wasn't fully aware of the significance of this first-time breakthrough for us, Goals for Dallas Group Leader Linda Wise's unusual sensitivity helped immensely. We are grateful for the whole experience."

Times changed by 1988. The economy was down. Anxiety was up. A commitment to a few goals, quickly established, that could provide a short-term sense of direction for the community was needed. Goals for Dallas responded with a new and streamlined plan. Following is a capsule description of the process:

Focus groups of community leaders and citizens identified specific solutions to issues facing Dallas. From these solutions, a Goals Poll of over 1,000 citizens established 20 priorities and a short-term vision for Dallas. Background papers were prepared on each of the 20 priorities from the Goals Poll. Based on these papers, 11 goals were adopted in 1990 by Goals for Dallas trustees.

Four goals were singled out by trustees for their own special attention: 1) economic development of southern Dallas; 2) a program to ensure jobs and scholarships for high school graduates; 3) preschool for 3- and 4-year olds in public elementary schools; and 4) a formal and continuing forum of community leaders to improve race relations. Achievement committees of trustees and others are now completing written plans for following through with these goals.

The early returns on this cycle show more agreement than disagreement among citizens, a willingness to try new ideas, and a renewed commitment to investing in public infrastructure and getting crime and drugs under control.

Results and Lessons

Since its inception, Goals for Dallas has had a hand in establishing Dallas–Fort Worth International Airport, a new downtown central library and city hall, a coordinating body for higher education, high standards for child care providers, and site-based management within the Dallas Independent School District. While Goals for Dallas is not solely responsible for achieving goals, action toward many of these was not made until they were specifically stated as goals by citizens.

As important as any concrete achievement of Goals for Dallas is that thousands of people have learned more about their community—what is good and ought to be preserved, and what is deficient and ought to be changed.

There are other lessons to be learned from the long history of the Goals for Dallas program:

• Some of the best ideas for goals do not emerge until there is wide citizen participation in a goals program—until there is a lot of "listening to the customer." For example, in the first round of Goals for Dallas in the 1960s, essays were written covering the different aspects of community life. A broad cross section of citizens studied them and then proposed a list of goals for consideration by all citizens in neighborhood meetings. One of the most important goals ever in the Dallas Goals program was never mentioned until one of these neighborhood meetings—the goal of an excellent library system, which got more specific with each succeeding round of Goals for Dallas.

• Fewer goals nowadays can be called glamor goals—such as building a new airport or a great community college system. Many goals today deal with decreasing domestic violence, housing the homeless, and drug abuse. A goals program needs glamorous goals to create excitement and a spillover effect in getting citizens interested in dealing with less glamorous goals, which are needed so that important community needs do not go unattended.

• Progress comes in incremental gains, especially in achieving many of the less glamorous goals. Unfortunately, many businesspersons who would be impressed with a 10 percent increase in company profits are totally unimpressed with 10 percent gains in achieving community goals—such as a 10 percent decrease in the number of homeless. This diminishes commitment by community leaders to important goals.

• A goals program should not be viewed as an organization separate from other organizations, or as an umbrella organization. It should build upon existing efforts and enhance those efforts.

• Ideas that seem good at the time should be thought about again. For example: "We need an independent and neutral organization to set goals, but we have good people at city hall, the chamber of commerce, and so forth. They will know what to do with the goals, so a goals program is not needed beyond arriving at the goals." Wrong. In our own lives, many of us feel that once we know what we want the rest is easy. But we find out that things do not always fall neatly into place. The same is true for a city. There needs to be follow-through by a goals program itself.

• The total number of goals should not exceed 20, and preferably be closer to 10—a small enough number to provide a focus, and a large enough number to deal with different aspects of the community. Too many goals is no goals.

Attention to these lessons at the early stage of implementing a community goals program can save frustration later and ensure that goals are achieved.

What we think of today as a failure of leadership is traceable in some measure to a lack of common goals, and to a subsequent breakdown in our sense of community. Goals for Dallas, by providing a vehicle through which elected, business, and civic leaders can listen to the desire of citizens for their community, is helping to provide the basis for strong leadership needed in an increasingly pluralistic community.

PHOENIX FUTURES FORUM
(By Rod Engelen)

Mayor Terry Goddard proposed the Phoenix Futures Forum in his State of The City message in the Spring of 1988, and in the 1988–89 Phoenix city budget. The first major Forum event was held in October, 1988. During the following 15 months, over 30 smaller workshops and forums and three more major forums were held, concluding in a report presented to the city council in January, 1990. Following presentation of the results of the Forum, the Phoenix City Council appointed an action committee to help carry out Forum recommendations. This committee is still active today.

Origins and Objectives

Early 1988 was an unlikely time for Phoenix to embark on an introspective "futures" project. The city and region were still feeling flush from the skyrocketing growth of the mid-1980s. From 1984 to 1988, area communities issued building permits for over 175,000 housing units. In-migration was routinely running at 120,000 or 130,000 persons per year. Projections were that the Phoenix area population would more than double by the turn of the century.

However, several factors were creating uneasiness. Although still high, growth slowed significantly in 1986 and 1987. Reports showed that for every four immigrants, three persons moved away. Rezoning was rampant. Speculators proposed whole neighborhoods for "buyout" and conversion to commercial use. Traffic was intimidating, and sometimes severely congested. Air quality was also perceived to be deteriorating rapidly.

By early 1987 these conditions had stimulated Pat Murphy, the publisher of the *Arizona Republic and Gazette,* to commission Neal Peirce to "provide a fresh and untinted view of our problems and opportunities." Peirce, a journalist now with *Newsweek,* and his colleagues for the project (Dr. John Hall, director of the School of Public Affairs at Arizona State University; Curtis Johnson, executive director of the Citizen's League of Minneapolis/St. Paul; and Christopher Gates of the National Civic League) produced a 20-page report acknowledging many positive features of the city, but also many troubling conditions and anxieties. The advantages of Phoenix included a "zestful dynamism," the outdoor lifestyle, and an absence of eastern crowds, California sprawl, and northern ice and snow. But the report also cited increasing air pollution, traffic, loss of open space, strained schools, and a lack of a sense of community as major and widespread concerns.

Despite prominent publication, most persons quickly forgot the Peirce observations. The community was still largely in denial regarding the downturn in growth and development that started in 1986. Many were not ready to face the need for a reevaluation of community directions and goals. As Peirce says: "The equation is relatively simple: Add together the forces of developers and land speculators and then consider their 'extended family'—from contractors to bankers, lawyers to title companies, sand and gravel operators to builders of schools, roadways and water mains. Mix in . . . a warm climate, a low cost of living and industrial expansion. . . . The equation provides an economic ebullience . . . that would make most regions green with envy."

Given this equation and the need to address the problems of growth, Peirce urged "more collective decision making, more cohesion among . . . competing businesses, and stronger and more effective government . . ." As the Peirce report noted, in days past a small group of business owners could be counted on to provide the leadership needed. However, growth, outside business ownership, and the increased isolation of business leadership had dramatically weakened this possibility.

This was the context in which Mayor Goddard proposed the undertaking of the Futures Forum. His goal was to make the community realize the need for social, economic, and environmental change. He also hoped that the Forum would produce a vision of the future that the community would support.

Futures Forum Planning Committee

At Mayor Goddard's request, the city council budgeted $100,000 to fund the Forum, for the fiscal year 1988 starting July 1. This was done with the understanding that city funding would be matched by private contributions. On July 8, the council appointed a Futures Forum Planning Committee of 14 persons with widely varied backgrounds. The council charged the committee to prepare a work plan, schedule, and budget for the Forum, to recommend the objectives of the Forum and ways of generating group and citizen involvement, and prepare guidelines for responding to requests from other jurisdictions to participate in the Forum.

The planning committee immediately took several actions with long-term significance. It set October 7 and 8, 1988, as the date of the first major Forum Workshop (subsequently to be known as Forum I). Until this Forum was done, its planning absorbed most of the time and attention of the committee and staff. Moreover, the breadth of the areas included and of persons involved helped frame the balance of the Forum.

The committee also received an unsolicited grant from the Honeywell Corporation of $50,000 to help fund the Forum. This, along with the participation of Honeywell personnel in planning, gave an immediate boost to the Forum and credibility in the business community.

Another action was to hire Chris Gates of the National Civic League as a consultant to help plan the Forum. Gates was active in a major goals-setting activity, the Front Range Project in Colorado, and was advising communities through the Civic League on similar projects. He provided the basic strategic planning framework questions that were used in structuring the Forum. These were:

> Where are we? Where are we going?;
> Where do we want to go?;
> How do we get there?; and
> What are our next steps?

These questions provided a basis for a work plan including three major "forums" beyond Forum I, and for work that would be done between these forums. Gates also recommended the creation of three subcommittees to work on public outreach, and coordination and development of alternate "visions."

The committee then hired a public relations firm to help in generating public awareness of the Forum and in distributing information generated through Forum activity. Skills in this area proved invaluable to the operations of the Forum and to its success in developing an identity and in generating support of the media.

Letters were sent to all other cities in the region and to many community groups inviting their participation in the Forum. One idea was that the Forum should bring community groups and cities together to create a sort of "council" to discuss community needs and opportunities. The lack of any significant formal response from other communities or from community organizations caused this approach to be deferred.

The next step was to establish a work plan and a budget of $392,000, with a private fund raising goal of $225,000. The basic work plan called for holding four major forums, starting in October, 1988, and ending in June, 1989.

The committee's best move was to work with a wide range of city, state and private agencies to compile basic background facts and projections for the region as input to the Forum. This generated a unique public-private effort resulting in an excellent publication.

Forum I, Phase One

The Forum "publicly" began with Forum I. It included general sessions with locals and leading speakers from across the country. Neal Peirce was the principal kickoff speaker. The Forum also included smaller workshops on five "breakout" topics, with dozens of expert panelists. Topics included Environment and Resources, Human Impacts and Needs, Technology, Transportation and Urban Form, and Paying for the Future. Questions and discussion were intended to follow the workshops. However, speaker presentations frequently used up all or most of the time available. Participants were excited about the topics, but frustrated that more time was not available for interaction with the speakers. Workshops were repeated four times to provide opportunities for many people to participate. A local cable television channel filmed one session on each topic for replay at later dates.

Over 700 persons registered for the event and well over 600 attended. It ran from noon through Friday evening and continued through noon

Saturday. Several hundred persons were still present as the final session closed.

Reactions to Forum I were very enthusiastic. People were excited about the future. They were stimulated by the speakers. They asked for more time for discussion, and wanted to get more deeply into the topics presented. The planning committee used these and other reactions to further develop its plans for the rest of the Forum.

The committee planned Phase Two of Forum I, a series of "mini-forums" to provide more opportunities for discussion. Each of these dealt with one "breakout" topic. Although there were only five "breakout" topics in Forum I, a sixth, "community," was added because of its prominence in discussion by speakers and participants.

The six mini-forums, one youth forum, and several other events were held between November of 1988 and February of 1989. Participants spent most of their time in groups of less than 30 persons. They responded to the question, "What are the most critical problems or opportunities to be faced by Phoenix in (specific topic) in the next 25 years?" Their brief answers were immediately recorded on large newsprint pads. After discussion, participants established priorities (voted) by marking their choices with colored stickers. Results were recorded for use in future phases of the Forum.

Forum II, Phase Two

Two things were done in Forum II. One was to present the results of the mini-forums. The second was to open discussion on the question of "Where would we like to go?"

Considerable preparation was done for this discussion. A focus group developed four alternative scenarios of the future. These were used to prepare brief dramatizations of life under each option that provided a basis for participants to answer the question, "What would you like to see in your ideal of Phoenix in 25 years?" Again, this was done in small, facilitated group meetings, and all comments and priorities were recorded.

Phase Two of Forum II then went forward with a flurry of workshops and meetings. These included eight "village" forums and a four-part film festival based on the work of Lewis Mumford and Edmund Bacon, at which Bacon spoke. It also included special presentations on issues of technology, based on work by the Federal Office of Technology Assessment, an urban design workshop organized by local chapters of APA, the

American Institute of Architects, the American Society of Landscape Architects, and the Phoenix Planning Department. Forum participants also organized a special workshop to discuss the future of the city's Hispanic community.

A drafting committee appointed by the policy committee assembled and analyzed the results of Forum II. This committee crafted what has become known as the Vision Statement, entitled "A Declaration of Commitment." The drafting committee derived the individual sections of the statement by integrating the many phrases offered by participants of Forum II to describe their "ideal" future city.

This process identified four values deemed to underlie all other elements of the vision. These were combined into the "Preamble." The drafting committee articulated the vision for nine areas: Community, Education, The Economy, Basic Human Needs, Urban Forum, Transportation and Communication, Governance, and Arts, Culture and Recreation. The policy committee drafted the Vision Statement for submission to Forum III.

Forum III, Phase Three

The principal activity of Forum III was the editing of the Vision Statement. The 350 participants, in groups of eight to 10, marked changes on which they could agree on large (17" by 22") copies of the statement. Table discussions were lively and produced significant proposals for change. However, most of the statement remained intact.

The drafting committee brought all proposed changes together and analyzed them for frequency and consistency, and then developed its proposals for the final wording of the Vision Statement. The policy committee reviewed proposed changes and adopted language to be carried forward in the process. Figure 5-1 shows the final statement.

The completed Vision Statement provided a basis for addressing the question, "How do we get there?" To develop answers, chairs were chosen from among members of the action committee and asked to form task forces to draft actions and strategies. One task force was created for each of the nine "elements" of the Vision Statement. Other members of the policy committee and all other Forum participants were invited to join the task force of their choice. Over 350 persons responded, a remarkable number considering it was midsummer.

The nine task force meetings were held simultaneously every other

Our Vision of the Future:
A DECLARATION OF COMMITMENT

The Preamble

We the people of Phoenix, having embarked upon a continuing, community-wide dialogue to reach a shared vision of our future, find that we hold these values in common:

- We have a duty to create and maintain an effective community. We are committed to each other and to an ethic which requires each individual, family and institution to act responsibly to meet our shared needs, dreams and aspirations.

- We believe that each person has an equal right to opportunities which allow full realization of that individual's potential.

- We acknowledge our responsibility to and dependence upon the healthy, natural world environment, and affirm that we must sustain and protect our Sonoran Desert.

- We have the obligation to learn from the past, to take responsibility for creating the future of Phoenix, and to affirm our role in the world community.

Being from diverse backgrounds and bound together by these shared values, we are committed to achieving the following vision of the future of Phoenix:

Our Vision

Community

OUR VISION is of a metropolitan region, made up of cooperative communities and strong, proud, stable and fully integrated neighborhoods and urban villages, with a high sense of community, caring and responsibility that permeates economic, social and family life and respects a wide variety of racial, ethnic and religious backgrounds.

Education

OUR VISION is of educational excellence exemplified by accessible educational systems that are innovative, diverse and fully integrated, dedicated to personal enrichment and the fulfillment of human potential, and responsive to the needs of the community. We believe that learning is a lifelong process which begins in childhood and continues as an integral part of family, community and business life.

The Economy

OUR VISION is of employment opportunities for all in a work environment that is sensitive to family needs. These opportunities are generated by a vibrant, diverse and sustainable economy based on our unique natural resources and regional location. This economy is fostered by the vigorous creation and application of technology, entrepreneurial business development, aggressive regional, national and global trade, and economic growth which supports community objectives and is compatible with our environment.

Basic Human Needs

OUR VISION is that every citizen enjoys good housing, food, health care, a clean environment, safety of person and property, and a community free of drug-abuse.

Natural Environment and Resources

OUR VISION is of a pollution-free city surrounded by beautiful mountains, blue sky, and a natural desert. The community is committed to improve and protect the environment, to manage and conserve resources, to preserve open space, and to direct growth to assure a healthy local and world environment for present and future generations.

Urban Form

OUR VISION is of a beautiful city with buildings and landscape that are appropriate to our climate, are framed by the grandeur of our setting, and are diverse in form, material and symbolism. Historic resources are preserved to protect our heritage as well as our urban environment. Our neighborhoods are attractive and safe for children, families and individuals. Our mixed-use, pedestrian-oriented village cores and neighborhood activity centers integrate open space, are convenient to housing and public transportation, and are built on a human scale. The heart of our city is a vibrant downtown core that provides a wide range of residential, cultural, business and entertainment opportunities.

Transportation and Communication

OUR VISION is of a fully accessible region where all destinations can be reached safely with or without an automobile. There is a broad choice of coordinated transportation alternatives which are convenient, efficient, affordable, safe, environmentally responsible and accessible to all. In addition, a network of affordable electronic communications provides an alternative to travel.

Arts, Culture and Recreation

OUR VISION is of an arts, recreational and cultural environment, supported by the community, which nurtures the expression and fulfillment of our best creative qualities. It encourages the enjoyment of our outdoor and urban settings, our entertainment activities, and the diversity of our ethnic, cultural and historic heritage. It enriches the lives of citizens and attracts visitors from throughout the world to enjoy the uniqueness of Arizona and the Southwest.

Governance

OUR VISION is of self-governance by informed citizens who create institutions which are fair and open, which balance responsibilities with resources, and which are responsive to the needs and rights of all citizens and of their communities. This open, grass-roots process encourages citizen involvement within neighborhoods, urban villages and the municipal government.

Our Commitment

AS PROUD CITIZENS OF PHOENIX, WE COMMIT our individual and collective effort to create a future for our city that reflects this vision. To this end, we dedicate our time, our resources and our talents, and we invite our neighboring communities to join with us in this endeavor.

FIGURE 5-1

week for three months. Some task forces met more often and even established subcommittees to complete portions of the work. Each task force developed its own report, which the Forum published and distributed. Most of these reports followed a similar format so they could be merged easily into a document for review by the policy committee and at Forum IV.

The results of task force work were distributed at Forum IV in both summary and complete versions. Selected elements of the report were discussed in small groups. Results were summarized for the policy committee, which decided on the final language of the report. Relatively few modifications from the earlier draft were required.

The Final Report and City Council Action

The time had come to prepare the report for the city council. The policy committee wanted its final report to be readable and interesting. Yet, it did not want the depth and richness of the recommendations of the task forces to be lost. The committee therefore chose to produce its basic report largely as fiction, from the perspective of a reporter writing about the Forum in the year 2015. This report, named Phoenix 2015, was written by an accomplished professional writer. To preserve task force recommendations, the committee also prepared a technical supplement.

As it approached the completion of its work, the committee also became aware of the need to plan for what would happen next. The policy committee chair appointed an "Action Task Force" to develop a plan of action to be included in the final report.

The task force recognized that the city council could not be expected to endorse all of the recommendations of the Forum. Yet, it wanted some action that would symbolize success and assure that Forum proposals would be carried out. The Action Plan asked the city council to not only adopt the Futures Forum Vision Statement, but also to establish the Futures Forum as a continuing action project charged to:

1.   Analyze the resources and resource needs of the community and develop recommendations concerning resource allocations.

2.   Build coalitions and commitments of support and involvement in the implementation of specific projects and programs.

3.   Publicize and provide information about the Forum and its recommendations.

4.   Monitor progress in the implementation of Forum proposals and

make periodic reports to the city council and public regarding their impact.

5. Assist in the interpretation and refinement of recommendations for implementation through current programs and projects and through the city's strategic plan and budget.

6. Encourage and support private, institutional, or educational organizations to work with the Action Project to fulfill objectives of the Forum.

7. Prepare proposals for ways to work with individual citizens, city boards and commissions, and private groups to carry out Forum recommendations.

8. Develop partnerships with educational institutions to work on the community challenges.

The policy committee approved the recommendations of the action task force for inclusion in the final report.

The chair of the policy committee also appointed a drafting committee to work with the professional writer in selecting the final report's basic format and to assure that the report accurately reflected the recommendations. The policy committee was also concerned that the report suggest priorities. To that end, the drafting committee identified a series of new "initiatives" that it believed were the most important things that could be done to achieve Forum goals. The final version of the report was reviewed and approved by the policy committee. These proposals, termed the 21 Initiatives, were incorporated into the Phoenix 2015 report.

The policy committee presented the recommendations of the Forum to the city council in January of 1990. About 300 persons attended the meeting, prompting Mayor Goddard to observe that it was probably the largest number of persons to ever appear in support of a proposal before the council.

The city council unanimously adopted the recommendations of the Action Plan. Specifically it:

• Adopted the Vision Statement
• Agreed to establish a Futures Forum action committee
• Directed this committee to work on the 21 Initiatives
• Directed city staff to look for recommendations that could be readily carried out.
• Directed city boards and commissions to look for recommendations that could be carried out through their programs.

Implementation

Several actions followed quickly. The chair of the policy committee appointed a planning committee to make recommendations to the council about implementation. This committee developed a Plan for Action, which included proposals for the organization and membership of the action committee.

An important part of this Plan was the formation of six "action groups" as subcommittees of the action committee. Each of these groups was assigned to carry out a few of the 21 Initiatives and to work on general proposals in these areas. The organizational plan calls for each group to "relate" to a corresponding subcommittee of the city council. This provides opportunities for action groups to talk directly with the city council and senior city staff.

Other organizational ideas included the creation of task forces to work on implementation of specific initiatives or other Forum projects, and the recognition of community organizations who are working to carry out major Forum proposals as "community partners."

Arizona State University also gave important support to the Forum. It established a position of "Loaned Executive" to work with the Forum and to link the resources of the university with the city and community. Professor Louis Weschler from the School of Urban Affairs was the first person assigned to this role. He not only worked directly with Forum action groups but also helped start research on several Forum projects.

As soon as it was established, the action committee started to prepare a "Work Plan" to provide focus to its work. A major event, called the Civic Summit, was organized to validate the draft Work Plan and to broaden community participation. Leaders of community organizations were invited to come together to discuss the plan and to "sign on" to help implement selected projects.

Several hundred persons responded and their discussion produced a list of 50 projects to be included in the Work Plan. Individuals and organizations were found to provide leadership on about 30 of these projects, some of which were already underway. In the excitement following completion of the final report, several task forces were created by Forum participants to start work on key projects and initiatives. Also, some proposed projects were found to be in early stages of development by other agencies during the preparation of the Work Plan.

The Forum is now working to implement the Work Plan by providing continued support to task forces and community partners who are working to carry out projects from the Work Plan.

It is also recruiting and training individuals and groups to work on projects already underway or other projects included in the Work Plan, as well as working with Arizona State University to complete and undertake several research projects.

Furthermore, the Forum continues to conduct a public relations and outreach program to provide a broader understanding of its objectives and to pave the way for implementation of more projects.

City staff also responded to Forum recommendations. Many projects that were relatively easy to carry out and for which political support was readily available were moved forward quickly. These included the establishment of a new office of "neighborhood notification," combining publication of all city notices on one page of a local newspaper one day of each week, incorporation of Forum proposals into the update of the city's general plan, which was and is still underway, and the establishment of other programs to give the public better access to city information.

The city manager appointed a departmental task force that recommended a process for systematic analysis of Forum proposals and for incorporating them into the city's corporate plan. This process is underway. It includes evaluation of the status of each Forum proposal (eg: done, under study, department responsible, etc.) and development of a monitoring system to follow up on work underway.

The manager also created a new Strategic Issues Department, which has greatly strengthened ties between the Forum and the Corporate Plan and has given the Forum status within the structure of the city. (During the first phase of the project, the Futures Forum was housed in the Office of the Mayor.)

What Has Been Learned?

The Phoenix Futures Forum has been a major effort. It has absorbed the enthusiasm, faith, and energy of thousands of citizens. It has cost a lot. It has consumed much of the energy and time of the city.

What has it produced? Many observers would say that it is too early to tell. They point out that the Forum proposed a 25 year vision, and that it will take years to tell whether that vision is being achieved. Emphasis of the Forum on fundamental causes—as compared with symptoms—is an argument for this view.

Success at this early stage needs to be measured in changes in the various plans of the city and the community, the motivation and involvement of people, the training of leadership and strengthening of institutions. In these terms it appears that the Forum has been very successful. The evidence includes the following:

• Many Forum recommendations are being incorporated into the city's corporate plan and the general plan.

• Many new people are being drawn into community leadership. These range from positions at the neighborhood level to seats on the city council.

• Many people and organizations are becoming more proficient in group planning and decision making, and in working with government and other community groups. Techniques being improved include meeting planning and facilitation, preparing proposals and "business plans" for projects, and building and maintaining community networks.

• Many new coalitions and groups have been and are being formed to work on opportunities and problems. These include "clearinghouse" and support groups in such areas as the environment, recycling, and neighborhood improvement.

The Forum is forging new techniques and methods that can be used by citizens to have a real impact on their future. To the extent that it is successful in this, this will more than justify its existence.

The Forum is being carried out in an atmosphere of innovation. As a result, there has been much to learn, and what has been learned should be valuable to others.

Five things that have worked well:

1. Facilitated Meetings: Methods used to facilitate meetings were effective, especially for the numbers of people who had to be accommodated. Techniques were developed especially for each of the Forums. Meetings were carefully planned, facilitators were trained, and materials were well prepared. This gave credibility to the process and increased confidence in its results. It also helped meetings go smoothly when the numbers of people involved could have meant chaos.

2. Four Question Format: Though the four question format for the phases of the Forum worked quite well, the questions were varied slightly to make them more useful to participants. For example, the question of "Where do we want to go?" was changed to "What would your ideal Phoenix be in 2015?" The questions were simple and understandable.

3. Vision Statement: Use of material from previous activities gave the drafting committee confidence that it was responding to concerns that had been expressed. Although the statement is longer than recommended, it appears to adequately express the will of the Forum.

4.   Task Forces: The work of the task forces in developing strategies and actions went smoothly because of several factors. One was effective work by the Task Force co-chairs and by other participants, many of whom were quite knowledgeable and quite dedicated to the process. Another is the concentrated schedule under which the work was done. This provided a discipline that led to decisions and completion. A third is the involvement of staff from the city and from other agencies in the area. Staff did not intrude into the process. But they did help significantly at this stage.

5.   Public Relations: The work done in public relations made people aware of the Forum in ways not otherwise possible. It provided clever ideas useful in making the Forum more fun. And it helped develop the Forum identity. While professional public relations help might be considered a frill, it is really a necessity.

Five things that did not work as well:

1.   Technical Input: After the initial background report and Forum I, very little technical input or background research came into the process. There was very little time to obtain such information and the process of active participation—as compared to passive absorption—did not allow for such input. Early plans to conduct a scientific poll of community attitudes and opinions were scrapped because it appeared that there would be no real use for the results.

Counteracting this is the fact that participants collectively brought tremendous knowledge and insight to the discussion. The proposals of the Forum were far richer and dealt with more issues than a professional study would likely have done.

2.   Repetition: Despite efforts to separate discussions of topics in the various workshops, suggestions were repeated in almost every workshop. For example, issues of human need were brought up in discussions of transportation, and transportation problems were brought up in workshops on paying for the future. If this had been anticipated, fewer forums might have been needed.

This redundancy did not seem to harm the process, but it added to the work and the volumes of material that had to be handled. It may have bored some participants as well.

3.   Confusion about staff involvement: Confusion developed at the first Forum because some staff was turned away as a result of high registrations. This and the fact that the process operated from the mayor's office, not under the city manager, created confusion about the extent to which staff was to participate. This resulted in resentment that still exists today. A clear, understood policy on staff involvement was needed.

4. Alternate Futures: Significant work was done in describing alternate futures as a stimulus to thinking about the future. However, there is little evidence that this had the impact desired. The results were entertaining, but did not generate any noticeable response.

5. Preparation of Work Plans: The preparation of work plans by action groups at the start of the implementation phase did not proceed smoothly. Although professional facilitators assisted, it became apparent that participants did not have sufficient knowledge of Forum recommendations or of the nature of a work plan to be efficient in this task. The experience was frustrating to everyone concerned.

The lesson is that people should have a better chance to review the Forum recommendations before they are asked to identify tasks, set priorities, and establish a plan of action. Also, it appears that much more time and effort must be put into orienting people for the implementation phase. Carrying out plans differs dramatically from planning.

SAVANNAH'S SHOWCASE NEIGHBORHOOD PROGRAM
(By Arthur A. Mendonsa)

The livability of a neighborhood is affected by many things: the condition of streets, sidewalks, and buildings; the cleanliness of yards, streets, and alleys; the availability of recreation facilities; and the level of crime and public disorder. These factors, however, inevitably depend on a community's social cohesion. If there is social deterioration, there is physical deterioration. In the past, Savannah, Georgia's response to socially disorganized and physically dilapidated neighborhoods was to increase services and facilities. This fact, however, produced marginal benefits at best. The explanation seemed to be that the city was working *for* the neighborhood residents instead of *with* them. It was accepting responsibility for making things right and placing none of the responsibility on the residents themselves. And it failed.

In 1987, the city tried a new strategy, one that is built on creating a partnership between neighborhood residents and the city. Called the Showcase Neighborhood Program, the plan used neighborhood organizers to develop neighborhood associations in some of the city's most troubled parts. Seven neighborhoods, predominantly black with a mixture of owner-occupied and tenant-occupied housing, are now in the program. All are low-income neighborhoods.

Under the Showcase Program, residents held a retreat to establish a vision for what they would like their neighborhood to become. Typically, neighborhood visions do not vary greatly. Residents tend to envision their neighborhood as one that is free of litter, debris, and junk cars; that has streets and sidewalks in good repair; that is free of vacant, dilapidated buildings; that has well-maintained yards; that is free of loiterers and criminals; that is well lighted; and that has many recreational opportunities for children.

Once the vision is adopted, the residents survey their neighborhood on a lot-by-lot, block-by-block basis to identify the conditions that must be changed if the vision is to be achieved. These surveys are conducted with the supervision of city staff. Street and sidewalk problems, dilapidated buildings, litter and debris problems, loitering spots and drug houses are all identified. The data is then consolidated, recorded on neighborhood base maps, and quantified in a printed profile of the neighborhood. Priorities and schedules are then set for making needed improvements.

Recently, job training and placement programs have been added to the Showcase Program. Other components include quarterly meetings between city department heads and the neighborhood associations, monthly briefings of the associations by city staff, annual picnics in each Showcase neighborhood, and awards for "house of the month" and the "block of the month" in given areas.

The Showcase Program has changed the relationship between the city and its disadvantaged neighborhoods. Now the city is viewed as a partner rather than as a provider. The residents have become empowered and, for the first time, are appearing before the city council to respond to issues that affect them.

Because of its measurable benefits, the Showcase concept is now being used in designing a comprehensive crime control strategy for Savannah. Studies have determined that neighborhoods with high levels of violent crimes also have the weakest physical and social programs. They also have the most dilapidated buildings, dwelling fires, infrastructure deterioration, child abuse and neglect, and teenage pregnancy and parenthood, but the fewest educational opportunities.

Therefore, the Showcase crime control strategy will not only focus on the crime issue, but also on the underlying social and physical conditions that foster crime and delinquency in the neighborhood.

REFERENCES

Bernard, L. 1989. "Granger seeks backing for East Side program." *Fort Worth Star-Telegram,* March 2.

Davidoff, P. 1965. "Advocacy and Pluralism in Planning." *Journal of the American* Institute of Certified Planners, Vol. 31, No. 5.

Denton, T., ed. 1990. "Goals program shows strong leadership." *Fort Worth Star-Telegram,* April 16.

6

Managing for Customer Service

IT STARTS AT THE TOP

Putting the customer first is a demanding challenge, but it is also an essential first step in positioning any planning organization to fully participate in, and benefit from, the surging demand for planning services. In taking their organization through the necessary transition, planners should model their behavior after that of other successful service providers. In *The Service Edge*, Ron Zemke and Dick Schaaf identify 101 outstanding frontline service organizations in both the public and private sectors (Zemke and Schaaf 1989). They report that these service providers share a number of common characteristics that have contributed to their success. In particular, each successful service organization has followed these five operating principles: listen to customers; define superior service and establish a service strategy; set standards and measure performance; select, train, and empower employees to work for the customers; and recognize and reward accomplishments.

Managing for superior customer service requires a total organizational approach to the development and delivery of products and services. The organization must have an unflinching commitment to service that starts at the top and is absorbed by the entire organization. In every public agency where there is an extraordinary dedication to customer service, I have found that the top administrator is responsible for this attitude.

One significant governmental unit that has received national recognition for its superior commitment to customer service is Montgomery

County, Ohio. It was selected by Zemke and Schaaf as one of the few examples of outstanding service in the public sector. They identify Montgomery County administrator Claude Malone as a "pacesetter," entrepreneur, and leader in the public sector. They note that Malone is committed to making Montgomery County government "the best there is in providing service." Malone asks, "If we aren't here to serve, what are we here for? We should do it to the best of our ability. And we should treat our fellow citizens with respect" (Zemke and Schaaf 1989).

To institute his vision of customer service, Malone developed a five-year "Service Excellence" program. The program has several key components. The first stage involves having each department identify its specific customers. Also, many of the departments surveyed the public to get a better understanding of their customers' perspectives. Zemke and Schaaf note that a number of very specific service-inspired changes have occurred under the Service Excellence program. According to Malone, the success of his program "has promoted a steady stream of phone calls from county governments nationwide who see in the Montgomery County model an image of how government can truly serve its constituents" (Zemke and Schaaf 1989).

FINDING THE RIGHT STUFF

Any good craftsman knows that you must start with the right kind of raw material to create a superior final product. The same principle applies with respect to people and customer service. In choosing employees for your organization, it is necessary to seek out individuals that naturally enjoy practicing planning and serving people. Of course this natural attraction should be supplemented and reinforced by solid technical knowledge and, most importantly, basic people skills.

John Friedmann argued in *Retracking America: A Theory of Transactive Planning* that "planning changes knowledge into action through an unbroken sequence of interpersonal relations" (Friedmann 1973). Over time, experience teaches us to value interpersonal skills as highly as technical skills. Friedmann, in his book, shared the following experience: "In recruiting the advisory staff, emphasis was given to the personal qualities of each advisor—his ability to be a person (not a role-playing professional alone), to establish direct relations with others that would not be perceived as threatening, to be sensitive to the needs of others, and to learn quickly from complex technical situations. Technical qualifications were also considered important, but they carried less weight" (Friedmann 1973).

Managers need to give careful attention to selecting employees in order to blend talents and personalities in the workplace. In selecting employees, it is much easier to hire planners that are naturally service-oriented than it is to try to change someone's personality and attitude. Unfortunately, if the organization does not have an existing commitment to customer service then no effort will be made to select people with a natural service attitude. Effective planning organizations include a commitment to customer service in their mission statements. Evidence of the growing recognition of the importance of conveying a service philosophy to employees and customers is provided by the trend to add the word "service" to the traditional title of the planning organization. For example, the planning department in Richardson, Texas, is now part of the development services department, just as it is in Aurora and Fort Collins, Colorado; Glendale, Arizona; Danville, California; and Farmington, New Mexico.

A customer-service selectivity must be practiced in filling *all* positions, with special attention directed toward lower paying, entry-level positions. In many large planning organizations, little interest is shown by upper management in the hiring of entry-level planners. Yet many of these beginning planners will often have initial contact on the phone or in person with the general public. The failure to recognize this is probably responsible for the negligent way in which some entry-level planners are hired and shoved behind the front desks. Though they are commonly expected to answer questions and serve the public while trying to learn their jobs, new employees frequently need months of training and practical experience before they can provide productive service. Yet the people that visit a planning office expect timely, high quality service and don't appreciate being used as training material for newly hired planners. Fortunately, the time has long since passed in the planning profession when a shortage of qualified planners forced organizations to "get somebody or anybody right now." There is no longer any excuse for hiring unqualified and unprepared planners at any level of your organization.

Roger Hedrick, the planning director of the Lafayette Areawide Planning Commission in Lafayette, Louisiana, values experience, education, and knowledge at all levels in his organization, but his first selection criteria are energy, enthusiasm, and a positive attitude. He has found it difficult to change attitudes, and almost impossible to energize passive, lethargic personalities. Furthermore, he notes that a negative or hostile attitude will cause far more disruption and damage to the organization than any benefits that can be obtained from that employee. Recently, three Georgia State University professors surveyed 122 supervisors and discovered that the number one personnel problem they had with subordinates was the lack of "the right attitude." They found that "most of the bosses said that they could put up with people who are not especially gifted or talented or even smart—as long as they are able to work well with others."

Many planning directors prefer hiring people they have previously worked with because they know them. Yet many a planner has been accused of showing favoritism by hiring a friend or former colleague. In most instances, what the hirer is looking for is not friendship but rather predictability and proven performance. The hirer is familiar with the individual's strengths and weaknesses and won't be surprised by this person's performance or behavior. Such knowledge is an important factor in the selection process because "the single most frequent reason new employees were fired," according to Carol Shorr, president of MKM Consultants, Inc., is "an inability to fit in with the corporate culture."

Even the most experienced planning director will sometimes have to choose from a pool of unknown applicants. The advantage in this situation goes to the employer who has established a network of trusting professional and personal contacts. Trusting written recommendations is dangerous because many individuals will not give a negative assessment for fear it could get back to the individual. Thus, honest assessments depend on establishing strong relationships with the individuals providing the assessments. Only if they can trust you to keep their remarks confidential will they confide in you.

I have hired a number of entry-level planners just out of graduate school and also have good relationships with the faculty at many schools. One professor, who I will call Will Rogers, never had a student he didn't like and always gave me a positive recommendation. Unfortunately, it was only after hiring a particularly psychopathic personality that I learned of Dr. Rogers's unique capacity to find goodness in everyone. Needless to say, I no longer seek his personal opinion.

When seeking to fill mid-range or higher level planning positions, I look with particular favor upon individuals that have worked with nonprofit organizations on either a paid or volunteer basis. I have emphasized throughout this book that volunteerism and self-help are essential components of effective planning. Individuals that have worked as volunteers or with volunteers are more appreciative of the value and potential benefits of volunteerism. They also have a perspective that lets them see things from the eye of the volunteer.

I have always prided myself in being involved in the hiring process for positions at all levels. The key word here is "involved." This does not mean I make the final decision. It only means that I fully participate in the process. I am an advocate of delegating authority and responsibility to the lowest possible levels. This even includes decision-making authority on hiring employees. But the effective manager does not leave the hiring process to chance. The hirer must also be adequately trained to make selections consistent with the goals, philosophies, and ideals of the organization. You can't just assume that the senior planner or chief planner knows how to evaluate and select employees.

The technical aspects of interviewing candidates are very sophisticated, but with proper training and guidance the critical responsibility of making hiring decisions can be delegated to lower echelons. Most large cities offer such training. I do recommend that hiring, particularly in medium or larger organizations, should be a team process. Rose Jacobsen, planning director for the City of Arlington, uses a team selection process that includes individuals from other city departments in addition to the planning staff. She wants the perspectives and opinions of other professions to be reflected in the interviewing and selecting process. Obviously, the opinions of individuals that will be working directly with the new hire are also important to consider.

A secondary benefit of the selection process is the chance it provides to identify and reinforce the corporate culture of the organization. The job description should go beyond the listing of education, knowledge, and experience requirements to include desirable personal attitudes and philosophies. Few employers bother to express such preferences, but a few do. The recent job announcement for the planning director position in a major city noted that the director would be responsible for installing a customer service orientation in the planning department. The announcement for a planning assistant for one Texas city stated that the "City seeks an individual with high customer service orientation." In a Wisconsin county, the announcement for the vacant assistant county planner position noted that it is desirable if the candidate has an "ability to interact effectively with the general public." In Virginia, a job announcement for a city planner asked for an individual who could "establish and maintain effective relationships with city officials, private business officials, neighborhood groups *and* coworkers." I recall the U.S.

Environmental Protection Agency advertising for a supervisory environmental protection specialist with a broad range of technical experience and "demonstrated effective interpersonal and communications skills."

But in reviewing recent job announcements and job descriptions, I was distressed by the lack of attempts to convey the corporate culture and working environment of the organization. Furthermore, except for a few isolated occurrences, there were seldom any references to personalities, attitudes, or interpersonal skills. Why should these things be taken for granted, especially when a recent survey showed that "most planners appear to feel stronger or more competent at intellectual than at interpersonal tasks" (Baum 1983). It may be that the absence of interpersonal skills in many senior level planners leads them to ignore this important trait when soliciting new employees.

Many job announcements are unclear. One has to wonder that when the job announcement calls for communications skills, does the employer want an oral, graphic, or written communicator and does this include being a good listener? Have you ever seen a job description that asked for listening skills? Why not? It is often noted that the applicant has to possess a drivers license, but no one ever asks for a sense of humor. Yet several planning directors I interviewed indicated that a sense of humor was one of the primary characteristics they looked for when hiring subordinates. And planning agency managers are not unique. I recall a column in *The Wall Street Journal* that reported chief executives look mostly for loyalty *and* a sense of humor when choosing subordinates.

I looked long and hard, but was unable to find any job announcements or descriptions asking for characteristics such as a pleasant personality, calm and unflappable behavior, empathic and caring attitude, positive outlook, patient and deferential behavior, nonargumentative personality, attentive listener, team player, cheerleader, risk taker, problem solver, lifelong learner, teacher, friendly, likeable, antibureaucracy, or just a fun person.

I particularly want planners who channel their feelings and emotions to help them service their customers, who will substitute emotion and enthusiasm for objectivity. Above all, I want human beings that wear their hearts on their sleeves and are moved when they see inequality and injustice.

Janusz Korczak was a legendary doctor, teacher, and protector of orphans in pre-war Poland. In the movie *Korczak,* there is a particularly moving scene where he is lecturing doctors at Warsaw's children's hospital. As part of his lecture, he brings a small boy to the podium, opens the childs shirt, places him under a fluoroscope, and turns off the overhead lights. In the darkened room, the only thing visible is the boy's rib cage and beating heart. Dr. Korczak pauses and then says, "Don't ever forget this sight. Remember always what a child's frightened heart looks like." Planners need to have the capacity to personally hurt for and care about all their customers, but especially those who cannot take care of themselves.

What else do planners need? James Heskett, in his 1986 book *Managing in the Service Economy,* cited research to the effect that "employee attributes of success in high-contact service situations include flexibility, tolerance for ambiguity, the ability to monitor and change behavior during the service encounter, and empathy with customers" (Heskett 1986). And while I could easily include a list of positive personality traits in a job announcement, what would happen if it was also suggested that the following types of people should not apply?
- Lazy, apathetic, and pleasant-to-your-face employees
- Time wasters, bathroom hiders, and lunch lizards
- Back stabbers, busybodies, and wedge drivers
- Employees with too many outside interests
- Consistently rude and socially disruptive types
- Boss underminers, uncooperative informal leaders, and disloyal individuals
- Change resisters and passive aggressives

Unless the employer formalizes the desirable characteristics that are being sought for the organization and includes them in job announcements, then the personalities of the applicants will not consistently be given sufficient weight during the evaluation process. With the availability of various personality assessment and personality type indicator tests there is no reason to continue to neglect the personality of the candidates. When your employees can't cut the mustard, you won't relish the outcome.

WHO ARE YOUR CUSTOMERS AND WHAT CAN YOU DO FOR THEM?

The lack of attention to the marketing aspects of planning is particularly disappointing because, as a general rule, no one in local government has more customer data than the planning department. Yet most planners fail to put this information to use when they prepare and prioritize their work programs, and they are not aggressive in packaging and promoting this information for use by other departments.

The first step in developing a customer-service strategy is the identification of the various existing and potential customers in the marketplace. According to George Wagenheim and John Reurink in a recent article in *Public Administration Review*, "Any organization that goes through the process of defining who its customers are automatically increases its effectiveness through a more precise focusing of organizational energy" (Wagenheim and Reurink 1991). Many planners are so busy, so comfortable, or so disinterested in people that they never even take time to find out who their customers are and what they might want from the planning department. The following is one of the exercises that Ray Quay and I ask participants to complete at our AICP-sponsored workshops on planning agency management:

> List your major client groups, first in order of their importance to you and your organization and, second, in the rank order which reflects the actual amount of staff time and resources which are committed to serving them.

> Ranking of clients in their order of importance to you

> Ranking of clients in amount of staff time they receive

> 1._____   1._____
> 2._____   2._____
> 3._____   3._____
> 4._____   4._____
> 5._____   5._____

> For your total work program, what percentage of your staff time is spent on serving your top two clients/groups? _____%.

After struggling with this question, some will respond that their top customer is the general public. At one recent workshop we suggested that planners who had trouble answering this question should go back to their organizations and have someone at the front desk take pictures of the people coming into their offices. I suspect many planners would be surprised by the results.

Some planners will identify their city manager, mayor, city council, or planning commission as their primary customer. While there is little consistency in the ranking of customers, there is uniformity with respect to the allocation of staff time. Most planning departments allocate only a very small or modest amount of staff time to their most important customers. When questioned about the logic behind this, planners' standard response is that they just never gave it much thought. Of course the real reason for neglecting this relationship is that most planners do not see their mission as delivering services to customers. They are planners, not customer-service providers.

The typical planning department develops and delivers a full range of planning products and services. The only real shortcoming I see when evaluating these organizations is a serious lack of customers or users for many of these services.

Several years ago, a major city conducted separate retreats for its city council and department heads. Each group was asked to list and prioritize the city's accomplishments for the past year and set goals for the coming year. One of the most shocking aspects of the retreats was the complete lack of consistency or agreement between the lists of the two groups. The city council's list of the top 10 accomplishments for the past year included only one project from the department heads' list, and it was ranked second on the council's list and ninth on the staff's. The only thing more shocking than this was the indifference of the department heads. Not one of them expressed any concern about the obvious inconsistencies in priorities between the two groups, and no one suggested that perhaps the staff should consider revising its proposed goals for next year to be more sensitive to the council's agenda.

In *Managing in the Service Economy*, James Heskett provides useful advice for helping service managers develop and deliver the right products and services (Heskett 1986). He argues that a service provider cannot be all things to all people and that "groups or 'segments' of customers must be singled out for a particular service." He explains how the "segmentation" process can be used to identify groups of customers with enough characteristics in common to make possible the design and presentation of a viable product or service.

Heskett also helps the planner answer that nagging question of "What is planning and what do planners do?" He correctly points out that the first step every organization must take if it wants to be successful is to decide "What business are we in?" or at least "What business do we want the customer to think we are in?" Successful service providers know the answer to these questions and communicate it to their customers and employees.

The concept of "strategic service vision" provides the primary focus for Heskett's book. This vision is a four-part blueprint for service managers—targeting a market segment, conceptualizing how the service will be perceived by consumers, focusing on an operating strategy, and designing an efficient service delivery system that transforms vision into action. Heskett explains each point with dozens of examples from a variety of service industries, and offers a structured set of management guidelines that can be used by almost any service provider.

In the typical city, less than one percent of the population is a real-world customer of the local planning department. Planners may argue that they serve the whole community, but in reality very few people ever have direct personal contact with a city planner or the specific products and services offered by the planning department. Think about it. How many legal notices do you mail? How many phone calls do you receive? How many people attend your public hearings? How many copies of your reports and plans are given out or sold? The typical planning department clearly has limited one-on-one contact with its customers. Under these conditions it is very difficult to tailor products to meet specific needs. But this situation does not have to be the norm. There are many ways for planners to increase contact with customers.

David Spencer, the director of community development for the city of Gillette, Wyoming, provides an outstanding example of what planners can accomplish when they have more direct contact with their customers. Spencer's customer-service philosophy is that by getting and staying in touch with customers, a planner is able to learn more about their needs and expectations and then use this information to develop more satisfying products and services. To uphold this philosophy, Spencer and his staff sought to answer the following four questions: What is our business and who are our customers? What counts most to our customers? What can we do with our services that customers would really notice? How do our customers see us now?

In response to the first question, the planning staff broke its customers into the following two groups:

Internal Customers
- City Council/Administration
- City Boards
- Fellow Employees/Other Departments/Each Other

External Customers
- Citizens of City/County
- Business Persons/Business Organizations
- Professionals including developers, contractors, architects and engineers, lawyers, and real estate people
- Other Governmental Agencies

The staff concluded that as a customer-oriented service business they should have the following service objectives:
- to see that the public and private sectors have the highest quality and safest development possible;
- to encourage better planning and compliance with the codes;
- to strike a balance between customer service and public safety;
- to ensure life safety standards in building construction; and,
- to provide guidance to the public in implementing *their* concept of community development.

The second important question was "What counts most to our customers?" The answers developed by the staff for each major client group are listed on the following pages:

Internal Customers

Council/Administration
- being informed about potential and ongoing problems; providing "insider" information;
- getting prompt assistance and timely information when requested;
- reduction of conflicts with external customer groups;
- provision of support which enhances image of being in control;
City Boards
- same as above list for council/administration;
- support and background information to make informed decisions;
- consistent and effective administration of policies developed by the board;
- good staff/citizen relationships.
Fellow Employees, Other Departments, Each Other
- timely response to requests for information and assistance;
- cooperative working relationships;
- accurate and consistent answers between departments.

External Customers

Citizens of City/County
- return phone calls and correspondence promptly;
- good listening skills;
- having human needs satisfied;
- getting a response when a problem occurs;
- being able to vent their problem;
- going to the site;
- consistent answers between individuals and departments;

  • providing construction advice and general guidance on technical matters;
    • explorations of options when a problem is encountered;
    • a clear explanation of the "bottom line."
Business Persons/Business Organizations
    • return phone calls and correspondence promptly;
    • respecting time tables which fit the particular business;
    • acknowledging and affirming their stature in the community;
    • profit/cost to be acknowledged in the process;
    • concern for disruption of customer relationships.
Professionals
    • dependable technical information;
    • consistency from one individual and department to another;
    • recognition of the fact that they have an informed opinion and want to be treated as colleagues;
    • comments framed so as not to discount the professional in front of a client.
Other Government Agencies
    • timely answers;
    • personable contact and cooperation;
    • more "ego" support;
    • recognition of having to respond to the same political pressures that we do.
  The third question was "What can we do with our service that customers would really notice?" Here are the Gillette staff's answers:

Internal Customers

Council/Administration
    • offer positive news releases;
    • provide well thought-out information in council packets;
    • participate in city newsletters, city circuit, etc.;
    • return phone calls promptly;
    • provide personalized service;
    • ask them to attend a board meeting;
    • hold a departmental open house.
City Boards
    • conduct training for them as a board;
    • ask for periodic input on the format of information presented to the board;

- provide "insider" information about operations that affect them
and the interest groups which they represent.

Fellow Employees/Other Departments/Each Other
- provide open communication;
- keep each other informed about policies and problems;
- be specific in communicating;
- hold staff meetings when required;
- be aware of others' functions and responsibilities;
- treat each other with respect and professionalism;
- offer services to one another whenever possible.

External Customers

Citizens of City/County
- practice customer skills in our "toolchest";
- publicize available services;
- strive to satisfy human needs;
- come as close as possible to meeting tangible needs as the rules
allow.

Business Persons/Business Organizations
- everything shown above for citizens;
- let them know that their project is important to you also;
- stress government's partnership with business;
- work to reduce the image of an adversary;
- provide an image of competence;
- acknowledge inequities;
- provide predictability to the process;
- keep them informed of developments and maintain realistic expectations;
- be available as required.

Professional
- promote colleague-to-colleague respect;
- if possible, give them the "big half" for their clients;
- don't discount them in front of clients;
- provide a feeling of preferred status;
- ask them for guidance and input on our projects;
- cultivate them as allies.

Other Government Agencies
- everything shown above under professionals;
- work to eliminate barriers and boundaries;

- socialize with them;
- strive to make each other look good.

When I talk at workshops about the need for planners to be more innovative and entrepreneurial, the response I often get is that most planning departments lack the financial resources to develop and market new products and services. When I suggest that the public should be expected to pay for improved services, the audience winces. Planners want to be allocated more funding from the city's general revenue stream in the annual budget. This is a nice wish, but it's also bad strategy. Reliance on general-purpose revenue protects planners from the often cruel realities of the marketplace. Most citizens don't know what city planners do, and they sure as heck don't want them to get any more of their local tax dollars. The solution to the revenue problem for city planners is not more subsidies, it is better marketing. It is marketing that develops significant political constituencies from among either targeted beneficiaries of their services or the general public.

Many planners want to serve the public interest and believe the best way to do so is to have mandatory planning legislation that requires local governments to meet strong planning requirements. Some older planners fondly remember Section 701 of the Housing Act of 1954, which over the years authorized millions of dollars in grants for general planning purposes. This act stimulated planning throughout the nation and led to the authorization of still more funds. Cities used these 701 funds to develop comprehensive plans that would make them eligible for various federal government grants for infrastructure improvements and additions. Most of these plans were very effective in helping local governments obtain these grants. Thus, high levels of customer satisfaction were reported and the planning profession grew and prospered. Unfortunately, when the unstable foundation of federal funding crumbled under the Reagan administration, so did local support for city planning. The message was loud and clear. Planning was an expensive luxury, and in tough fiscal times it was an easy target for budget cuts.

While some planners are calling again for more federal assistance, others want mandatory planning legislation. But it is interesting to note that in California, which has mandatory planning requirements, regulation is still the dominant activity for planning agencies. Linda Dalton surveyed 270 city planning agencies in California in 1986, and found that they allocated only 9.4 percent of their time to general plan preparation, in contrast to 48.3 percent for land-use permit processing.

Furthermore, the adopted general plans did not withstand development pressures, says Dalton, who found that these cities approved "three-fourths of all zone change requests and two-thirds of the general plan amendments that private parties initiated" (Dalton 1989). Nothing in the California experience suggests that planning is any more effective or that planners are any more secure or protected from budget pressures in California cities because of mandatory planning requirements.

The foundation of effective planning should be marketing and customer service, not slavery. Planners do not own their customers or their jobs.

SETTING QUALITY STANDARDS AND MEASURING PERFORMANCE

As stated in *The Game of Work* by Charles Coonradt, "scorekeeping is the heart of athletics, and it must be the heart of every successful business" (Coonradt 1985). Coonradt believes that the primary responsibility of managers is to set the rules, create the scorecards, and to manage by measurement. It is a recognized management adage that what gets measured gets done, and when performance is measured, performance improves. Conversely, areas without specific objectives will be neglected. Keeping score is an incredible motivator. If you don't believe it then just ask any planning director that is required to set departmental goals as part of an annual budgeting or performance evaluation process.

It is increasingly rare to find a planning department that does not have an annual work program. Salem, Oregon, is cited in the book, *Management of Local Planning*, by David Slater, AICP, as having successfully implemented an employee work planning process based on management by objectives (Slater 1984). The Lafayette Areawide Planning Commission is another excellent model. As previously mentioned, in Lafayette, Louisiana, the planning staff meets with the planning commissioners in an annual retreat to jointly develop the following year's goals. Their resulting objectives are measurable, very specific, and highly publicized. Al Neuharth, founder of *USA Today*, argues that objectives that are only abstract ideals or good intentions are almost worthless and that private objectives are for wimps (Neuharth 1989). Objectives must translate into work with clear measurable results, deadlines, and accountability. Figures 6–1 (a) and (b) from the Central City Plan for Portland, Oregon, illustrate the necessary linkage between planning proposals, implementation, and accountability (Portland 1988).

Policy 2: THE WILLAMETTE RIVERFRONT

Enhance the Willamette River as the focal point for views, public activities, and development which knits the city together.

FURTHER:

A. Recapture the east bank of the Willamette Riverfront between the Marquam and Steel Bridges by expanding and enhancing the space available for non-vehicular uses.

B. Locate a wide range of affordable and attractive public activities and attractors along the riverbank and create frequent pedestrian access to the water's edge.

C. Encourage a mixture of land uses along the river, while protecting opportunities for water-dependent uses, especially north of the Broadway Bridge.

D. Maintain and improve public views to and from the river.

E. Improve the Central City's bridges for pedestrians and bicyclists and enhance the bridges role as connections between the two sides of the Willamette.

F. Encourage development of facilities that provide access to and from the water's surface throughout the Central City.

G. Foster opportunities for touching and entering the Willamette River.

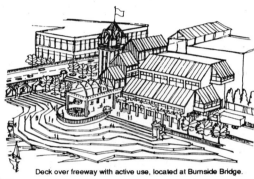

Deck over freeway with active use, located at Burnside Bridge.

Water taxi

FIGURE 6-1 (a)

To return to a recurring theme, whose quality standards are we trying to meet? Quality should be a direct function of the clients' needs and not be dictated by staff. All too often, however, planners equate quality with extensive data collection and lengthy analysis. Yet there is no causal relationship between data collection/analysis and product effectiveness. Carol Weiss, editor of *Using Social Research in Public Policy Making*, concludes that researchers can seldom show that data plays a key role in decision making (Weiss 1977).

Terry Moore, in the Department of Planning, Public Policy, and Management at the University of Oregon, wrote an article on this subject, entitled "Planning without Preliminaries," that was particularly critical of the goal-setting and data-collection phase of the planning

ACTION CHART

#	PROPOSALS FOR ACTION	TIMING: ADOPT WITH PLAN	NEXT FIVE YEARS	SIX TO 20 YEARS	POSSIBLE IMPLEMENTING AGENCY	INDEX TO ACTION DETAIL
	PROJECTS					
R1	Include a riverfront section in a Central City Developer's Handbook.		+ + + +		Planning	P 84
R2	Create a river taxi system with stops at public attractions and existing piers.			+ + + +	PDC/Parks/Pvt. Port/GPCVA	P 84
R3	Enhance the bridge walkways for pedestrians and bicyclists. Construct new features and maintain existing paths.		+ + + +		PDOT	P 84
R4	Improve connections for pedestrians and bicycles to the bridges and from the bridges to the east bank waterfront.		+ + + +		PDOT	
R5	Establish a public aquarium as a major attraction on or near the river.		+ + + +		PDC/METRO	
R6	Illuminate Portland's bridges with night lighting.		+ + + +		Mult. County/ MAC	P 84
R7	Enlarge the Oregon Maritime Museum on or near the riverfront.		+ + + +		Pvt./PDC/OMSI	
R8	Study and make recommendations on feasibility and location of a bridge for pedestrians and bicyclists.			+ + + +	Planning/PDOT	P 84
R9	Complete the development of the Greenway Trail within the Central City.		+ + + +		PDOT/ODOT/Parks	
R10	Build a full size working replica of one of the tall ships important to Portland's history and dock it in the Central City.		+ + + +		PDC/Private	P 85
R11	Create an inner-city riverfront loop trail between the Hawthorne and Steel Bridges, with a new rail level crossing on the Steel Bridge.		+ + + +		Parks	P85
R12	Establish facilities that access the water's surface; temporary boat tie-ups, swimming areas, a light craft center, and moorages.		+ + + +		Parks/PDC Planning/Pvt.	
R13	Establish rivercraft tie-up facilities to allow access fom the river to the river bank.		+ + + +		PDC/Parks	P 85
R14	Encourage riverfront tours, particularly on a renovated Steamer Portland.		+ + + +		Port/Pvt.	
	PROGRAMS					
R15	Preserve and enhance existing rights-of-way which extend to the river. Encourage the dedication of additional rights-of-way, especially where they line up with existing rights-of-way to provide access to the river through donations, condemnations, etc.		+ + + +		PDOT	
R16	Protect views of the river on existing rights-of-way.		+ + + +		Planning	P 85
R17	Enhance the role of the Central City bridges as gateways.		+ + + +		Multnomah County	P 86
R18	Encourage recreationally-oriented retail uses along the river.		+ + + +		BOP/Parks/PDC	
R19	Develop and distribute brochures and maps on riverfront recreation.		+ + + +		Parks Bureau	
R20	Enhance fish and wildlife habitat along the river.		+ + + +		Planning/Parks	P 86
R21	Preserve opportunities for river-dependent industrial uses.	+ + + +			Planning	

NOTE: Proposals for actions shown on the Action Charts and maps were adopted through City Council Resolution. The projects, programs and regulations listed are a starting place. As studies are undertaken, some actions will need to be amended, or in some cases, replaced with other proposals found to be better or more feasible.

FIGURE 6-1 (b)

process. He contends that planners spend too much time reconfirming and documenting the obvious. Moore recommends significantly reducing data collection and analysis, which would speed up the planning process and encourage more citizen involvement.

It is often difficult to reduce data-collection activities because for many planning organizations it is the only thing they do well. It is a simple, safe activity that gives the appearance of knowledge and expertise. Excessive data also relieves the manager from having to use foresight or to be held accountable for efficiently targeting data collection and analysis. But customers are becoming increasingly critical of wasteful planning activities that do not meet their expectations.

Customer participation should always be an integral part of the performance measurement process. But not everyone understands this. Stephen Morgan, assistant city auditor for the City of Austin, Texas, recently detailed the "performance measurement auditing and productivity improvements program" being implemented by Austin at the 1989 Region VIII Annual Conference of the American Society for Public Administration. He described a comprehensive and rigorous performance evaluation system, but upon questioning, he acknowledged that there was no customer involvement in the design or implementation of the program. His defense was that Austin had an aggressive city council and a number of active boards and commissions, and therefore there was no need for additional public involvement. Unfortunately, he and the management structure in the city of Austin will learn the hard way that there is no substitute for customer involvement in evaluating service and performance.

MANAGING FOR MOMENTS OF TRUTH

Jan Carlzon, president of Scandinavian Airline Systems (SAS), coined the phrase "moments of truth" in regards to customer service, and described the concept in detail in his best-selling book *Moments of Truth.* Every time a customer comes into direct contact with an employee, he says, it shapes the customer's perception of the quality of service and products offered by SAS. By managing for these moments of truth, Carlzon was able to turn a near-bankrupt airline into a highly profitable carrier (Carlzon 1987).

Each day every service business, from an airline to a planning department, has countless moments of truth. Albrecht and Bradford recommend that service providers should develop a graphic illustration of the moments of truth, or the cycle of service, for each product or service (Albrecht and Bradford 1990). Figure 6-2 is a service cycle model that we prepared for the map room in the Fort Worth planning department.

Diagraming the cycle of service is simple. In the Fort Worth example, I found over a dozen contact points that occur from something as simple as an individual purchasing a common map from the planning department. I was surprised by the large number of moments of truth, and suspect that you will be too when you diagram the service cycle for some activity in your organization.

The perceived quality of service that is received from the map room will obviously be influenced by the quality of the map that the customer

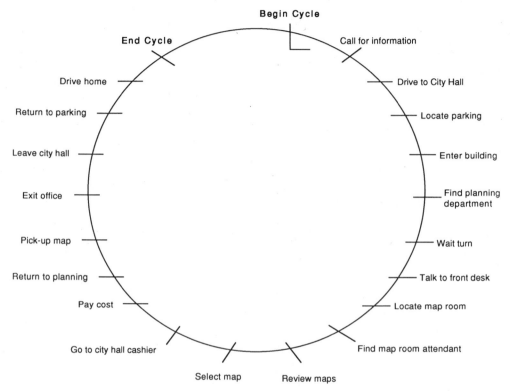

The Cycle of Service Model
Fort Worth Map Room

Begin Cycle

End Cycle

Call for information

Drive home

Drive to City Hall

Return to parking

Locate parking

Leave city hall

Enter building

Exit office

Find planning department

Pick-up map

Wait turn

Return to planning

Talk to front desk

Pay cost

Locate map room

Go to city hall cashier

Find map room attendant

Select map

Review maps

FIGURE 6-2

purchases, but it will also be influenced by: the staff that answers the initial phone inquiry; the customer's ease or difficulty in finding city hall, the planning department, and the map room; the availability and cost of parking; the hours during which the map room is open; the cost of the map; the attitude and helpfulness of the map room attendant; the convenience of payment (cash only, check, charge card, etc.); and the length of time it takes to transact business.

There is a cycle of service for every product and diagraming the cycle helps identify the various moments of truth which are going to determine the satisfaction levels of your customers. Service managers cannot afford to neglect any of these moments of truth. Nor can they afford to ignore the customer's perspective. For example, when I played the role of the customer going through the cycle of service with the map room, I found out for the first time that customers in the waiting area could hear sounds coming from the men's restroom.

Customer perceptions are based on a series of cumulative experiences. The totaling of all the moments of truth is what determines the customer's final assessment. A failure or breakdown at any one point can poison this assessment and undermine what was otherwise a positive experience.

While the service provider must be aware that all moments of truth are important, some moments are more critical to the formation of a positive overall experience. In the case of the map room, I have already indicated that the quality, usefulness and availability of a particular map is obviously important. Another critically important factor is the initial phone contact with the customer. The person handling this call must be personable and knowledgeable of the products in the map room. If you have a useful product, you want the customer to know about it. And you sure don't want to misinform someone and have them come down to city hall to find that what you have is not what he or she needed.

Critical moments of truth vary for each product and each organization, but, according to Albrecht and Bradford, there is one thing in common for all critical moments of truth: "The critical moments of truth, if left unmanaged, invariably lead to loss of customer confidence. Once you lose your customer's confidence, loss of loyalty and loss of repeat business quickly follow" (Albrecht and Bradford 1990).

Successful planning programs will be those that make the customer the primary focus of everything they do. At no time is this more important than at each moment of truth.

DECENTRALIZATION, AUTONOMY AND MOTIVATION

In the final analysis, superior customer service is going to depend on delegating authority, autonomy, and responsibility to front-line employees that have direct contact with the public. Planners at the lowest levels and extreme periphery of the organization must have the authority and motivation to solve problems that they know about and understand better than those that are higher up in the organization. Each planner must have the responsibility for helping customers to solve their problems. According to John Gardner, in his outstanding book *On Leadership*, "individuals in all segments and at all levels must be prepared to exercise leaderlike initiative and responsibility, using their local knowledge to solve problems at their level" (Gardner 1990). Unfortunately, there are still many employees at all levels in government that do not understand the need to produce results. In one community, an apartment complex had a flaw in its sewer lines that resulted in frequent spills into the street and parking lot of the local high school. Several times a year for a period of over 10 years, the code enforcement staff would issue a citation to the apartment manager. These violations continued at little cost to the apartment owners until a local television station made it a significant news story. With public pressure, the city forced the owners to reconstruct the sewer lines, which cost them around $12,000. In talking with the code enforcement staff, it was easy to find the cause of their ineffectiveness. They believed their only responsibility as inspectors was to issue citations. They never understood the need to resolve the violations so the problem would go away. Job performance must be based on results, not citations, and employees at all levels must accept personal responsibility for the problems they find. "I did my job" is not an acceptable defense for poor customer service.

Employees must have the support and the backing of their managers as they attempt to provide satisfying customer services. George Wagenheim and John Reurink argue that, "(t)hose organizations with a customer-service perspective provide their employees with the capability of bringing all the necessary resources of the organization to bear on solving the customers' problems and serving their needs" (Wagenheim and Reurink 1991). Remember, our customers want solutions and results now—not citations, studies, reports, and plans or buck-passing bureaucratic delays. Customer satisfaction should be our ultimate objective, not bureaucratic efficiency.

Too much of what we call management consists of making it difficult for people to work. Many planning organizations need to reduce their bureaucracies and streamline their operations. Tom Peters, author of the best-selling book *In Search of Excellence*, contends that all organizations need to move toward "life without hierarchy" (Peters 1989). A good example of the application of this principle is provided by Costis Toregas, president of Public Technology, Inc. (PTI). If you ask Toregas for an organizational chart of PTI, he'll admit he doesn't have one. He explains that PTI creates unique work teams for each specific project it undertakes and, as a result, has a different organization chart for each project.

Flexibility is essential for responsive management and effective problem solving. Inside and outside barriers to flexibility must be broken down. Planners should not work for divisions, but rather with other members of a multidisciplinary team assembled to serve the needs of specific clients. Managers must be able to freely move the right people for a particular assignment into a team created specifically to meet the unique needs of the situation. This flexibility has the added benefit of also providing for more enriching experiences for staff planners.

In *Mastering Change,* I wrote about the planning organizations that were streamlining their vertical organizational structures to promote more flexibility, teamwork, and responsiveness to customers. It was reported that in recent years the hierarchical structure of the Fort Worth planning department was slimmed down and compressed so as to decrease supervisory responsibilities and increase responsibility and authority for lower level planners. The number of core divisions or management modules was increased from two to four and a strategy of interdivisional team building for aggressively attacking emerging problems was established. The book included an illustration of the organization chart for the Fort Worth planning department that showed the horizontal structure of the department.

I often receive requests for more information about the Fort Worth situation. Not much has changed since my earlier writings. As shown in Figure 6-3, a similar organizational structure is in place that emphasizes teamwork and flexibility, but the size of the department has declined over the years. Since 1984, there has been more than a 50 percent reduction in staffing levels while production and service has actually increased. The department was able to achieve these improvements primarily because of the commitment to decentralization and autonomy for all of its professional employees.

Superior customer service demands a brave new world where accountable front-line professional planners with specialized knowledge and expertise are free to operate without general supervision. Devolution of authority is required. The ancient Romans had a unique practice for assuming accountability. When they finished building an arch, the engineer in charge was expected to stand below when the scaffolding was removed. Not surprisingly, many of these arches are still standing today.

People, the actual service providers, are the strength of any service organization. The latest equipment and technology, the best physical plant, and superior knowledge are of little value if you are not able to successfully deliver personalized products and services that meet the

Organizational Chart

Department of Planning and
Growth Management Services

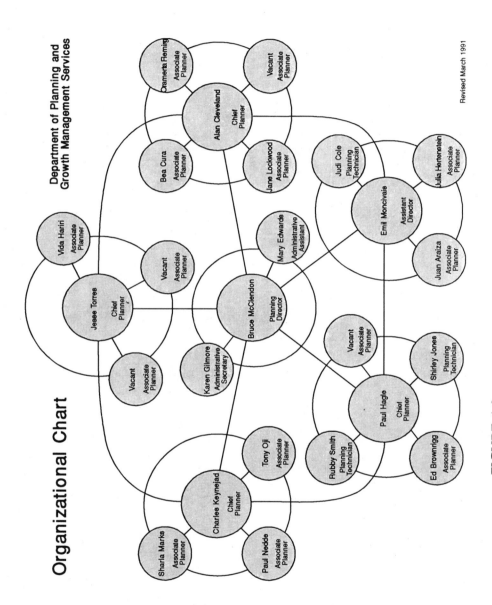

Revised March 1991

FIGURE 6-3

specific needs of your clients. Select people that fit the philosophy of your organization and then train and empower them to becoming winning service providers. Create a work environment where people feel motivated, committed, and happy to give their best to their customers and to their organization. Encourage all of your employees to put forth their best effort and to receive the biggest possible satisfaction from helping others.

REFERENCES

Albrecht, K. and Bradford, L. 1990. *The Service Advantage.* Homewood, Illinois: Dow Jones-Irwin.

Baum, H. 1983. *Planners and Public Expectations.* Cambridge, Massachusetts: Schenkman Publishing Company.

Carlzon, J. 1987. *Moments of Truth.* Cambridge, Mass: Ballinger.

Coonradt, C. 1985. *The Game of Work: How to Enjoy Work as Much as Play.* Salt Lake City, Utah: Desert Book Company.

Dalton, L. 1989. "The Limits of Regulation." *Journal of the American Planning Association* Vol. 55, No. 2.

Friedmann, J. 1973. *Retracking America: A Theory of Transactive Planning.* Garden City, New York: Anchor Press/Doubleday.

Gardner, J. 1990. *On Leadership.* New York: The Free Press.

Heskett, J. 1986. *Managing in the Service Economy.* Boston, Mass: Harvard Business School Press.

Neuharth, A. 1989. *Confessions of an S.O.B.* New York: Doubleday.

Peters, T. 1989. "Time to head back to school if you flunk this quiz." *Dallas Business Journal.* January 30.

Portland 1988. *Central City Plan.* Portland, Oregon: Bureau of Planning.

Slater, D. 1984. *Management of Local Planning.* Washington, DC: International City Management Association.

Wagenheim, G. and Reurink, J. 1991. "Customer Service in Public Administration." *Public Administration Review* Vol. 51, No. 3.

Weiss, C. 1977. *Using Social Research in Public Policy Making.* Lexington, Massachusetts: Lexington Books.

Zemke, R. and Schaaf, D. 1989. *The Service Edge.* New York: NAL Books.

Appendix A

The Arlington Action Plan

[Information for this appendix has been provided by the City of Arlington.]

In *Mastering Change*, Ray Quay and I identified the city of Arlington, Texas, as having one of the best examples of a comprehensive customer-service program and philosophy. The program was started in Arlington by Bill Kirchhoff, now the city manager of Redondo Beach, California, and then continued by George Campbell, the new city manager. The following mission statement of Arlington reflects that city's strong support for customer service: "The mission of the Arlington City Corporation is to provide excellent service delivery programs to the citizens of Arlington. The organization exists for the single purpose of providing the best possible services to the people who reside in this community."

Each employee in Arlington has been given the following guidelines to help establish good public relations and provide quality personalized services to the local residents:

1. The citizen's problem, complaint or request for information deserves your undivided attention, interest and concern. Be sure to listen carefully and ask questions.

2. Citizens need to have their questions answered clearly and in a language they can understand. This means elimination of complicated technical jargon or slang whenever possible.

3. Citizens expect to receive accurate, thorough, and complete information in a timely fashion. (An employee may not like to admit that he/she "doesn't know," but this is preferable to giving a wrong or incomplete answer.)

4. Citizens deserve a prompt response to their questions or requests. Nothing is worse than "passing the buck." If you do not know the answer, you should accept responsibility for finding the person who does. Whenever possible, obtain the information for the citizen by making a call or talking to another employee in person. Refer citizens to another city employee only if you do not know the answer and are positive that the employee you are referring the person to will be able to solve their problem.

5. Citizens expect courteous treatment. Not everyone an employee meets in the course of their duties will be courteous, but a part of your job is to maintain good relations in spite of these difficult situations. Do not make an issue a personal matter, maintain a professional attitude, and keep the conversation on the facts.

6. Citizens should feel that every attempt has been made to assist them by the time they leave the city building.

Five years after our last review we returned to Arlington and were not disappointed. The city of Arlington has not only maintained its original commitment to customer service, but it has also expanded on it in the city's new

Mission 90s Customer Service Action Plan. The stated purpose of the plan is to "create a strong Customer Service orientation in the collective and individual attitudes of the City's work force. This service attitude will become an objective of every employee of the City of Arlington."

In developing the short term action plan, each department in the city was required to prepare and submit a list of recommendations to maintain, improve, or create a positive customer service attitude by its employees. The second kind of recommendations were those relating to the operating processes of each individual department—the nuts and bolts of the bureaucratic functions that might be modified to create a more *convenient* way for customers (either employees or citizens) to complete *their* transactions with the city. Many of these suggestions included ways to measure customer satisfaction and dissatisfaction and ways to inform them about the various services which the city delivers.

The recommendations relating to city-wide training programs and attitude reinforcement efforts that were accepted and incorporated into the action plan are summarized below:

• The "Service Is Our Business" training program will be modified and become two seminars. One will be directed toward professional, technical, and office employees and the other toward field service employees in the various operating departments. The seminars, as in the past, will address the importance of good service and impart techniques for creating positive rapport with our customers. Program attendance will be mandatory for persons holding identified "high public contact" positions by December 1990. All employees will be required to participate by December 1991. All new employees will attend classes within six months of their employment date.

• The City Manager's Office is currently previewing the ICMA's new training program specifically designed for cities and emphasizing customer service. Use and applicability of this program will be determined in the next 60 to 90 days.

• At least one and possibly two videos are being purchased for the Human Resources library and will be available to department heads and supervisors for use in staff meetings to reinforce the importance of customer service. Supervisors are *expected* to periodically discuss customer service with all levels of staff to maintain enthusiasm among the work force and to motivate employees to become part of this work objective. The videos are being made available as one tool to help achieve that objective.

• Once a motto has been selected for this program ("Service Is Our Business" or some other motto) all departments will begin having that motto printed on selected forms, documents and business cards. The intent is to not only inform our customers of our new commitment to customer service, but to constantly remind the employee of his/her commitment and obligation.

• The Human Resources Department will distribute to all supervisors tips about characteristics and personality traits to look for when interviewing candidates for city jobs. If persons are hired with natural inclinations to be friendly, positive and creative, *in addition to* being technically qualified, the long-term impact on the organization will be positive.

• The Human Resources Department is evaluating the Performance Evaluation instruments to determine the best way to ensure that "maintaining and exhibiting a customer service attitude" becomes a part of the valuation process for both exempt and nonexempt employees.

• The Support Services Department will determine appropriate locations throughout city buildings where well-designed signs can be placed reminding citizens and employees of our commitment to "public service."

• A manual will be prepared which will list the questions most commonly asked by citizens for each department of the city. This reference manual will be made available to all departments and in particular to PBX operators and receptionists in an attempt to allow the citizen to get answers to questions immediately or be referred, if absolutely necessary, directly to the person most likely to provide the proper answer or information.

• A comprehensive telephone training program is being developed to address the issues of telephone technique and telephone equipment capabilities. Numerous departments and employees have identified problems associated with telephone usage. Problems cited range from the tone of the employee's voice to our inability to respond to questions being asked or frequently misdirecting the caller to third and fourth parties. The Communications Services Department along with Human Resources is developing this training program.

• The Human Resources Department is making modifications to the New Employee Orientation Program to provide greater emphasis on the importance of "Customer Service." New Employees will be able to better understand the commitment and expectations of the city's management team and the enthusiasm of all employees for friendly, positive service delivery.

Even more impressive than the list of citywide training programs and attitude reinforcement efforts was the list of specific short term actions to be taken by individual departments in support of the city's expanded commitment to customer service. The following is a summary for each department of the actions they were going to be taking in the immediate future to provide improved customer service to their customers:

Development Group—Planning

Enhanced Customer Service Environment. All work activities of the Department will be examined from the perspective of the client to determine if current procedures may be intimidating, confrontational or otherwise impose unnecessary constraints on the customer. Examples might include the Development Review Committee process, environment for personal meetings with clients, telephone procedures, returning of phone calls, etc.

Customer Surveys and Response Cards. Surveys would be conducted on a more regular basis than in the past and satisfaction response cards can be monitored continuously. An analysis of these instruments should produce specific recommendations for improving customer service.

Simplification of Ordinances. As ordinances are written or rewritten, particular attention will be given to producing ordinances which are easier for the lay person to understand. This could be accomplished by minimizing legalese jargon, reformatting, and utilizing graphics when possible.

Review Content of Forms and Letters. Standardized forms and letters will be reviewed to ensure that they are necessary and, if so, that they are user friendly and do not require more information than is necessary. The "Service Is Our Business" motto should appear on such forms and letters.

Establish Development Services Desk. The Development Services Desk provides centralized information related to development processes, fees, schedules, etc. in an open, user-oriented environment. Qualified staff will be cross-trained with other departments to further reduce need to refer clients to others.

Establish Centralized Permit System. The Program provides a designated staff "watchdog" and contact person to ensure that building permits, plats and zoning cases are processed smoothly; that processes are viewed as user-friendly; that alternative approaches are examined; red tape is cut when possible; etc.

Zoning Ordinance Rewrite. The Zoning Ordinance is being rewritten with particular attention being paid to simplifying the ordinance and making it easier for the lay person to understand. This will be accomplished by reducing the number of districts, focusing more on development standards and less on land use, and using graphics when appropriate.

Development Information Flyers. Simple, straightforward, one-page flyers will be written about development processes and other city procedures for free distribution to the public.

Revise the Development Handbook. Make the handbook more user-friendly by reducing its size through eliminating unnecessary text, expanding graphics and soft-binding the document. Underwrite the new handbook for one year by distributing it free to the development community and neighborhood associations.

Designate a "Hot Spot" Planner. This program will result in one senior planner being designated to respond to direction from Council on special reports, ordinance revisions, etc. as the position's number one priority. This should reduce response delays caused by conflicting priorities.

Expansion of Planning Referral Program (PRP). Currently the PRP is a subscription service that provides advanced notice of upcoming rezoning applications and ordinance revisions. It is targeted to neighborhood associations and business community subscribers. Though the annual subscription fee is nominal, many neighborhood associations have no dues. The PRP will be expanded to include other topics of general interest (i.e. street closings, construction schedules, public meeting announcements, etc.). The delivery of this information could be expanded significantly if the PRP becomes a free service to qualified neighborhoods and business associations for one year. It would also aid the City in identifying neighborhood associations and their officers—an important service to rezoning clients who generally attempt to contact adjoining neighborhood leaders.

City Charter Amendments. The Arlington City Charter has a provision, not mandated by state law, that requires two readings for ordinance adoption. Approval of a Charter amendment to require only one reading would stream-line several development processes (i.e., rezoning, easement abandonment, etc.).

Development Group—Transportation

Transportation "Help Desk". This desk would be staffed by a receptionist/ information person who would be the first citizen contact. This person would be trained in basic department policies and could provide answers to simple questions and provide information and publications such as the Visibility Ordinance, traffic count maps, traffic study procedures, thoroughfare plan maps, etc.

Customer Service Brochures. Develop general information brochures on those items of routine interest to the public. Possible topics include traffic signals, traffic signs, street light requests, driveway requests, block parties/ race/parade permits, the school crossing safety program, Handitran, Arlington Municipal Airport, and traffic/drainage maintenance. These brochures would be made available at the Help Desk and at the Customer Service Desk on the second floor.

Dress Code. To ensure a neat and professional image for all employees, a dress code will be developed for employees performing various types of public contact jobs. Such a dress code will provide employees with a definite set of expectations for their dress and appearance and will be included as an integral part of the performance review process.

Public Information/Street Maintenance Activities. Newspaper articles, mail-outs and door hangers will be used to promote and inform the public regarding various street maintenance activities prior to project implementation. The purpose will be to provide answers to citizen questions and provide pertinent information to area residents regarding the projects.

Schedule Staff Meetings. Staff meetings, at all levels, will be held to reinforce employee awareness of service needs, recognize employees setting good customer-service examples, and to discuss improvements in service delivery and employee incentives.

Establish "Quality Circle" Committees. "Quality circle" committees with representatives from each part of the Department will be established. Their task will be to review operations of the Department and establish goals and objectives to improve customer service and productivity. These committees will provide another opportunity to reinforce the objectives of the Mission '90s program.

Customer Service Evaluation Cards. Evaluation cards will be made available at all public service desks. Customers will be encouraged to turn in the evaluations or return them by mail.

Mailing of Service Questionnaires. Periodic mail-out of questionnaires with prestamped, return addressed envelopes will be mailed to customers for feedback on service delivery of office staff, field inspections, and administrative systems.

Development Group—Capital Improvements

Restructure Pre–Development Review Committee (DRC) Process. Staff will meet with developers and consultants in a Pre-DRC format to discuss problems on plats before the formal submittal date and final comments are due. This would require division head level attendance since decisions requiring division or department head approval would be necessary.

Consolidate Street Cuts Permit Process. Presently an applicant must make contact with three different departments regarding street cuts. Consolidation under one department's authority would reduce the time that the applicant must spend in City Hall, thus providing a more efficient service to the public.

Public Contact and Notification Prior to Capital Improvements Projects. Depending on the size of the project, a public meeting and/or notice regarding street, drainage, sidewalk or street rebuild projects would be provided to area residents. The public meeting or notice would include the answers to frequently asked questions regarding the project scope and would provide reassurance to property owners regarding the length of time they would be inconvenienced. The meetings would better inform the public and reduce or eliminate misinformation about the projects.

Preconstruction Notification to Property Owners. The division will require that contractors distribute "door hangers" for capital improvements projects approximately 1 week prior to the start of construction. The door hangers would have the contractor's name and phone number, the city inspector's name and phone number and the Assistant Director of Capital Improvements's name and phone number.

Development Display. Investigate development of a display showing proposed capital improvements construction projects. Such a display could be placed in a public place such as the City Council Chambers' foyer, a heavy traffic area at the Parks Mall or other suitable location. The display would show proposed capital improvements projects along with the names and phone numbers of the project engineers. The public would become better informed about these projects and be provided a source for answering their questions.

Development Group—Community Development

Conduct Self Evaluations. Employees will be asked to conduct a self evaluation to determine their own impressions of their strengths and weaknesses. The purpose of the self evaluation is simply to afford employees the opportunity to know where they need to concentrate their efforts to meet the objectives of providing a greater customer service awareness.

Regularly Scheduled Staff Meetings. Division managers will be expected to hold regular staff meetings wherein customer service efforts can occasionally be discussed. Top department managers will be expected to attend division meetings to stress the importance of customer service and other Mission '90s objectives.

Establish "Quality Circle" Committees. The establishment of standing "quality circle" committees will allow representatives from each part of the Department to meet in a risk-free environment and discuss the operations, goals and objectives of their division or the department.

Conduct Monthly Field Surveys. Mid-managers will conduct field surveys of contractors and citizens in an effort to gauge the quality of service being provided by our employees. These surveys will be conducted verbally and in a casual atmosphere.

Establish a Development Services Desk. Establish a development services desk to assist developers, builders, design professionals and the general public with the development process. The purpose of this program is to provide immediate service to customers seeking assistance. The desk will be staffed with employees who will have broad decision-making ability and knowledge of most development activities.

Mailing of Service Questionnaires. Periodic mail-outs will be sent to random customers and will include prestamped, preaddressed questionnaires concerning service delivery by office staff, field inspections and administrative systems.

Quality Control on Incoming Calls. Complainants will be contacted at random and asked to answer a brief service-oriented questionnaire. The purpose is to determine from the complainants how they were treated upon initial contact with city staff.

Public Service Questionnaire Cards. Evaluation cards will be placed at all public service desks. These cards will be provided to seek responses regarding customer service either at location or by return mail.

"Centralized Service System". The key feature of the program is that a plans examiner will take the lead role in processing plans through all departments of the city's review process. This will include regular telephone contact with permit applicants, monitoring of the progress of plan review in other departments, and checking all departments' plan review comments for clarity, reasonableness and consistency with other departments' comments.

Extend Customer Services to Multi-family and Single-family Rehabilitation Projects. Inspectors will perform a "courtesy walk-through" for contractors and property owners to identify required building standards for rehabilitation projects as well as required permits for proceeding to reconstruction.

Provide List of Mowing Contractors. A list of contractors available to provide mowing services for citizens will be submitted with all weeds and grass "notice to mow" correspondence from the city.

Establish a Proactive Approach to Weed and Grass Abatement. A letter will be submitted to the ownership of those properties that have had a history of recurrent high weed and grass and/or unclean premises violations. This practice will reduce unnecessary advertising and other costs to both the citizens and the city.

Publish a Quarterly Newsletter. The newsletter to the development industry and community will provide information regarding code changes or other specific issues. Information included in the newsletter will come from various development departments.

Brochure for Apartment Owners and Managers. The brochure will explain the format of property inspections and the impact of existing ordinances on apartment properties. Helpful guidelines for compliance and maintenance will be included.

Development Group—Convention Center

Redesign the Present Client Evaluation Form. The evaluation form will be redesigned to include questions regarding catering and other contract services provided by the Center's contractors. Evaluation results will be provided to those contractors. A letter stressing the center's goals of making customer satisfaction the highest priority will accompany the evaluation instrument.

Critique and Follow-Up of Client Evaluations. The Center's division managers and subcontractor managers will be required to follow up with personal phone calls regarding clients complaints. Those managers will listen, respond and evaluate situations so that issues will not arise again in the future.

Installation of House "Service Telephones" in the Exhibit Hall Areas. House phones will promote immediate service response, thus eliminating customer frustration and valuable time loss in locating proper staff assistance.

Employee Evaluations. The proposed forms will be composed of questions on how the employee perceives the quality of the work environment at the Center. Through this evaluation process, internal problems and issues will be addressed so that customer service attitudes among the employees can be maximized.

Development Group—Convention and Visitors Bureau

"Company's Coming". The "Company's Coming" Program has worked extremely well in the Bureau's efforts to get front-line employees of local hotels and restaurants to be aware of the importance of customer service. The "Company's Coming" seminar will be modified and adapted to the sales and support staff of the Bureau itself.

Visitor Information Center (VIC) Hotline. Visitors to Arlington need a 24-hour hotline to get information concerning attractions, festivals, and other events that are important to the tourist. Such a system would reduce the number of general information calls to the Bureau office or VIC and would create a 24-hour a day way the visitor could get information he needs to enjoy his stay.

Produce a "What is the Bureau?" Brochure. The brochure will familiarize the customer or meeting planner as well as the local community, hotels, and restaurants with the services provided by the Convention and Visitors Bureau.

Customer Surveys for Visitors. Customer satisfaction surveys will be distributed in our Visitor Information Center and eventually by area hotels, restaurants and attractions in an effort to evaluate the level of service being provided by both the Bureau and the industry.

Industry Survey. A survey would be provided to the hotels, restaurants, and attractions in Arlington for the specific purpose of evaluating the effectiveness and service delivery of the Convention and Visitors Bureau.

Upgrade of Computer and Word Processing Systems. High quality and prompt responses to customer needs is essential to the Bureau. Improved word processing capabilities will enable the Bureau to provide that high quality and timely information to customers.

Training for Handling Customer Complaints by Hotels and Attractions. A training program directed at hotel and attraction employees regarding the handling of customer complaints will enhance the image of both the city and the industry. Many times the customer comes to the Bureau out of desperation to get problems resolved when in fact the Bureau has no ability to cure those problems. Such a program could be implemented in a manner similar to the "Company's Coming" Program.

Human Resources

Employment Fact Sheets. Fact sheets will be prepared to provide applicants and employees with information regarding the employment process and answers to frequently asked questions regarding employment with the City of Arlington.

Notification to Applicants. The Department will send cards to applicants informing them of the status of their employment application with the city of Arlington. Previously letters were sent only to those persons applying for exempt positions. The new cards will be sent to those applying for nonexempt positions as well.

"Position Interest" Cards. These cards will be placed in booths within the Human Resources Department along with a listing of all city positions. The intent is to encourage use of the "Position Interest" cards by the public in order that potential applicants may be notified when positions of interest to them become available.

Extended Hours. In March of this year, Human Resources offices began remaining open until 6:00 p.m. one night per week. The purpose is to accommodate applicants who are employed and cannot make applications during normal working hours.

Applicant Pools. In an attempt to accommodate hiring supervisors, the Department will develop applicant pools for high turnover, nonexempt positions. This pool of qualified applicants will be available for immediate referral to supervisors and cut the controllable time for these positions from fifteen days to eight days.

Customer Satisfaction Cards. An evaluation card will be provided to applicants requesting that they evaluate the staff regarding interpersonal skills, attitude, helpfulness and image. This questionnaire will supplement annual efforts to make such determinations through meetings with Department Heads and Division Managers.

Develop a Computer Program for Employees. A program will be developed to calculate retirement benefits. A computer terminal will be made available in the Human Resources Department in order that employees may access information regarding retirement eligibility, benefits, etc.

Drop Box. A drop box will be located at the Human Resources Department allowing employees to leave paperwork before or after normal working hours.

Employee Work Schedules. Schedules will be adjusted to assure that adequate staffing is available during lunch hours between 11:30 a.m. and 1:00 p.m.

Finance—Tax Office

Public Access to Tax Data. Increase the number of computer terminals available to the public. Idle terminals are available. Benefits to be derived include:

- Reduce time required of Tax Office employees to access data.
- Allow regular customers to easily access tax and property information.
- Provide additional work stations for use by volunteers.

Tax Data Subscription Service. Study possibility of modem link to tax data base for use by tax services and title companies. Tax service and mortgage companies could be allowed access to the city's tax data base via modem. Cost for this service could be recovered with a subscription fee.

Finance—Risk Management

Increased Visibility of Risk Management. Risk Management will develop a structured training schedule and orientation process to introduce departments to Risk Management functions. The purpose will be to inform departments of how and when to utilize Risk Management functions and to more aggressively address safety issues before they become claims.

Personalized Letters to Claimants. Improved correspondence to claimants will explain city's position on claim issues. The purpose is to provide a greater sense of personal treatment and minimize bureaucratic and form letter responses.

Implementation of a Formal Diary System. For follow-up on liability and subrogation claims. A computer-based claims diary system will provide a more systematic work flow and prompt follow-up on claims. The system will result in more efficient, orderly processing of claims to the public and to third parties involved in claims against the City.

Management Services—Data Processing

Terminal User Contacts. The Data Processing Department will become more proactive with terminal users by visiting all users and the managers during the year. These visits will allow DP and the user to better understand each other and will allow problems and misunderstandings to be identified. The visits will also facilitate better training of terminal users.

PC Management. Data Processing will examine current procedures for approving purchasing, installing, maintaining and repairing personal computer systems. This review will include analysis of the current committee system of evaluating PC needs.

Utilization of Electronic Mail System.   This new system potentially reduces telephone tag, allows easier meeting scheduling, more efficient document review by the departments, and has the potential to substantially reduce paperwork.

Management Services—Internal Audit

Improve Service Request Procedures.   The Internal Audit Office will conduct a preliminary interview with persons requesting a service from their division. This interview will replace the current requirement that all requests for service be submitted in writing. Essential information will be gathered by the auditor during the interview process and will provide the requesting party with expectations of the audit review.

Management Services—Budget

Name Tags.   Management Services will, upon request from other departments, order name tags for high public contact employees. Department heads would be expected to identify employees for whom they believe name tags would provide a customer service and submit those names to the management services department.

Staff Assignments.   The Budget Division will assign various staff members to the tasks of processing travel advances, expense reports, and appropriation adjustments in order that processing of these documents will not be delayed when key staff members are on vacation or out of the office. The multiple assignments will improve the delivery of this service to the employees of operating departments.

Automated BAR and Budget Salary Accounts.   The Budget Office will generate salary account information for use in BAR reports in order that various departments will not have to generate that information. Provision of this information will significantly enhance the other department's ability to complete BAR reports in a timely manner.

Improved Description of Budget Accounts.   With the development of a new budget instruction manual, an updated chart of accounts will be provided to the departments of the city. In recent years, several new budget accounts have been established and others have been renamed. The updated descriptions, particularly for nonsalary accounts, would improve service to the user departments.

Support Services Department

Special Training.   Because divisions including Fleet Services, General Services, Communications Services and Building Maintenance provide frequent services to other departments and personnel in the city, those employees must develop and maintain permanent and positive working relationships. A special training seminar may be developed to assist personnel to learn how to better serve other city employees.

Customer Satisfaction Cards. Cards will be passed to city employees as they receive a product or service from Support Services divisions. The card will inquire as to the level of satisfaction with repair work, whether the job was performed in a timely, professional, and cost-effective manner.

Support Services—Fleet

Establishment of a Heavy Equipment Pool. A pool of heavy equipment will be established by holding heavy equipment back from auction. The availability of this equipment will assist departments in obtaining needed vehicles when their units are down for major repairs.

A Customer Services Representative. A representative has been designated within the Fleet Services Division. That person is totally responsible for interfacing with departments about problems, complaints, or other issues of importance.

Establish Job Completion Dates. The Division will make every attempt to give reasonable and accurate due dates for vehicle repairs. If unable to meet deadlines the customer will be called and informed of the problems and new target date for completion.

Professional Appearance. The creation of a more professional appearance for both the Fleet personnel and facilities has been implemented to create a greater appreciation of the Division's capabilities.

Quality Repair Services. Through training, standardization of vehicle types, better quality control, better organized facilities and access to proper tools and parts the Division is giving special attention to the quality of repairs made to vehicles of the user departments. The ability to repair vehicles and equipment properly and prevent follow-up repairs for the same problem will improve the Division's service delivery.

Support Services—General Services

Quick and Positive Problem Solving. General Service employees and their supervisors will be held accountable for providing quick and positive resolutions to problems or complaints from other city departments. All General Services employees will be regularly counseled regarding the emphasis on "user friendliness."

General Services Information Brochure. The Division will produce a brochure summarizing services provided by General Services. The brochure will be distributed to all departments and to new employees during orientation. This brochure will be a quick reference about where to acquire a particular service and who to call with questions or problems.

Quality Circles.   The Division will explore the concept of creating "quality circles" to improve the quality of products produced by the General Services Division. If successful, this concept may be extended to Fleet Services and Building Maintenance since they also produce a "product."

Support Services—Building Maintenance

Outside Contractors.   Where feasible and cost effective, Building Maintenance will assist other departments in using an outside contractor to do assignments that cannot be done in a timely manner by Building Maintenance.

Support Services—Communications Services

Training PBX Operators.   Training will be provided to operators on how to better assist employees seeking help on telephone problems or equipment failure.

Explore the Feasibility of a 24-hour City Hall Telephone Information System.   Such a system would allow citizens to call in at any time to get questions answered about selected topics. It would require funds for equipment and advertising but would provide a valuable service to citizens after normal working hours and on weekends.

Study of Kiosks.   Examine the feasibility and cost of placing "Kiosks" in shopping malls and/or other public places that get a great deal of citizen traffic. By touching a screen on a personal computer, a citizen could get information about a variety of topics ranging from Council meetings to garbage pickup. The possibility exists that this system could be used to poll citizens regarding their thoughts on any particular subject.

Develop a Citizen Handbook.   A handbook would be developed that explains City government in Arlington and includes the processes followed by the City Council, Planning and Zoning Commission, etc. This information could be made available to citizens at the Customer Service desk on the second floor of City Hall.

Develop a brochure that explains what Communication Services does. Self explanatory.

Operations Group—Library

Combine Customer Service Desks.   Rearrange the second floor of the Central Library so that the four existing customer service areas can be combined into one new public service center. The Library would experience better use of materials and staff assistance to library patrons would be improved.

Move the Children's Service Desk.   Relocate this service desk to near the entrance to this area. Moving the service desk would allow the librarian to better supervise children left unattended.

Training for Support Groups.   Provide special training to groups such as the Friends of the Library and the Library Board of Trustees so that they may better represent the Library in the community.

Suggestion Boxes.   Place suggestion boxes in strategic places with pre-printed "We Are Here To Help You" cards for citizen input.

Bookstore.   Permit the Friends of the Library to operate a "bookstore" within the Library to sell material not normally returned once checked out by a patron. Examples might include GED Study Books, Civil Service Exam Study Guides, and Postal Exam Books. Other items might include paperback classics used for school assignments, and books on pregnancy and childbirth. Additionally, such items as pens, pencils, paper, correction fluid, paper clips, etc. would be available in the store.

Revise Library Card Policies.   Examine the feasibility of having a single library card for both adults and children or whether a library card is even necessary.

Operations Group—Municipal Library

Staffing Allocation Analysis.   Perform a study comparing availability of staff with customer service demand. The study would compare staffing availability with time and frequency of telephone calls, walk-in customers, etc., during various hours of the day. A redistribution of the staff could then accommodate service demands.

Customer Service Satisfaction Surveys.   The surveys will be accomplished and used as a basis to determine needed improvements to customer service delivery and to measure the degree of success of customer service efforts.

Information Board.   An information board will be located in the lobby which will contain specific easy to read information pamphlets on certain designated subjects (i.e. defensive driving school, teen court, deferred adjudication, appeals, seat belt safety classes, alcohol awareness program and trial settings.) This is the same type of information that could be adaptable to an automated digital telephone information system and it addresses the most commonly asked questions.

Customer Service Award Program.   Develop an ongoing customer service campaign to encourage and promote good customer relations. The department will develop and implement an award program to recognize employees for consistently promoting good customer relations. The administration staff will assume the selection of the awardee based upon customer service performance. Awards will continue to include special parking privileges and photo displays.

Police

Office Space for Department of Human Services Child Abuse Case Workers. Having case workers housed in the public safety building will greatly enhance cooperation in the investigations for victims and witnesses in child abuse cases. Essentially citizens will only have to tell their story one time as these two agencies work together on each case.

Full Service Facility. The establishment of an independent 24-hour "full service" facility in the southern part of the city would increase community responsiveness and relationships. The goal of decentralization of standard patrol and investigative services to the south half of the city is recognized as appropriate by the resource utilization analysis.

Extension of Jail Visiting Hours. Current visiting hours of Wednesday and Saturday from 1:00—5:00 p.m. greatly limit the availability of citizens to visit inmates within the jail facility. Due to the rapid turnover in prisoner population and greatly diminished length of stay, an extension of visitor hours should have minimal impact on jail operations.

Elimination of Report Copy Charges. Only a small loss of revenue will result if charges for some report copies are eliminated. Speed, however, of each transaction will be improved and dropping the charge will permit our police employees to promptly assist more citizens than is currently possible. The loss of revenue should be recovered by labor savings.

Citizen Access. Movement within the police facility will be expedited to improve customer service by having visitors escorted to secure areas of the police building rather than requiring that they leave important identification at a monitoring point.

Fire

Code Book Availability. The Department will print sufficient copies of Fire Code books to make them available for purchase by developers and contractors. The code books will also be made available at the Central Library along with the National Electric Code, Plumbing Code, Mechanical Code, and NFPA Standards.

Non-Fire Related Services. The Department will begin to provide simple non-fire related services to nonprofit organizations. Examples might be the installation of halyards on flagpoles or other services that can be performed by the Fire Department but for which there is little or no resource for the general public.

Parks and Recreation

Park Facility Information. Develop and distribute park facility brochures for the interested public. These will also greatly assist front-line staff in responding to numerous daily inquiries from the public.

Direct Mail Promotions. Increased direct mail efforts will be made to better inform the general public of Parks and Recreation programs and services.

Preferred Customer Discounts. Initiate preferred customer discounts as an incentive for continued citizen participation and interest in the various recreation programs. Discounts will be offered to repeat participants in various activities.

Customer Relations. Develop a program to improve customer relations and ultimately regain customers who have expressed dissatisfaction with the process or quality of program services. Personal contact and follow-up will highlight the program and will be conducted by the responsible program managers.

Telephone Hotline. Continue public service efforts with a parks and recreation telephone hotline which relays timely program information and other related public service announcements.

Program Focus Group. Implement a focus group concept to oversee and enhance recreation center services and operations. This would provide a process for direct feedback from participants.

Job Factor Assessment. Conduct a department-wide survey of full-time employees to gain better insight into the factors employees feel are important in their jobs. This survey instrument will also provide results which will help departmental managers better understand the work force.

Public Service Announcements. Include information in the *FunTimes* magazine concerning the City of Arlington that may have appeal and value to the general public. Public service announcements or special interest articles could be distributed through the 55,000 magazines published four times each year. The program is estimated to cost $20,000.

Performance Work Plan—FY 1989–90. The following customer service objectives are established in the Parks and Recreation Department 1989—90 Performance Work Plan.

1. *Computerized Park Reservation Scheduling.*
2. *Enhanced Marketing Efforts.* To better identify the profile or program users in an effort to respond to the needs of recreation center, golf, aquatics, athletics and lake customers.
3. *Trail System Brochure.* A parks trail system brochure has been developed for public distribution to identify trail location and distances in the parks system.

4. *Public Awareness.* Coordinate the "Don't Bag It" grass clippings program and implement as a public awareness program addressing environmental concerns.

Utilities

Cross-training. Cross-training to enable employees to work in other divisions. Employees are assisting in other divisions at times when shortages of personnel or work load increases occur to maximize efficiency and provide better service to the public.

Regularly Scheduled Staff Meetings. Regularly scheduled staff meetings at all levels will be used to reinforce customer service objectives and the Mission '90s program. During these meetings employees will be encouraged to make further suggestions and become participants in promoting the objectives of Mission '90s.

Impromptu Visits of Division Heads and Department Heads. These impromptu visits to various work sites within the Water Department would provide the managers with an opportunity to personally express the importance of customer service and provide a forum for employees to demonstrate their successes to higher level supervisors.

Telephone Message for Customer Services. A new recorded message providing additional information concerning the location of the Water Office, operations hours, etc. has been added to the answering recording from the Customer Services Division.

Comments Added to Water Bill Reflecting Concern for Unusually High Water Consumption. A note will be listed on the customer's water bill notifying the customer when dramatic changes in water consumption have occurred. The customer is thereby alerted to a potential problem and arrangements can be made to assist the customer in payment of unusually high water bills.

Comments Added to Water Bills Regarding Good Payment History. Customers who are in good standing and have achieved a good payment history will receive comments on their water bill commending them for their payment history.

Employee Evaluations. An evaluation of all employees will be conducted to identify areas of strengths and weaknesses relating to communication skills, knowledge of public relations, interaction and customer services. Once identified these items will be used to determine necessary training for employees and will be shown on performance evaluations.

Service Rating Card. A service rating postcard will be distributed by field crews to those individuals who have been in contact with the Utility Department. The cards will allow customers to identify the person who served them, the type of contact made, and their rating of the service provided. The card would additionally provide for the customer to rate the quality of the water.

Customer Service Surveys. Surveys will be conducted by both mail and in person to determine the level and quality of service provided by the Water Department. The survey results will be the basis for training programs and service improvements.

Complaint Follow-up. Any customer who contacts the Utility Department with a complaint will receive a letter or telephone call from the appropriate division head responding to the complaint. The Customer Water Quality Brochure and service rating card will be enclosed with any correspondence.

Taste and Odor Survey. Periodic telephone taste and odor surveys from a representative portion of Arlington's population will be conducted. The survey would improve our knowledge of customer rating of the water's palatability. Survey participants will be encouraged to notify the city anytime they perceive a disagreeable change in the water's quality.

Water Conservation Audit. This program will, at the customer's request, provide an individualized water conservation service to customers which would include an onsite inspection and specific recommendations for improvement in water conservation and water consumption habits.

Adjustments for Water Leaks. Currently, adjustments are not made for water leaks. Customers therefore try to prove that water meters are faulty, necessitating an investigation of the water meter or water lines. Upon documentation that water leaks have been repaired, adjustments may be made to the customer's water bill. Eligibility guidelines for such a program would be necessary.

Telephone Applications for Water Service. An analysis will be made to determine if applications for water service can be taken over the telephone instead of requiring all customers to come to the office. The feasibility of such a program will be researched to address additional staffing needs, noncollectable deposits, unpaid bills, increased bad debt ratio, and the ability to acquire valid information over the phone before the program is implemented.

Proactive Meter Downsizing. Customers who have oversized meters will be notified as to the cost savings available through meter downsizing. This program has the potential for the city to recover revenues from currently unmetered water and to reduce costs to many customers.

Implement a Four Day/Ten Hour Work Shift. A feasibility study will be conducted to determine possible costs savings and convenience to customers that would be achieved by the revised work schedules. Work that is now left unfinished at the end of a normal work day could be completed the same day without overtime expense.

Customer Notification of Water Main Repairs. By installing public address speakers on crew trucks, customers could be notified of unscheduled water main repairs that will interrupt water service. If used, the comment section of the work order would be used to note that outside notification was used rather than written notification.

Street Patching by Water Department. The Department will study the feasibility of purchasing a one-ton roller in order that water repair crews can make street repairs immediately following work in the street area.

Central Telephone Answering for Water Utilities. An analysis of the potential for a central switchboard operator within the utilities will be made. The potential exists that such a central operator could respond to many questions from customers in a more timely fashion and without interruption to professional staff.

On-line Main Frame Data Base for After Hours Call Takers. After hours contact personnel for all departments would be included on an on-line main frame data base to be updated by the individual departments. After hours dispatchers could then have access to current standby personnel in each city operating department.

Making "Service Is Our Business" the Business of Our Contractors and Vendors. The program will be developed to ensure that contractors and vendors who perform services under the city's direction are held to the city's high standards of customer satisfaction and service. Contracts and bid specifications will include a description of service expectations. Contractors will be required to distribute service rating cards to customers and these cards will be used to document satisfactory or unsatisfactory performance by the city's contractors.

Anyone that has been able to read through this list has to be excited about the possibilities of using some of these ideas in his or her own operation. The city of Arlington truly has a unique and extraordinary commitment to customer service. Arlington's commitment starts at the top with its city manager. In a personal memo accompanying the Action Plan, former city manager Kirchhoff stated, "no deputy manager, department head, assistant department head or division head can make the required contribution to this organization without clearly demonstrating that his or her employee units have been successful in improving relations with our citizen customers." The memo added:

We need to treat citizens as our valued 'customers' and recognize that our continued existence depends on their satisfaction. It is important that all of us recognize that we represent the city every time we answer the phone, or walk into a house or place of business. Each time we do so we must be conveying the image that "we, your staff, are here to help." Management and supervisory commitment, training for all levels of the work force and reinforcement (rewards, performance evaluations and feedback) will be required to upgrade the current level of customer service. . . . The employment, compensation and promotional opportunities of the deputy managers, department heads, assistant department heads and division heads will be dependent upon their individual and collective success as it relates to the enhancement of a customer service culture . . .

Ted Tedesco, the former longtime city manager of San Jose, California, and vice-president of strategic planning for American Airlines, tells me that Arlington's Mission 90s Action Plan is "at the cutting edge of city management practice."

Kirchhoff contends that any plan to improve customer service must remain dynamic and can never be considered finished. He warns that the long-term success of such efforts will depend on the ability of the management staff to: 1) set a good example; 2) continue reinforcing their own commitment directly to other employees; and 3) implement hiring practices that attract employees with natural inclinations toward positive public customer service.

Index